THE POWER TO DESTROY

THE POWER TO DESTROY

William V. Roth, Jr.
William H. Nixon

Atlantic Monthly Press
New York

Copyright © 1999 by William V. Roth, Jr., and William H. Nixon

Published simultaneously in Canada
Printed in the United States of America

FIRST EDITION

Library of Congress Cataloging-in-Publication Data

Roth, William V., 1921–
     The power to destroy : how the IRS became America's most powerful
agency, how Congress is taking control, and what you can do to
protect yourself under the new law / by William V. Roth, Jr. and
William H. Nixon.
          p.   cm.
     Includes bibliographical references.
     ISBN 0-87113-748-8
     1. United States. Internal Revenue Service.   2. Tax collection—
United States.   3. Tax administration and procedure—United States.
I. Title.   II. Title: How the IRS became America's most powerful
agency.
HJ2361.R67   1999
352.4'4'0973—dc21   98-52234
                                                                CIP

Atlantic Monthly Press
841 Broadway
New York, NY 10003

99 00 01 02   10 9 8 7 6 5 4 3 2 1

For Jane, Bud, Katy, Eunhee, Chris, Bobby, and Charlie—
Tammy, Brittany, Billy, and Joseph.

"If the true number of incidents of taxpayer abuse were ever known, the public would be appalled. If the public also ever knew the number of abuses 'covered up' by the IRS, there could be a taxpayer revolt."

Witness Number One
IRS revenue officer with over
two decades of experience,
sworn testimony

Contents

Acknowledgments

While it is impossible to grasp the causes of events in their entirety, the authors gratefully acknowledge the compelling circumstances and many individuals who contributed to this work, as well as to the restructuring and on-going reform of the Internal Revenue Service.

The Power to Destroy was written during late nights, early mornings, long weekends, and holidays. For the most part, it was a labor of love, driven by the conviction that real change will take place within the IRS only when Americans are fully aware of how the agency works and possess the knowledge necessary to protect themselves. It is also our hope that this book, in pointing out the critical need for continued vigilance and reform, will keep the issue of improving the Internal Revenue Service alive well into the future.

This work makes it clear that the successful Congressional hearings and unanimous passage of the Internal Revenue

Service Restructuring and Reform Act of 1998 would have been impossible without the courageous men and women of the Service. Many of their stories are contained in these pages, and we are most grateful for their candor and desire to constructively change the culture of their agency. Much of the information in this book is new, and we appreciate the time these employees took—most often in their off hours—to meet with us, to answer additional questions, to provide illustrative material, and greater detail than was available in the public hearings. We express profound appreciation to Charles Rossotti, the agency's new commissioner and want him to know that we support his agenda, admire his leadership, and esteem his association.

We acknowledge the invaluable contributions of the senators and staff members who contributed to the Senate investigation, the Finance Committee hearings, and successful passage of the Restructuring and Reform Act. Particularly, we want to mention Eric Thorson, the chief investigator; investigators Debbie McMahon, Kathryn Quinn, and Maureen Barry; Frank Polk and Lindy Paull, Finance Committee staff directors; Mark Prater and Tom Roesser, staff counsels; Jane Butterfield, the committee's chief clerk; as well as Virginia Flynn, Brian Tassinari, and Christina Pearson, press representatives.

We are also grateful to John Duncan, Carol Petty, and Susie Cohen who worked not only toward the success of the IRS hearings, but who encouraged the writing and publication of this book. As great care was taken to keep this project separate and apart from official life on Capitol Hill, we are grateful to those who on their own time graciously read portions of the manuscript and offered their constructive criticisms.

We thank the many tax professionals and legal experts who spoke with us, particularly Bruce Strauss, John Behrens, David Keating, Richard Beck, and Jay Freireich. Special gratitude goes to Robert Schriebman, a good friend, experienced advocate, and eloquent counselor. And we are grateful for the willingness of their clients to share their stories. This book is written for them, for the taxpayers who made their cases public, and for all those who have come up against less than fair treatment in their experiences with the IRS. We hope this work gives these men and women the encouragement they need to carry on.

As with all important efforts, this one builds on what has gone before. There are several books and many articles written about the Internal Revenue Service. These were used not only as the Senate Finance Committee prepared its hearings, but for the composition of this manuscript, and we want to acknowledge many of the sources we relied upon and quoted: David Burnham, and his seminal book, *A Law Unto Itself: The IRS and the Abuse of Power* (we also appreciate the time David took to work with us personally on this project); journalist James Bovard, and his book, *Lost Rights: The Destruction of American Liberty;* Shelley Davis, former IRS historian and author of *Unbridled Power,* a compelling inside view of the agency (Shelley, too, spent many hours meeting with us, increasing our understanding of the history and inner workings of the agency); Michael Josephson and the Josephson Institute on Ethics; Charles Adams and *Those Dirty Rotten Taxes,* his excellent history of America's relationship with the tax man; Dr. James Hill Shelton, and his unpublished dissertation, "The Tax Scandals of the 1950s"; the General Accounting Office and many of its reports related to the IRS; the Joint Committee on Taxation, and its excellent summary of the Restructuring and Reform Act; the National Commission on Restructuring the Internal Revenue Service, and its 1997 report, "A Vision for a New IRS." These were only a few of the many resources we came to rely on. We also appreciate the countless employees and taxpayers who kept our fax machine busy both night and day.

Finally, we wish to express our gratitude to Richard Barber, our enthusiastic agent who championed this project from beginning to end, and to Morgan Entrekin, Amy Hundley, and Brendan Cahill who caught the vision at Atlantic Monthly Press. Each was instrumental in helping us take a huge subject and presenting it in an understandable and engaging way.

Introduction

"More tax is collected by fear and intimidation than by the law. People are afraid of the IRS."

David Patnoe
Enrolled agent and former
IRS revenue officer

Bruce Barron died in the prime of his life. On a hot night in August 1996, he pulled his Mercury Grand Marquis station wagon into the garage of a Cape Cod summer house that he and his wife shared with family. Resolved that he could fight no longer, Bruce closed the garage door, left the engine running, and waited for his life to end. Two hours away, at their home in East Derry, New Hampshire, his wife, Shirley, slept restlessly, waiting for him to return from his law office in Salem. Their 16-year-old daughter, Carrie, had invited friends for a sleep-over. Bruce was scheduled to take the girls on a road trip the following morning to visit college campuses in Vermont.

Shirley and Carrie were accustomed to Bruce's hard schedule, his late nights and weekends spent at the office. He was a lawyer in a small town, working only blocks from the home where he grew up, the street where his father, grandfather, and great-grandfather had lived. Everyone knew Bruce Barron, and many came to him with their legal problems. Some could pay; others could not. It didn't matter. According to Shirley, he turned no one away. So nothing seemed out of the ordinary when Bruce told his wife and daughter that he had to return to work after the three of them had spent the evening at a birthday party for his 74-year-old father.

At 10:00 P.M., Bruce called to hear his wife's voice one last time. He told her to go to sleep. Standing almost six and a half feet tall, with brown hair and a confident face, Bruce had learned that with broad shoulders come responsibility. His parents were aging—he visited them daily, taking care of chores around their home—and he was the guardian and protector of his wife and daughter. On that final call, he told Shirley that everything was going to be okay. His mood was up, just as it had been at the party earlier that evening. Shirley knew he was under pressure, but it didn't show, and after growing up together, attending high school, and sharing 23 years of marriage, she believed she could read him better than anyone.

"That night he was as jovial as always," Shirley recalled, as we spoke about those fateful final hours. "He was lighthearted—a natural-born clown who loved to have fun." At the party, and even on the telephone, "he sounded happy."

Shirley went to bed, but awakened at 5:00 A.M. Bruce had not returned. She called his office, but there was no answer. She tried his cellular telephone, then his pager. Still nothing. Thinking that he might have fallen asleep in his office, she drove to Salem. His car was not in the parking lot. The office was locked. "I had absolutely no idea where he could have gone," she remembered. "I was troubled. He had promised to take Carrie and her friends to Vermont. We had talked about it that evening, and he had never stayed out like this before. Still, it didn't enter my mind that things would end this way."

Shirley returned home and waited. Around 10:00 A.M. she received a call from Cape Cod. Bruce's mother and sister, planning to spend a few days at the beach, had arrived at the summer house that morning. The house smelled of carbon monoxide. They entered the garage and discovered his body slumped over in his car. "You can't imagine what it's like to get that telephone call," Shirley told me. "I'm incapable of describing how it feels. We had absolutely no idea why."

The mystery was solved when Bruce's secretary opened the office later that day. A note he had left on his desk made it clear that he had resigned himself to believing there was no other way out of a conundrum he had been placed in by the Internal Revenue Service. "The IRS and PB&T [Pelham Bank and Trust] are bigger than me," the note began. "One sits, does nothing, and watches you die. One needs to clear its books. . . . Killing myself is much harder than I thought it would be. Carrie will need everyone's love. I wish I could stay and see her continue to grow. There is no good solution. I'm sorry for hurting everyone by doing this. I hope there is enough insurance money."

Bruce Barron's problems had begun when a recycling company in which he had invested heavily was forced to close its doors in 1986. The family's certified public accountant reflected the loss on the couple's joint tax return that year. Bruce, however, did not lose heart. He redirected his efforts into building his law practice. Tragedy struck the family again in 1990, when a malfunctioning telephone answering machine caught fire, and the Barrons' home burned to the ground. The family lost everything. "We didn't have a penny," Shirley said. "Our home was gone. We had to buy a car from Bruce's parents." Yet once again he was resilient, trying a few cases for pay, working others *pro bono*.

Then, in 1992, the IRS showed up with questions concerning the '86 tax return. Bruce and his CPA went in for an audit that ended with the agency denying $80,000 of the losses the accountant had listed six years earlier. "Bruce had lost hundreds of thousands on the plant," his wife explained. "The New Hampshire economy was down. His legal practice wasn't generating much money. Still, he didn't burden me with concerns. Bruce figured he could take care of the problem."

That was until the IRS told him about penalties and interest.

Because six years had passed since the return had been filed, the disallowance of Bruce's $80,000 business loss had turned into an assessment well over $200,000. "It was impossible for us to pay," Shirley told me. "One helpful agency employee told us we were eligible for the offer-in-compromise program." An offer-in-compromise takes place when a tax assessment is beyond the taxpayer's means. The agency allows the offer to substitute a smaller amount for the full assessment and erase the liability. This was the answer Bruce was looking for. He thanked the officer and worked cooperatively with his CPA and the agency to make an offer of $30,000.

Enter the IRS collection revenue officer, a woman, who according to Shirley did not want to bring closure to the case. "She began to play with us," Shirley recalled. "She did not want to work toward resolution like the first officer. She just wanted to go through the motions." According to Shirley, the collector rejected the Barrons' offer without explanation. "Our accountant asked why," Shirley said. "But she insisted she didn't have to give a reason. The answer was just, 'No.'" It was discovered later that the revenue officer believed the offer was only

$2,600 too light. "Had she told us, we would have agreed to the difference immediately," Shirley said, explaining that instead of communicating, the woman began to levy bank accounts, giving the IRS control over money in the family's checking and savings accounts. She placed liens against the Barrons' property, notifying business associates, banks, lenders, clients, and others that the agency had claims against the family's property to satisfy tax debts. And she garnished Shirley's salary, forcing Shirley's employer to withhold a portion of her salary and pay it over to the agency. Each of these methods—levies, liens, and garnishments—is an enforcement tool that, according to the Internal Revenue Manual, is not to be used while a good faith effort is being made to settle a case through an offer-in-compromise.

The Barrons appeared to be making such an effort, but that didn't seem to matter. The revenue officer even seized $300 from 13-year-old Carrie Barron's savings account. According to Shirley, the collector went from courthouse to courthouse, talking to Bruce's clients and to other attorneys, demanding that any money due him be sent to her. "Here was this lawyer in a very small town," Shirley explained. "The only thing he has is his reputation. And here was a government employee—someone who was supposed to be a servant—going around, trying to destroy him." Bruce told Shirley that the woman had openly admitted that "she was going to put him out of business."

The Barrons appealed her rejection of their offer-in-compromise. While the appeal was in process, the collector allegedly violated internal guidelines once again by seizing Shirley's Individual Retirement Account. "She was out of control," Shirley said, holding back her anger. "She was a real rogue officer. Impossible to deal with. We pleaded with her not to garnish my wages. I'm the librarian in Londonderry—a public employee. We even offered her more money than what she was going to garnish to spare the embarrassment, but she wanted to embarrass us. She even called and harassed Bruce's elderly mother."

In September 1995, the Barrons' appeal was heard; their offer-in-compromise was accepted. The revenue officer was transferred to another state and things looked to be getting better for the family. They began to make plans for the future. Carrie's college. Family vacation. Bruce's law practice. Their nightmare with the IRS appeared to be over.

Then came the bureaucracy.

"We asked how to proceed with the payment, but nothing happened," Shirley told me, her voice reflecting the soft, polite whisper of a librarian. "For the next eleven months we were consistently told that they would send paperwork and a bill. But it never came. When we contacted them they would either say, 'We have too many cases we're working on. We don't have time to get that to you.' Or they wouldn't return our phone calls."

Collection activity had stopped. Bruce Barron continued his efforts to bring the matter to a close. "At one point he was told that the person who was working on our case had more important cases to work on," Shirley said. Bruce's urgency was justified by the fact that liens against the family's property were still filed at Pelham Bank and Trust, a small financial institution that was being sold to a larger and more aggressive bank in Massachusetts. Without clearing up the liens, the new bank would foreclose on the Barrons' home and property.

"Bruce kept telling the loan officers that it was being cleared up," Shirley said. "But the IRS never moved."

With the liens still attached, the new bank would not accept the Barrons' mortgages, and during the first week of August 1996, the foreclosure notice arrived. "Bruce didn't even tell me," Shirley explained. Her face is gentle, with sensitive eyes and a kind, tenderly turned mouth. "It must be terrible for a man who is the provider to come to feel that he can no longer provide." Bruce was tired. Worn down. Pushed past the breaking point. "The revenue officer would tell him that if you get me this, this, and this, I won't levy your account," Shirley said. "But by the time he'd drive from her office in Nashua back to Salem, he'd discover that she would have already taken money out of our account." Now, because the IRS would not send the paperwork, the bank was taking his family's home. According to Shirley, "Bruce believed there was no way out." Perhaps with the life insurance money, he reasoned, his wife and daughter would be able to put things back together.

Even that was not to happen.

Following Bruce's death, the family attorney called the IRS. "We want the damn bill so Shirley can pay it and get on with her life," he told the Collections Division, explaining the tragedy that had taken place. The IRS employee expressed condolences and then flatly added that "according to the manual, when a taxpayer dies the offer is automatically rejected." Eleven months after the Barrons' offer-in-compromise had been accepted, and despite the agency's own apparent negligence in processing the paperwork, the agreement was being withdrawn. Why? "Because the widow now had money."

The Barrons' file was transferred back to collections and a new agent went after the insurance policy. "He came to my home at eight o'clock one morning," Shirley remembered. "He put a badge in my face, told me who he was, and said I had better cooperate with the IRS. He refused to acknowledge power of attorney. He was tall and imposing. I told him I couldn't believe he was standing in front of me when the IRS had killed my husband. He didn't say anything, as I proceeded to tell him how wonderful Bruce was. He said, 'I have a subpoena here, do you want to read it.' My power of attorney was only a few blocks away from where his office was located and yet here he was at my door. It was a deliberate attempt to scare the life out of me. And it worked."

The new collections officer proceeded to levy the insurance money. The agency placed another lien against the home and sent a notice to the town clerk in Londonderry telling her that with penalties and interest still mounting on the original assessment, Shirley Barron now owed the agency $350,000. "I wrote letters to everyone," Shirley said. "The regional problem resolution officer did not respond. Everyone kept moving my case. It went from Portsmouth to Boston to Manchester. Nobody wanted to handle it. I wrote a letter to President Clinton. I wrote a letter to Hillary. I wrote a letter to my senators. Only Senator Judd Gregg listened."

As if the liens and levies weren't enough, a few days before Christmas—four months after her husband's death—a letter from the Internal Revenue Service arrived at the family home. It was addressed to Bruce. It threatened that if the agency didn't hear from him in ten days it was going to garnish his wages and levy his bank accounts. Shirley called immediately. "I asked, 'How do you send a letter to that effect? My husband's dead. You killed him, and you won't stop the harassment." A Service employee looked up Bruce's Social Security number on the computer and informed Shirley that, yes, her husband was in fact deceased. Then, two weeks later—on January 2, 1997—she received another notice stating that since the IRS had not heard from Bruce, the agency was going to begin levying all his bank accounts. Merry Christmas, Shirley thought. "By that point our case had become a joke. But I can't describe the pain."

No federal agency touches the lives of more Americans than the Internal Revenue Service. None strikes as much fear into the hearts of honest taxpayers. The threat of an audit, pronounced by the awesome power of the IRS, looms over the head of every individual who files a return. With an army of over 100,000 employees, and a budget exceeding $7 billion, the Internal Revenue Service has more manpower than all other federal law enforcement agencies combined.

During the time the Barrons were going through their ordeal, two thousand Americans were waking up each morning to find liens placed against their homes and other personal property. Another nine thousand were having their assets levied. Seizures of private property, which had increased 400 percent since 1980, were rocking the lives of families everywhere, and over 300,000 households a day were receiving requests for more information, and notices of audits. Many innocent taxpayers, denied due process and living lives on the edge of financial ruin, were forced and even bullied into paying more taxes than they owed, and the perpetrators of this abuse were being promoted, given cash awards, and allowed to carry on within a federal agency that is shrouded in more secrecy than the CIA.

As Chairman of the Senate Finance Committee, one of only two congressional panels authorized to conduct thorough oversight of the Internal Revenue Service, I made the decision in 1996 to use my authority to launch a full-blooded investigation into the agency's policies, practices, and culture. My objective was to be fair and open-minded, to listen to the IRS' defenders and detractors, to explore the need for reform, and to begin a process of restructuring that would strike the necessary, but long-lost, balance between service and enforcement.

At the time of my decision, I was unaware of its historical significance.

Only two members of Congress possess authority under Section 6103 of the Internal Revenue Code to conduct a top-to-bottom investigation of the agency—the Chairman of the

Senate Finance Committee and the Chairman of the House
Ways and Means Committee. Upon my appointment in 1995,
I discovered to my dismay and disappointment that Section
6103 authority had never been used by the Senate to investigate the agency, nor had either full committee ever held oversight hearings. In other words, throughout its history, the IRS
had largely been able to escape from complete, consistent, and
constructive congressional examination.

This changed the week of September 21, 1997.

After a year-long investigation led by Eric Thorson (a
former Assistant Secretary of the Air Force and Chief Investigator on the Senate Permanent Subcommittee on Investigations), our committee began the first in a series of hearings to
audit the Internal Revenue Service from its frontline employees to the Office of the Commissioner. We looked at every division of the agency, checked into its daily operations, its dark
secrets and well-hidden past. We studied its culture, mores, and
the unspoken rules that govern the conduct of its agents and
officers. For the first time ever, we used the authority necessary to request that the Internal Revenue Service hand over its
files concerning taxpayers who complained of unfair and even
outrageously abusive treatment.

What we discovered was as startling as it was disconcerting.

As NBC's lead news story reported on September 23, our
hearings were disclosing "nightmarish scenarios" that ran right
to the core of the problems affecting the agency. We were in-
troducing Americans to a new lexicon of frightening terms that
described tactics used by revenue agents and collection officers who, as we discovered, could become brutal in their battle
with the taxpayer: "browsing," "blue sky assessments," the
"whipsaw technique," "chase and scare."

What we uncovered was an agency in crisis, caused by a
breakdown in management, a lack of accountability of IRS

employees for their actions—both against taxpayers and internally against each other—and a tax code so confusing that even the foremost tax experts are left angry, bewildered, and prone to mistakes.

We discovered that this lack of accountability not only facilitated the abuse of power and denial of due process for taxpayers, but it demoralized employees. The problems we found manifest themselves in an unworkable bureaucracy, the inability of the IRS to address and resolve taxpayer problems within a reasonable amount of time, a despairing breakdown in the administration of the laws now on the books, and in many cases a complete lack of fairness and concern for the welfare of the taxpayer and frontline agency employees.

Directing a handful of investigators and professional staff, and working in coordination with the General Accounting Office, Eric Thorson began an investigation that, while still ongoing, has already become the most extensive oversight effort in the history of the Internal Revenue Service. The investigation has led to the most comprehensive agency restructuring and reform effort ever—dozens of legislative proposals, many of which have been embraced, others that have not. Tearing down the walls of partisan politics, the investigation went to the core of the troubled agency, verifying and disclosing abuses that were more egregious than anything we had anticipated. In the process, it brought Republicans and Democrats together to work on solutions that, in the end, received near-unanimous support.

When we initiated our undertaking in late 1996, many within the IRS and even on Capitol Hill were quick to discourage and even undermine our efforts. They cautioned us against catastrophic consequences. From within the agency came dire warnings of taxpayer revolt, violence against employees, and disillusionment with government in general. There was a purpose for secrecy inside the Service, we were told, a need for isolation. The revenue was being collected. Leave us alone!

Their voices reminded me of a stanza from W. H. Auden's Pulitzer–winning *The Age of Anxiety:*

> We would rather be ruined than changed
> We would rather die in our dread
> Than climb the cross of the moment
> And let our illusions die.

I disagreed. It is in our common interest to gain the knowledge and make the reforms that will not only serve us today but will prepare America for the future. When it comes to government, change is always difficult, and often perilous and uncertain. As Woodrow Wilson admonished, it is the surest way to make enemies. But change is necessary, and to be of consequence it must be complete and founded upon truth and a clear understanding of what must be done. While it might be easier to take smaller steps—as Congress had done with the Taxpayer Bill of Rights (1989) and the Taxpayer Bill of Rights II (1996)—incremental change is often insufficient for necessary and lasting reform. And the failure to make permanent improvements in a system as relevant to Americans as the IRS results in unavoidable sacrifices as taxpayers, in their daily lives, discover painful evidence of IRS' shortcomings. This, in turn, leads to skepticism, an attitude of abandonment, and eroding confidence in national leaders.

Early in our investigation we discovered two valuable insights that increased my resolve to probe deep into the heart of the IRS. First, our efforts, rather than engendering anger and hostility among ordinary citizens, appeared instead to defuse frustration. Letters of gratitude poured into my office, as did faxes and phone calls. People felt that Washington was listening, that government was working the way it should. There was an immediate feeling of optimism; with consistent over-sight, something could be done to correct the behavior of an agency that for too long had been allowed to play judge, jury, and executioner in the lives of taxpayers. There was a feeling of hope in the country. The IRS—or as one reporter had called it, "the biggest bully on the block"—had, by the end of our first three days of hearings, apologized and admitted that change was necessary.

The second insight we gained in the initial phase of the investigation was of equal importance, not only because it helped us proceed in a constructive and engaging way, but because it allowed us to share a valuable truth with the taxpayer: the vast majority of IRS employees are good men and women. When we speak of abuses and shortcomings, we do not mean to indict honest and hardworking employees, or even the Ser-vice itself. Rather, we offer a candid assessment of consequences that can befall innocent families when any organization has near-absolute authority, and when even just a few of the individuals within that organization wield such authority without being accountable or even cautious concerning its use. We speak of structural deficiencies, overbearing bureaucracies, conflicting regulations and priorities—many caused by Congress—and antiquated information systems.

Each of these deficiencies proved catastrophic in the life of Shirley Barron and her family. It is of little consequence that the agency has now admitted to a violation of procedures in the process of collecting against an honest mistake made by the family's CPA. Where were the checks and balances that should have protected the Barrons in the first place? Where were the managers who should have been watching their employees? Where was the Taxpayer Advocate and the appeals officers? What compelled the revenue agent to proceed with liens, lev-ies, and seizures in violation of agency regulations? How was it that Shirley Barron, still reeling from the loss of her husband, had to open not one but two threatening letters addressed to him months after he had died and the agency had knowledge of his death?

It might even be said that given the structural deficiencies that are beyond the control of most IRS employees, the men and women of the agency have done a remarkably good job in overseeing the highest voluntary tax compliance rate in the world. The problem is that the unchecked power given to the Internal Revenue Service, and the culture of isolation that protects it against interference and oversight, succeeds in providing cover for a handful of malicious or overzealous employees as they engage in renegade agendas. And these individuals are allowed to carry on by managers who are under extreme pressure to "keep the numbers up"—managers inclined to look the other way and even to respond with cash awards and promotions, as long as the work is getting done. Not only are many of these managers inadequately trained themselves, but they are also out of touch with the ongoing actions of the people they are supposed to manage.

This state of affairs cannot stand.

I am heartened by the changes the IRS has made in reaction to the initial phase of our investigation and subsequent hearings. I am encouraged by Congress's very real attempt at structural reform. The Internal Revenue Service Restructuring and Reform Act of 1998, which was signed into law on July 22, 1998, is a good bill, one that brings greater balance to the relationship between the IRS and the taxpayer—offering tools that taxpayers can use to ensure fairness for themselves and tools the Service can use to better police and protect the integrity of its operations.

These represent a beginning. But they are only that. As Charles Rossotti, the agency's new commissioner, told me, changing the culture of the IRS will require more than legislation. It will take a decade of training and oversight, vigilance by Congress, and zero tolerance for abuse and mismanagement within the Service. I admire Commissioner Rossotti and believe he can do great things to correct the Service from inside. There has already been marked improvement in self-inspection and taxpayer services, not to mention a bold new mission statement that places emphasis on service and fair treatment to the taxpayer. But much more needs to be done. After decades of unchecked growth, increasing authority to interfere in the lives of taxpayers, and the ability to systematically shroud its activities, the IRS is a monolith, standing like a testament to Lord Acton's adage concerning absolute power.

Such an organization cannot be expected to change quickly and unilaterally, despite the will of the taxpayer, Congress, and how well the restructuring laws might be written. Certainly the legislation we passed will provide the foundation upon which the Internal Revenue Service must govern its behavior, now and in the future. But as we discovered in our investigation, many of the abuses committed by Service personnel were in violation of laws that were already on the books. And many of those who perpetrated the abuses did so despite the disapproval of their peers. On many occasions, their actions were reported to mid- and upper-level managers; yet abuse continued.

This book springs from an insight that kept recurring throughout our investigation, hearings, and legislative process: for real and lasting change to take place within an organization like the Internal Revenue Service, we need to go beyond laws and regulations to make certain that a paradigm shift occurs at the very heart of the agency. This must be a mighty change of heart—one that destroys old icons and perverse incentives, rewrites misguided priorities, and reforms destructive attitudes.

It must be serious change taken seriously—embraced by agency employees, from the GS-2 clerk who opens tax return envelopes to the Office of the Commissioner—and it must be understood by the taxpayer. For such change to take effect will require the direct participation of Congress, leaders who are not afraid to joust with a giant; it will require a well-informed public, one that knows its rights and refuses to be led blindly into submission; and it will require the continued willingness of men and women within the organization who, remarkable in their valor, stand for justice and customer service.

It is my hope that this book provides the information necessary for these conditions to coalesce: a brief history of how the IRS' culture went terribly wrong as the agency grew in scope and power; an outline of the events that led to the most aggressive congressional investigation in the agency's history; profiles of the courageous individuals—taxpayers, government officials, and agency employees—who came forward to cooperate; the ever-consolidating will of Congress leading up to the passage of the Restructuring and Reform Act of 1998; the protections included in that legislation; the rights and responsibilities of taxpayers under the new law; and the need for taxpayers, Congress, and well-intentioned agency employees to remain ever-watchful.

I also hope this books serves as a reminder that Congress must never again neglect its duty for oversight. A world of internal reforms and legislative mandates will not alter the course of the Internal Revenue Service, unless the Senate and the House of Representatives use their full authority to remain aggressive in the responsibility they have to consistently monitor the agency, and let its commissioner, executives, managers, and employees know in unmistakable terms that in the hierarchy of priorities service comes first and abuse will not be tolerated.

At this writing, the Internal Revenue Service is still in trouble. For too many decades, power and insufficient accountability have corrupted. For more than forty years, congressional emphasis has been on giving the IRS whatever authority and enforcement tools were considered necessary to collect the last dollar. And these tools have been incorporated without a counter-balancing policy: intolerance of their misuse. Any organization that has such authority must possess a culture marked by the highest standards of ethics and integrity. Anything short of this is dangerous.

As the Barrons' case demonstrates, the abuse or mistreatment of even one taxpayer is unconscionable. The consequences can be devastating. Ultimately, Congress must assume responsibility, as it alone is given power, under the Constitution, to lay and collect taxes. If Congress wants to delegate authority to execute that commission to the Department of Treasury and the Internal Revenue Service, it may, but then it must have an aggressive system in place to see that such awesome authority is exercised appropriately. I intend to follow through to see that the process we began in 1997 becomes a continuing practice. There is no alternative. Congress must not be satisfied until Americans feel that they are going to get fair and civil treatment by the Internal Revenue Service.

Let our investigation, our hearings, our legislation, and this book offer the first layer of a broad foundation—a foundation that will provide the support for what must be done, one that cements solid proposals in place and offers the structure needed to build a balanced and abuse-intolerant agency, but, what is more important, a foundation that remains viable and strong well into the future. We see from past efforts at reform that after a few years even the best intentions are most often forgotten, new rules are swept aside, vigilance wanes, and old forces return from solitary confinement, where they've been biding their time, and once again consolidate their power. Then, before countervailing forces can place them under control, the agency returns to business as usual.

This time things can be different. They must be different.

The climate is right for change. We have seen progress already. Now, with the continued support and determination of Americans, we can not only continue our effort to reform the Internal Revenue Service, we can make sure that Congress never again takes its eye off of the agency and the unimaginable power it has been given.

1

Anatomy of an Investigation

"For far too long the IRS, with its incredible power,
has operated with anonymity and total immunity
from oversight."
—Senator William V. Roth, Jr.

If my career is remembered for any one thing it will more
than likely be my penchant for tax cuts. This is how I would
want it. The most fitting epitaph for my headstone—the one I
would choose, as Jefferson chose the accomplishments etched
in marble above his grave—would be simple: "Here lies Bill
Roth . . . the taxpayer's best friend."

For more than thirty years on Capitol Hill I have fought
against overbearing taxation and runaway federal spending,
believing, like Cicero, that there are those who, "greedy for
renown and glory, steal from one group the very money that
they lavish on another." In order to be liberal to some, they
harm others, and "fall into the same injustice as if they had converted someone else's possessions to their own account."

This is dangerous and counterproductive. Giving too much money and power to government, we're reminded, is like giving whiskey and car keys to teenage boys. Whether the transfer of wealth is done out of genuine altruism, or out of a sincere belief that government has not only the right but the responsibility to balance the fortunes of Americans, or whether it results from the desire of a politician to consolidate power by serving one constituency over another, makes little difference. Either way, excessive taxation harms the very individuals it is meant to help.

And Americans are excessively taxed.

Congress's inability to curb spending has resulted in a condition where taxes have steadily eaten away at family income, and the unchecked growth of government—with burdensome regulations to compound excessive taxation—has diminished economic vitality, cutting away even more of the family's buying power.

The adverse economic consequences associated with overbearing taxation give us reason enough to declare—as 70 percent of Americans do—that taxes are too high, and the complexities of the tax code give us additional reason to demand a change in the status quo, as the vast majority of us are now demanding.

But these reasons do not stand alone.

In his best-selling book, *Values Matter Most*, Ben Wattenberg explains how the real problem with taxes is that they bite not once but several times. "Taxes are not a single-bullet theory of politics," he writes. "Taxes are important, but they are seen by voters in a context of other issues, very much including the social ones, and particularly in the context of *how the tax money is spent*. When government programs are seen to be not only expensive, not only wasteful, but also *harmful*, then taxes hit voters several times: once when their dollar leaves their pocket to go to

Washington and once again when it comes back home in a way that hurts."

In other words, not only are taxes too high, not only is the tax code too complex, but Americans are incensed by how their money is being spent.

So the question: How bad can things get?

We have an income tax, something Americans aren't too fond of in the first place. Seventy percent believe it's excessive. It's applied by a code so complex that on April 15 most folks don't know whether they're cheats or martyrs. And then it's too often spent on things they don't want.

Could the equation get any worse?

As a matter of fact, it could.

Add to these valid concerns a tax collection agency where even just a few of the employees resemble the kind of characters vividly described in the old vaudeville routine—"The income tax people are very nice. They're letting me keep my own mother"—and you have a combustible mix crying out for wholesale reform.

To be fair, tax collectors have never been popular. Scripture lumps them in with heathens and sinners. Yet, in society, they have always been necessary. We must "render unto Caesar that which is Caesar's," Christ taught, and he chose Matthew, a tax collector, or publican, as one of his apostles.

Why the unpopularity? Because at its heart, the income tax itself is a dichotomy. While the power to tax is the power to destroy, it is equally true that taxes are what we pay for a civilized society. Given this, it stands to reason that the feelings Americans have toward the people assigned to collect the taxes—to extract from their wallets the money they earned—would be as ambivalent as they are volatile.

And yet value cannot be measured by popularity. The fact that tax collectors and the agency responsible for gathering the revenue are less than esteemed in the realm of public opinion means little in the context of their critical role in the function of government, and in government's ability to meet the legitimate needs and demands of the people. The truth is, the same can be said of Congress, the President, or any other institution, organization, or individual put in place to create, maintain, and enforce conditions that balance the rights and responsibilities of citizens in any social order. They are seldom popular, but most often necessary.

It is my belief that the Internal Revenue Service and the vast majority of its employees are doing an extremely good job under very difficult conditions. When I made the decision in early 1996 to use the authority of the Senate Finance Committee to conduct oversight of the IRS, I made it clear to our chief investigator that above all else our investigation would be fair. This didn't mean that we couldn't be the taxpayer's advocate. I find that just like H. L. Mencken, "in any dispute between a citizen and the government, it is my instinct to side with the citizen." It is also my firm belief that the interests of the individual—the taxpayer—come before the interests of Washington. This conviction is borne by the fact that anything serving the taxpayer's best interest also serves the government, as the latter derives its strength and very survival from the former. Balanced against my philosophy that the taxpayer comes first, however, is my belief that outside of those who serve in our armed services and law enforcement agencies no other federal employee has a job as difficult, and certainly no job as thankless, as those who work for the IRS.

One unforgettable moment that occurred early in our investigation was a conversation I had with one of the agency's group managers, a man visibly shaken by the revelations that were being disclosed to our investigators. "You have no idea how difficult it is for us to perform our jobs," he told me. "You have no idea how demoralizing it can be, how we hesitate to tell people we meet what we do for a living. When I'm at a party with doctors and lawyers—educated people who should know better—I hear their caustic remarks. I'm offended by their critical asides. Anymore, I won't even tell people what I do. The most I'll say is that I work for the Treasury Department."

That night, following our conversation, I tried to imagine dedicating my professional life to a job that could have such a dispiriting influence. I realized that the vast majority of IRS employees, like this man, are concerned about the welfare of the taxpayers whom they serve. However, I wondered how the self-conscious malaise and pessimism he described affected his family, his colleagues, and the taxpayers. How pervasive were these feelings? One former IRS commissioner actually admitted similar emotions, stating that he, too, would not tell people where he worked.

What would it be like to face each morning with the prospect of confronting such a job? What would the consequences be in the lives of others? Our attitudes, choices, and actions cannot be separated. More than anything, they influence the way we work, how we feel about ourselves and those around us. In the end, they determine the outcome of our lives. Yet, here was a man with a very important job who was uncomfortable—even unable—to tell others what he did for a living.

At the time this conversation took place, I was receiving almost daily reports concerning what our investigation was uncovering. Story after story described horrible abuses by IRS personnel and disturbing trends within the agency's culture. We heard tales of despair, loss, and abandonment from taxpayers who had run up against irresponsible, uninformed, or even malicious employees—taxpayers who had been stymied by incomprehensible regulations and bureaucracies, or who had found their once-quiet lives hopelessly entangled in a system weighted heavily against them. I wondered how the negative feelings of this fine group manager reflected the feelings of others who worked within the Internal Revenue Service, and how those feelings collectively influenced the clients of the agency: the taxpayers.

What struck me most is that of all those who contacted our investigators—taxpayers, IRS employees, academics, and authors—the group most desirous to report and correct abuses and mismanagement were the employees themselves.

Nobody knows the weaknesses of a family better than its members, those who live each day intimately acquainted with, and influenced by, its shortcomings. Like most employees with whom we talked, this group manager felt a need to share his perspective concerning the troubles that, in his words, "plague the agency." His criticisms were thoughtful, yet gushed out with such force that I found him at times struggling for words that he believed might make his case sound more persuasive.

As he spoke, I was reminded of Razumihin's observation in *Crime and Punishment,* "In wine there is truth, and the truth had all come out." Inebriated with emotion, this manager from the trenches had given me not only insight into the agency, but an understanding of how the culture of the IRS affected him and his colleagues, and how their attitudes influenced their interaction with the taxpayer.

The Decision
My decision to conduct oversight of the Internal Revenue Service was not easy in coming. Since its inception in 1862,* the agency assigned to collect federal taxes has largely avoided se-

---

*In response to the rising costs associated with the Civil War, the Bureau of Revenue was established by Abraham Lincoln to levy the first American tax on

rious examination by Congress. The reasons why are as varied as they are numerous, and some even have a legitimate ring to them. For its part, the IRS insists that investigations into its activities, and public disclosure of those investigations, give heart to tax protesters and could result in violence against its employees. The agency tries to attach a patriotic rationale to its desire to be left alone, maintaining that compliance with tax laws will decline if the veil of secrecy is torn away and light is allowed to illuminate the inner workings of the Service.

Another argument is that mystery and confusion are actually useful to the agency's enforcement efforts. This line of reasoning holds that people are frightened by what they don't know, by what they can't see and understand. Fear leads to submission. Frightened Americans will more readily pay their taxes. Tell us too much and we may actually begin to believe that the IRS is run by mortals who have feelings and are prone to mercy as well as mistakes. This, in turn, may embolden us in our opposition to their tax collecting efforts.

As adamant as I am in my fight against excessive taxation and my belief that government has a responsibility to control spending, I am equally emphatic about the responsibility all

---

income. Until 1862, the Treasury Department raised revenue primarily through tariffs, duties on imports, and excise taxes. The income tax was repealed in 1872, though the bureau and its revenue officers continued to collect excise and regulatory taxes. The income tax reappeared in 1894 as part of the Wilson Tariff Act, but was ruled unconstitutional a year later. The Supreme Court held that the income tax, levied on the wealthiest one percent of Americans, violated Article 1, Section VIII of the Constitution, which states that while Congress has the power "to lay and collect taxes, duties, imposts, and excises," they must "be uniform throughout the United States." The Court ruled the tax was a "direct" tax unequally apportioned. In February 1913, Congress passed the Sixteenth Amendment to permit a "direct" tax. Ratification followed eight months later, and in 1914 a little more than 350,000 Americans—representing only one percent of the population—filed their 1040s. In 1955, following the disclosure of rampant corruption, the bureau changed its name to the Internal Revenue Service.

citizens have to provide for the common defense and general welfare of the United States. There's no excuse for those who refuse to pay their fair share of taxes, and it's contemptible that anyone would seek to harm or harass a government servant charged with the stewardship of collecting revenue—or performing any other duty, for that matter.

Taxation is a responsibility shared by everyone who enjoys the blessings of America. Those who refuse to contribute only place a greater burden on the rest of us as they minimize their ability to function constructively within the law. And this is where change, if it is to be lasting, must take place: within the inspired constitutional framework given us by the Founders.

It did concern me that an investigation of the Internal Revenue Service might send a signal to the 17 percent of Americans who refuse to comply with the law that they are somehow justified in their illegal behavior. For several weeks, I weighed this concern against the responsibility I had as Chairman of the Senate Finance Committee to conduct oversight of the agency. As I contemplated the possible repercussions in this area, I was taken aback by a startling statistic: the 83 percent compliance rate today is the lowest in recent history.

In 1962, when the IRS had only 60,000 employees, a full 97 percent of Americans paid their taxes. Today, even though the agency has roughly 102,000 employees (a 70 percent increase) and our population has grown just over 40 percent, compliance has dropped to where almost two out of ten Americans refuse or fail to pay. In other words, as the size, power, and reach of the agency has increased at a rate far outpacing the growth of our population in general, and as the advent of information technologies has given those employees exponentially more capability to perform their duties, the rate of taxpayer compliance has dropped sharply. This, despite the fact that

Congress has: (1) vastly strengthened the agency's enforcement power; (2) increased its budget every year except two over the last four decades; and (3) never conducted full and consistent oversight.

There are statistical and demographic reasons to explain a portion of the decline in compliance. Current data are more accurate, reflecting taxpaying individuals, families, and businesses that may have been overlooked in 1962, and a larger portion of Americans are taxpayers today as the baby boomers have come of age. However, these reasons are insufficient to warrant such a steep drop. I began to wonder whether the IRS' defense that oversight results in noncompliance was little more than a convenient theory to ward off congressional attention. Until our current oversight efforts began, the most far-reaching congressional investigation into the heart of the agency had taken place in the early 1950s, when Senator John Williams of Delaware and Congressman Cecil King of California exposed widespread misconduct, including bribery, embezzlement, influence peddling, and rampant conflict of interest. Their efforts led to public outcry and sweeping reform, but compliance rates remained high.

Between the King hearings and the beginning of our investigation, Congress had undertaken only a few smaller attempts to look at anecdotal concerns, and even these didn't get too far as senators, representatives, and their committees were limited in authority by Section 6103 of the Internal Revenue Code. Originally intended to safeguard privacy, 6103 prohibits the IRS from disclosing information about taxpayers to anyone other than agency employees who are essential to process returns and conduct audits, oversight, and collections. While protecting taxpayer privacy has long been part of the code, 6103 was dramatically tightened after Watergate, in response to public perception that the IRS had shared information with the White House concerning the names listed on President Nixon's "enemies list."*

In the aftermath of Watergate, Congress railed against the Internal Revenue Service, promising, as Senator Lloyd Bentsen declared, to stop the agency from being used as a "lending library" for the White House. Unfortunately, in strengthening the privacy laws, Congress inadvertently gave the Service a formidable weapon in its ongoing war against congressional oversight. Former Georgia Congressman Douglas Barnard, who attempted to look into alleged abuses in the late '80s and early '90s, complained that "6103 was used as a moat to hide information." Unable to see the IRS' side of reported cases of taxpayer mistreatment, Barnard could not get to the root of actual wrongdoing, which, he said, "typically did not involve taxpayer information at all." The IRS used Section 6103 to cut off the flow of information it perceived to be damaging to the agency or its top-level managers, a practice that continues today.

More recently, William A. Dobrovir, a lawyer for Tax Analysts, the publisher of *Tax Notes,* told *The New York Times* that the agency has long abused the law to "deny the public access to information it rightfully needs." The strident use of 6103, he said, leads to "intransigence" and the lack of appropriate oversight. Senators Charles Grassley and Bob Kerrey, both in-

---

*The word "perception" is used because the truth is that to his credit IRS Commissioner Johnnie Walters refused to act on the "enemies list" sent to him by John Dean. However, at the same time that the Nixon administration was cultivating the list of left-wing organizations it wanted the IRS to audit, inside the agency a top-secret group known as the Special Services Staff (SSS) was amassing a list of its own, thousands of names of assumed protesters and tax evaders. The work done by the SSS and President Nixon's "enemies list" is often confused, but the distinction is important to understand. It was not until after Watergate that the SSS was said to have been abolished.

strumental to the success of the National IRS Restructuring
Commission, explained to the Finance Committee how the
agency used Section 6103 to keep the commission in the dark
on issues that were critically important in their effort to draft
restructuring legislation. "We just do not get a sufficient amount
of information across the board to know what is going on over
there," Senator Kerrey told us. Senator Grassley described how
their efforts were often "derailed" by "a cloak of secrecy more
potent than even the most elaborate secrecy arrangements at
Langley," headquarters of the CIA. The IRS, he explained, even
uses 6103 protection to "mislead Congress."

The evidence simply did not support the agency's argument that sunshine wilts compliance. When Senator Williams
and Congressman King disclosed the crimes rocking the agency
in the '50s, compliance increased. On the other hand, once
Congress strengthened Section 6103, inadvertently giving the
IRS a shield against effective oversight, compliance declined.

With that argument gone, my next concern was one best
expressed the way I heard it from a Montana cowboy when I
was a boy growing up in the Big Sky country. "Never shoot
the horse you're riding." Tax collecting is an essential requirement for any government. It's understandable that Congress,
which has come to depend on the ability of the IRS to raise ever-
increasing revenue for the programs that come out of Washington, would be averse to careful scrutiny. It's understandable that
when it comes to holding the agency accountable for its actions,
any Congress possessing a genuine tax-and-spend mentality
would be more inclined to focus on weaknesses in the areas of
collections and enforcement rather than weaknesses in service
and taxpayer satisfaction.

I was disturbed to discover that in the last quarter century
the vast majority of studies conducted by the General Accounting Office, Congress' investigative agency, focused on short-

comings and inefficiencies in raising revenue rather than on meeting taxpayer needs and correcting abuses. "What seemed to matter most was that the taxes were getting collected," explained my good friend Senator Daniel Patrick Moynihan, my predecessor as chairman of the Finance Committee and its current ranking member. "We have never paid attention either to the organization or to the job we were giving it."

For the last thirty years, whether or not the IRS was succeeding in its mission was based almost exclusively on its annual revenue figures: had the agency raised sufficiently more money in the current year than it had the year before? If it had, then Congress appeared to be satisfied. Congratulations and agency bonuses abounded. If it hadn't, then Capitol Hill would throw still more money at the agency and pass stiffer enforcement laws, strengthening its ability to—as I recently heard one revenue officer cheerfully tell his colleagues—"bring the taxpayer to his knees."

When the occasional congressional investigation *was* launched, outrage and formal inquiry focused more on specific cases and relied almost exclusively on anecdotal evidence. As far as I could determine, there had been no thorough oversight, no examination of systemic abuses and cultural pathologies. This concerned me.

The years I had served as Chairman of the Senate Governmental Affairs Committee, as well as Chairman of the Permanent Subcommittee on Investigations, taught me that constant oversight is necessary for all government agencies. Power not only corrupts but can become menacing when it's allowed to consolidate its strength in darkness. I had overseen many investigations into the Department of Defense, particularly its procurement practices. Now, as Chairman of the Finance Committee, possessing the authority necessary for thorough oversight of the IRS, there didn't seem to be any question concerning my responsibility.

My only other hesitation in launching the investigation was one that I really should not have taken seriously. Yet I wouldn't be honest if I didn't say that it lodged itself in the back of my mind, often finding its way into dinner table conversations with my wife, Jane. This centered on the fates of the few senators and congressmen in history who had dared look at the agency. One of the countless political cartoons that appeared during the course of our first series of hearings crystallized this concern. It showed an IRS bureaucrat sitting at the witness table, facing our Finance Committee panel, his eyebrows peaked, his mouth stern. "The IRS is not mean and vindictive, Senator," he responds into the microphone, "and you'll be sorry you asked that!"

In the mid-1920s, James Couzens, U.S. senator from Michigan, was one of the first legislators in this century to investigate charges of graft within the Bureau of Internal Revenue. As author David Burnham describes in his seminal investigative book about the agency, *A Law Unto Itself: Power, Politics, and the IRS,* Couzens believed that "widespread corruption and secret deal making in the federal tax agency were destroying its ability to collect taxes." His concern led to the creation of a select committee to look into allegations that had come to his attention, and he was appointed its chairman.

A year later—with his investigation in full swing—the tenacious Senator Couzens was summoned off the Senate floor by Internal Revenue Commissioner David Blair and one of Blair's assistants. In a crowd of legislators, lobbyists, and reporters, the commissioner had the audacity to hand Senator Couzens a letter demanding that he immediately pay $11 million in back taxes. It was a direct act of retaliation. The truth, which emerged only after a long, bitter, and costly fight, was that the Bureau actually owed the senator a million-dollar refund. It was an attempt, according to Burnham, "to bully the senator into abandoning his investigation of the agency and the corrupt deals it was cutting."

In the late '60s, Senator Edward Long of Missouri held hearings to look at specific allegations of abuse, particularly an accusation that the agency had been used by the Kennedy administration to carry out a political agenda. In retaliation to Long's efforts, individuals within the IRS leaked false information to *Life* magazine linking the senator to Teamsters president Jimmy Hoffa. Unable to contain the damaging rumors, Senator Long lost his seat the following year.

In 1972, Senator Joe Montoya of New Mexico announced to the media that he would be looking into charges that many of his constituents were making against the agency. Before he even had the chance to begin his investigation, the IRS launched a counteroffensive with an investigation of its own. Within days, the Service leaked information concerning the senator's tax status to the *Washington Post*. Like Senator Long, Joe Montoya went down to defeat after an opponent used the illegally disclosed information to campaign against him.

The list goes on, and as I listened to each story, I wondered whether this was another reason why the agency had been largely left alone by Congress. No one is beyond the influence of the IRS. Presidents and vice presidents have been audited. Senators and congressmen have been threatened and intimidated. The agency has even retaliated against its own commissioners and employees. "This is one area that makes the IRS distinct from every other agency in our government," Shelley Davis, the IRS' first and only historian, told me. "It has the power not only to reach out and touch us, but to grab us around the throat, and nobody is beyond its reach." According to Davis, anyone who has studied the history of the agency in the twentieth century realizes there's far more to lose on a personal basis than there is to gain by trying to make the Internal Revenue Service better for the American people. "Even the media tend to ignore the IRS," she told me. "Either they're frightened, or they don't believe taxpayers are all that interested. I think they're frightened."

Honest John Williams

One senator, however, *was* able to break through the redoubt of secrecy and retaliation that kept others at bay. It was his courage and dedication to public integrity that led to the King Hearings and the most thorough reorganization of the agency so far in this century. His name was John Williams, a tenacious defender of the truth whom I was honored to call my mentor and friend.

On December 19, 1947, less than a year after taking office, the man Delawareans came to call Honest John went to the floor of the Senate with a startling accusation: an Internal Revenue employee in Wilmington had been embezzling money from tax payments. Approximately 2,000 transactions from Delaware taxpayers had been manipulated in an effort to cover up stolen or misappropriated tax payments, including payments the senator and his wife had posted to their own account.

None then listening would have guessed that Senator Williams' report of illegalities in the agency's Delaware operation would eventually rattle the walls of the Oval Office. In the beginning, National Headquarters lobbied furiously against the senator, Bureau Commissioner George Schoeneman insisting that pursing an investigation "would serve the interests neither of the government nor the taxpayers of Delaware." It was an isolated incident, Schoeneman claimed. The senator's information led to the embezzler's suspension and admission of guilt. Now, according to the bureau, there was no need to dig any deeper. But Williams disagreed. He wanted to know why disciplinary action had not been taken against other employees and managers who had known of the illegal activities but had refused to respond. He angrily pointed out the bureau's disturbing habit of trying to ignore and then hide mistakes rather than resolve them—a habit that remains stubbornly to this day.

National Headquarters' attempt to stonewall was too little, too late. Williams had gained the confidence of Internal Revenue employees everywhere. At last, they believed, someone was listening. Letters documenting similar abuses poured in, as did reports of official cover-ups taking place in offices throughout America. At first, the senator had no intention of expanding his investigation beyond Delaware, but in March 1949, a bureau employee shared the sordid account of an organized tax-fixing scheme, implicating managers at the highest levels of government. Judiciously, Williams pondered his course of action. He gathered evidence for more than a year. Then, in June 1950, he went to the floor again. This time the bureau would not be able to dismiss the charges as being isolated or unusual occurrences.

While Commissioner Schoeneman protested that it takes more than idle rumors and the unverified mumblings of disgruntled former employees to produce indictments, John's intuition and evidence were dead on. There was a cancer in the Bureau of Internal Revenue, and before the scandal was over, hundreds of careers ended in disgrace, including lengthy prison terms for bureau collectors in Boston, San Francisco, New York, and St. Louis. Schoeneman himself resigned. His predecessor, Joseph Nunan, was convicted of tax evasion.

I've heard it said that civilizations can only revive when there comes into being a number of individuals with a new tone of mind, a mind independent of the one prevalent among the crowd and in opposition to it, a tone of mind that will gradually win influence over the collective one, and in the end determine its character. The same can be said of governments and, for that matter, any organization. John Williams had an independent mind. In the many years that I had the opportunity to work with him, he made it clear to me that the most important trust we have as the people's elected representatives is to know what must be done, to be able to articulate it, to love our country, and to be incorruptible.

John was incorruptible, and I must say that I pondered his example as I made my decision to move forward with our investigation. Just as a concerned clerk in the Wilmington Collector's Office had reported lawless behavior to Senator Williams, I received several letters from agency employees following my appointment as Chairman of the Senate Finance Committee in September of 1995.

Responsible for 97 percent of all federal income and 70 percent of the outlays, the Finance Committee spends the majority of its time on tax-related issues, international trade, Social Security, Medicare, and welfare policy. An important part of its stewardship is to oversee the Internal Revenue Service. For this reason, the Chairman of the Committee is given the authority to examine all taxpayer-related records necessary to monitor the agency. Unfortunately, it had never been used. John Williams, James Couzens, and Edward Long never had the authority. In the House of Representatives, Cecil King went as far as he could, but still ran into obstacles, and when Doug Barnard sought 6103 authority from Dan Rostenkowski for an investigation in 1988, the powerful chairman of the House Ways and Means Committee refused to cooperate. Another senator who attempted to investigate the agency without 6103 authority lamented that "we probably know more about the KGB in the Soviet Union than we do about our own Internal Revenue Service."

There are only a few times in life when the fates line up so concisely that they dictate our course of action. The more I considered my responsibility, the more I realized that all arguments against proceeding were vacuous against the powerful forces demanding that I move forward: the thousands of letters I had received from constituents and agency employees, over the years, sharing everything from minor complaints to outrageous horror stories; the commitment I made at the beginning of my career to be an advocate of the taxpayer; my experiences on the Governmental Affairs Committee and the Permanent Subcommittee on Investigations, teaching me not only that bureaucracy requires oversight, but also helping me understand that to be effective you must first be constructive, prudent, tempered, and fair; the legacy left to me by John Williams; and finally, the authority necessary to move beyond the otherwise impenetrable veil hiding the IRS.

The Investigation Begins

Lack of consistent congressional oversight concerning the Internal Revenue Service the last half century had a profound and unexpected influence on our initiative. First, it made our decision to launch an investigation newsworthy. Second, seeing Congress as their last hope and believing that the Finance Committee was willing to undertake a sincere examination of an agency that for too long had engendered feelings of helplessness, frustration, and anger, countless Americans rushed forward with their harrowing stories. After the *Wall Street Journal* ran a page-one notice announcing that the Senate Finance Committee was going to look into "recurring complaints of harassment and intimidation by the IRS," our office was inundated with letters, faxes, and telephone calls. Several people drove to Washington, D.C., from hundreds of miles away to hand-deliver their messages. Each case was compelling; many were decades old.

Maryland State Senator John J. Hafer wrote to remind me of how the IRS had destroyed his father's life and harassed his family in the 1960s. From California, I received a letter that began: "My loving husband left me last November, the day after Thanksgiving, when I received a notice of intent to levy from the IRS. It was, given the history of this particular tax assessment, an understandable response. My husband concluded, probably rightly, that my tax problems were too severe to allow us to remain husband and wife." From Arkansas came a letter written by a small businessman whose company was seized after his bank failed to pay the employment and withholding taxes he had been depositing for payment. A single mother from Connecticut wrote to tell me how she was shackled with excessive penalties and interest because of a mistake she had made after following the advice of an IRS service representative. From Texas came the humble petition from a 62-year-old man who had served in the military for 22 years. For more than a decade, and despite repeated correspondence and reassurances from the IRS stating he owed no taxes, the agency continued to file liens against his property, his paychecks, and his military retirement.

And this was only the beginning.

From Muskogee, Oklahoma, I received a troubling letter from a small businessman who after being audited seven years in a row, and discovering that for every year in question the IRS actually owed him refunds for overpayment, was informed that the agency wanted to audit him yet again. Allowing him only eight days to prepare for an examination that would require dozens of ledgers, journals, and documents, the taxpayer was told that the IRS was concerned about records related to the contract labor he used to conduct his business.

Despite consistent rulings in the seven previous audits that the businessman had always abided by the law in his treatment of independent contractors, a new examiner determined that the laborers should be treated as employees. He dismissed the businessman with a vague statement about being notified later concerning the assessment.

When the bill finally arrived after what the taxpayer described as "the longest four months of my life," it totaled $18,959.02. "I was told that this figure was calculated with about $6,000 in penalties dropped, which would only be done if I immediately agreed to sign the assessment."

Frightened, intimidated, and unable to afford a CPA or tax attorney to represent him, the businessman agreed to pay $1,500 down and $700 a month, an agreement he kept until, once again, the IRS changed its mind. "I received four different sets of instructions on ways to make these payments," he wrote. "I believe this was done to make my payments more difficult on me than they already were. I was notified after [making the first four payments] that they would not accept any more, that I had to pay up in full, because there was a new supervisor who did not like the credit business."

According to his letter, paying such a debt in full was impossible. He wrote that in an honest effort to remain faithful to the original agreement, he continued to send the IRS $700 a month. While the agency accepted the payments, the taxpayer explained that his attempts to be faithful to the original installment agreement angered the supervisor. A few months later, the case was sent to collections. A lien was filed. "They got one of their better collecting agents after me," he continued. "She put a levy on my bank account for $17,474.95." In response, the bank surrendered everything he had: $56.09.

Undeterred, the revenue officer showed up at the tax-payer's home with a summons, demanding that he meet her in her office with all of his records or risk going to jail. "It didn't take me long to convince her that I was broke and, thanks to the IRS, had absolutely no credit anywhere. All I had was my Social Security check in the amount of $750 a month."

What was the result of this nightmare? The revenue officer demanded that the taxpayer sign a new installment agreement, this time in the amount of $19,123.88. Where would he get the money? The IRS put him on an installment plan. How much would his payments be? Seven hundred dollars a month!

"I hope," he wrote, "that this new payment plan doesn't make the new supervisor any madder."

As I read the letter, I felt the frustration of this hardworking taxpayer, a small businessman whose future had been mortgaged by a seemingly arbitrary decision made by one auditor concerning the status of the laborers the taxpayer had used in the conduct of his business. I had heard on many occasions that the agency had long before declared war on contract labor, pushing to have as many taxpayers as possible listed as employees rather than contractors, thereby making tax collection easier. Here was a tragic example of that strategy.

I grew angry as I read about what had been done to this man and his family. "The IRS has audited, levied, summoned, liened, and threatened me with jail for the last 15 years," he wrote. "They have destroyed my credit, harassed me, and severely damaged my health because of an increased blood pressure problem. They have greatly weakened my belief in the American free enterprise system. My health and my credit will never recover, no matter what happens from this point on. I only hope that there is a way to get some form of justice for myself and others in my situation."

Letter upon letter contained similar stories of taxpayers—often trying to work with the IRS without professional assistance—coming up against bureaucrats whose absolute authority in pronouncing judgment was not mitigated by the possibility that they might be wrong, misinformed, having a bad day, or even willfully and wantonly abusive. The sheer volume of complaints we were receiving confirmed to me that shortcomings within the IRS were more than anecdotal, and they were occurring not in one or two recreant districts, but throughout America.

I realized the authority that came with the chairmanship of the Finance Committee also came with responsibility. I wanted to know if these stories had merit. Without 6103, it would be impossible. With the authority it was paramount that I do something. Case by case, I began to make my requests for the agency's documents.

The other indication I had that the troubles reported by the taxpayers were more than just random stories, that they reflected deficiencies in IRS management and culture, was the number of telephone calls our investigation received from employees within the agency, and the troubling experiences they related.

I found it interesting that while the taxpayers—generally desperate in the position they had been placed in—were careful in their correspondence to document their cases and share information about themselves rather freely, the IRS agents and officers who contacted us—especially in the beginning—were hesitant to put anything down on paper. Some would not even share their names with our investigators.

This hesitancy, I came to realize, resulted from several factors.

First, there was a "wait and see" attitude. Many had heard of well-intentioned investigations that were never carried out, or, when they were, fell far short of mandating change. As a consequence, there was a genuine and even warranted suspicion about congressional intervention.

Second, there was concern about retaliation. Without exception, every employee expressed fear of reprisals. Many even made it known in the course of their conversation that they were calling from a pay telephone, fearing that their offices and home phones might be tapped or that their calls would be traced.

Third, agency employees were worried about "disclosure," a word repeated like a mantra within the IRS, and possessing more definitions than the *Oxford English Dictionary*. One veteran employee, who did eventually dare put her concerns on paper, began her letter explaining that when she joined the Service and went through early orientation meetings the trainers made it clear to her class that "if we discussed procedures or the workplace with anyone outside the Service that Internal Security would view it as a disclosure violation as serious as revealing taxpayer information and that we would be prosecuted.

"They were dead serious," she wrote. "They told us how much they hate publicity and told us that under no circumstances were we ever to create any publicity surrounding ourselves as IRS employees or the Service as an entity. They said that the last thing they needed was publicity to bring them under scrutiny of Congress or the Executive Branch. They made it plain that if we focused attention on them in any way other than those approved by the Disclosure Office we would be the ones to suffer."

In the beginning, few letters arrived from employees, but the phone calls were overwhelming. Nights, weekends, and holidays, the calls came in, each validating the complaints filed by the taxpayers, building a case that here was an agency, perhaps the most powerful agency in America, in dire need of reform and oversight.

One revenue agent crystallized the concerns: "I have been horrified at the situations I have seen," she wrote. "Some IRS personnel seem to have forgotten we are there to enforce the law, not break the law. If we destroy someone's life it defeats our purpose. They will never again be taxpayers. You cannot just run over someone with hope that they won't know the law and their rights. I cannot begin to imagine the amounts of taxpayer dollars that have been wasted because of derogatory behavior by the IRS. I really don't want my tax dollars going for this. Someone in charge needs to get the message across that the most efficient way to collect tax is not by treating people like dogs."

By the evidence we were collecting, it was clear: problems existed in every area of the Internal Revenue Service—Examinations, Collections, Inspections, Criminal Investigations, and Management.

2

When Things Are Worse than You Expect

"I can personally attest to the use of egregious tactics by IRS revenue agents which are encouraged by members of the IRS management. These tactics—which appear nowhere in the IRS manual—are used to extract unfairly assessed taxes from taxpayers, literally ruining families, lives, and businesses—all unnecessarily and sometimes illegally."

Jennifer Long
IRS Revenue Agent
September 24, 1997

Beth Barlow is 88 years old, widowed, legally blind, confined to a wheelchair, and now—thanks to questionable tactics used by IRS auditors—she has lost her home.

On paper, Mrs. Barlow's tragedy began in tax year 1981, the first year the IRS claims she and her husband, Bill, failed to file their 1040. A photograph in their local paper shows a be-spectacled round-faced woman bearing a striking resemblance to Aunt Bee, the sweet matron of *Mayberry, R.F.D.* Her husband, dressed in his Sunday best, stands at her side, a shy smile, large ears, and tall forehead. "Barlows Epitomize Modern-day Pioneers," the headline reads, and the story documents a pull-yourself-up-by-the-bootstraps kind of life that began with the couple working in the beet fields of Utah. From there it was labor in a copper mine, then construction, and finally the American Dream—ownership of a plumbing, heating, and wiring firm in Pocatello, Idaho

Bill served as a leader in his church, as a member of the city council, and was nominated "Man of the Year" by the National Contractors Association. By all accounts, they were fierce patriots—faith in God, country, and the Bill of Rights. Ironically, this patriotism, friends and supporters of the Barlows will tell you, is what in fact led to their run-in with the Internal Revenue Service.

It started in 1975, when a representative of the Occupational Safety and Health Administration showed up unannounced on the doorstep of Bill Barlow's small business. Though the 4,900-square-foot fabricating shop had a spotless safety record, OSHA demanded entry to conduct an inspection. "They just wanted to come in here fishing and nit-picking to find something wrong," Barlow told reporters, and he wouldn't stand for it. Starting a battle that would take him all the way to the Supreme Court, the businessman refused to let the inspector enter his establishment, maintaining that an unwarranted search violated his constitutional rights under the Fourth Amendment.

In 1977, the Supreme Court agreed, and like a scene out of *Meet John Doe,* Bill Barlow was hailed as the champion of the little guy, indomitable against an increasingly overbearing bureaucracy. "Technically, Bill Barlow was the winner," touted one editorial. "But, really, we all won, for it was our freedom he sought to protect. . . . It was an entire approach to government regulation that lost, an approach which held that individual rights are of no consequence when government seeks to achieve a democratically agreed to public goal."

The editorial concluded by stating that as OSHA and "other federal agencies come to grips with *Barlow*, we expect a general reaffirmation that government regulatory agencies must be concerned with the rights of those they seek to regulate. Pursuit of a public good does not warrant intrusion on constitutionally protected rights. This is the real message of *Barlow*."

Evidently, it was a message heard loud and clear not only by the business community and civil libertarians, but by the Internal Revenue Service as well, another federal agency whose conduct would be affected by the decision handed down by the Court. According to an affidavit signed by a former IRS senior agent, a man with over 20 years in the Service, the Barlow case was like a burr under the saddle of the agency. When, during a meeting with the staff of the agency's Pocatello office, the subject of the Barlow case came up, the district director for Idaho who was visiting from Boise reported that the director of the state's office of OSHA had been "crying on my shoulder every month at our Federal Executive luncheon meeting."

The district director indicated that he believed the Barlow case was a clear challenge to government authority, and that it carried adverse consequences for the IRS. According to the affidavit, the director "finished his discussion of the Barlow/ OSHA matter by slamming his fist on the table and stating,

'This family has no respect for government authority and [expletive deleted] we're going to teach these people a lesson.'" The director indicated that he was going to brand Bill Barlow a protest leader on agency records, and that the family "would be dealt with accordingly."

Illegal Tax Protesters?

Shortly thereafter, Bill Barlow's name did turn up on the IRS' list of "Illegal Tax Protesters," where it remained until his death in 1993. Members of his family were also designated as protesters by the three-digit code—*148*—placed by the agency on the IRS' master file next to the names of all those suspected of participating in tax evasion schemes or fomenting rebellion. And while the IRS certainly disagrees with the sworn affidavit by one of its former employees concerning how and why Bill Barlow and his wife received the dubious designation, there is universal understanding about the way it can immediately turn the life of a taxpayer upside down. As one senior IRS official told our investigators, "Once you're labeled an 'Illegal Tax Protester,' God help you."

According to the Internal Revenue Manual, "Illegal Tax Protesters" are placed under increased scrutiny by the agency. "Priority consideration" is assigned to their tax returns, and greater burden is placed on the auditor to get them in line "as expeditiously as possible to achieve compliance with the tax laws." The designation of "Illegal Tax Protester" all but guarantees that subsequent returns will be automatically screened by a special team of agents and auditors working out of the agency's national service centers. According to one employee interviewed by our staff, in practice the designation "Illegal Tax Protester" results in the "loss of the taxpayer's rights," including the opportunity to appeal.

Another auditor with the courage to testify before our committee explained that having a taxpayer designated as a protester can be a boon to the agency. She described how IRS management actually encourages examiners to incite anger in taxpayers in an effort to get them branded as protesters. "When a taxpayer comes to the IRS to negotiate a tax payment issue in good faith, they are subjected to provocative behavior on the part of the IRS in order to 'set them off,'" she explained. "Management will then use the taxpayer's response as proof that they are, in fact, a reactionary, saying, 'See, this person's a troublemaker, a real hothead.' Based on this pretext, the IRS can then justify taking severe action contrary to the law in order to pursue the collection. The immediate and direct consequence of these actions is the deprivation of the taxpayer's lawful rights." This, of course, makes the agency's job that much easier as it proceeds with assessments and collections.

So how does one become an "Illegal Tax Protester"? What sort of heinous crime must one commit? How many public rallies must one lead on the steps of IRS headquarters? How strident must one be in refusing to pay one's taxes? How belligerent toward the agency and its employees? How uncontrollable and dangerous?

Unfortunately, it doesn't take much. "IRS Management automatically assumes that everyone is a criminal," says Jennifer Long, a veteran revenue agent, and herself the daughter of lifelong employees of the Service. According to the IRS' former historian Shelley Davis, "anyone who offers even legitimate criticism of the tax collector" is labeled a "tax protester." Another witness before our committee—a field collection officer with over 35 years of experience in the Internal Revenue Service—testified how one person was designated a protester for simply writing a letter to the editor.

I was troubled not only by how easily one can be tagged an "Illegal Tax Protester," but by the fact that the designation—as well as that of "Potentially Dangerous Taxpayer" (designated by the code *168*)—can be applied without the taxpayer's knowledge and without the right to appeal. Indeed, there is no due process or grievance procedure available for a person branded a protester or dangerous taxpayer. According to one veteran revenue agent, "The most hardened criminal would have more rights. Any Internal Revenue Service employee can convince their manager that a taxpayer is dangerous and should be marked as such. I have seen taxpayers receive the title for doing nothing more than being emotional or upset."

Taxpayers are deemed illegal protesters or potentially dangerous for joining protest organizations or other political groups that might be considered out of the mainstream. Some have received the designation for doing little more than attending a meeting with friends and being spotted by IRS employees who are sent to secretly monitor these kinds of groups. According to those with whom I spoke, it is a completely discretionary and arbitrary process.

"Imagine this scenario," one tax attorney told me. "A revenue officer comes to your home to collect taxes. You say, 'Get out of my house, or I'll throw you out.' He goes back to his manager. He's angry. You've given him an unproductive afternoon. What's he going to do? He'll classify you a potentially dangerous taxpayer. After all, you threatened him. You may have said the same thing to the guy who came over trying to sell magazine subscriptions. It may be your personality to be brusque. But the guy selling the subscriptions doesn't have the power to destroy you. The tax collector does. He labels you a protester or potentially dangerous, and as far as the IRS is concerned, you're ruined. There is no procedure for removing the codes from your master file. You can try to petition the district director and prove a negative—that you're not as bad as the collector says you are—but it's not going to work.

"From then on, when you deal with the revenue officer, he's coming with an armed escort. You have no more credibility with the agency. IRS employees will see *148* or *168* and they won't cooperate. You will never be given the benefit of the doubt. Tax protesters get no breaks. Even years of good behavior won't get you off the list. Most often, you won't even know you're classified."

While there can be no excusing anyone who breaks the law, and there must be strong measures in place to protect IRS employees from the few who might cause them harm, there is no excuse for destroying a taxpayer's reputation and stripping him of his civil rights.

Designating people as "Illegal Tax Protesters" simply because they exercised their right of free speech, or because they express frustration during an audit, is unconscionable. Not only does it place the taxpayer in an untenable position that serves to legitimize anger against the agency, but it weakens, if not destroys, the legitimate designation of a tax protester. Words and labels have consequences. We cannot be indifferent to their use without paying a price in the end. If an individual is designated an "Illegal Tax Protester" for writing a letter to the editor, what do we call the man or woman who truly seeks to undermine the system? How do we treat the two differently? If we do not, then that is the very definition of injustice.

Were the Barlows, aging and infirm, really "Illegal Tax Protesters?" The IRS said yes, regardless of how they had been branded such, and the designation did, indeed, result in painful consequences to them and their family.

Retired and living on savings and a meager pension, Bill and Beth did not have enough income in any one year to require that they file tax returns between 1982 and 1993. Both were over the age of 65. Beth was blind, fighting diabetes, and amassing large medical bills. According to their CPA, neither had been employed nor had they received any wages or other income since 1980. Independent to the end, they had even refused to accept Social Security.

Then came the auditors.

Blue Skies, Box Cars' and Water

Believing the Barlows were evading their taxes by hiding income, the examiners used a tool they call a "substitute for return." Exactly what its name implies, a substitute for return is a return filed by the IRS for a taxpayer who, the agency believes, should have filed an income tax return but did not. On a substitute for return, the agency tends to inflate the taxpayer's liability by excluding exemptions, exclusions, dependents, deductions, and credits. The IRS will then use the substitute for return to get an assessment and proceed to collection. In the Barlows' case, taking Bureau of Labor Statistics data, revenue agents assigned income to each of the years in question, in this case tax years 1982 through 1993, and filed returns for the Barlows. They averaged the income earned by folks living in the Pocatello, Idaho area, making the assumption that the average income earned in that region accurately reflected the income the Barlows must have earned but had not reported.

That the IRS has the authority to use Bureau of Labor Statistics data to assign additional income to a taxpayer at its discretion, without any basis in fact, is, as one former agency division chief told me, "frightening and absolutely unacceptable." This 31-year veteran of the Internal Revenue Service claimed, however, that using BLS data to inflate tax returns was becoming more common. Not only was BLS data used to file substitutes for return, but the agency actually used it to add tax liability to returns that had already been filed.

In one case detailed to our committee, the IRS actually used Bureau of Labor Statistics data to assess a tax *twice* for the same 1040. The tactic involved accepting Schedule C income (earned business income), but disallowing all the related business expenses. When the taxpayer requested the case to be reopened, the IRS reversed itself and the deductions were allowed. But then to offset the deductions the IRS reopened the income issue, which was a violation of law, and assessed additional taxes based on Bureau of Labor Statistics information to boost the taxpayer's income. According to the witness, the taxpayer was then "informed he had no appeal rights to contest the additional resulting tax."

As the Barlows painfully discovered, for an "Illegal Tax Protester" to appeal a substitute for return prepared by an auditor using BLS statistics is next to impossible. Not only will the IRS maintain that the taxpayer has lost his rights as a protester, but the agency places him into the indefensible position of trying to prove a negative. How can you produce a check never received, or a bank deposit never made? Unfortunately, we learned that IRS auditors not only had the authority, but that many were actually taught to place taxpayers in that exact conundrum. They did it to the Barlows, filing a $60,000 assessment against them, and—when the retired couple couldn't pay—sending it on to collections.

What happened to the Barlows is what employees of the Internal Revenue Service call a blue sky or box car assessment, an assessment that has no basis in fact or in tax law, but which is levied in an effort to intentionally hurt the taxpayer or simply to raise the individual statistics of an IRS employee. Our investigation and subsequent hearings taught us a great deal about statistics and quotas, the use of which was supposed to have been outlawed in the late 1980s. It became apparent that while the IRS reserves the right to be unyielding in its enforcement of the law, some within the agency have no problem bending it when bending serves their interests.

We discovered that despite laws against the practice, goals and quotas still drive the performance of auditors, groups, divisions, and even districts. They serve as measurements of an agent's effectiveness, a manager's worth, and a district's success. Tangible, and lending themselves to consistent analysis, goals and quotas can be reflected in statistical benchmarks that are easy to understand and easily implemented for motivational purposes and personnel evaluations.

But they are dangerous.

Imagine how a traffic cop would behave if his job security depended on a ticket quota, with the mark being raised each month to encourage him to issue more than he had the month before. Consider the influence quotas would have on a judge if he received bonuses and even promotions based on the number of guilty verdicts he decreed from the bench.

We discovered that within the IRS the establishment of quotas and goals was still pervasive, and far too many taxpayers were falling victim to statistics. We saw case after case where managers looked the other way or condoned unethical and even illegal practices used by examiners chasing numbers rather than fair assessments. The practice of inflating a taxpayer's liability beyond what is just and fair is so well known that employees of the Internal Revenue Service refer to it euphemistically as "adding water." It is a practice that results not in reprimands but in awards and career advancement.

Another story powerfully illustrates how tax auditors and revenue agents go to great lengths to "add water" to their assessments, including ignoring evidence and records. This story concerned a restaurant operator whose entire business income was determined to be taxable despite the fact that the businessman had provided receipts and records indicating otherwise. Rather than adjusting the income to reflect the costs of doing business—expenses incurred to buy food, equipment, and necessary materials—the agent ignored the evidence and treated the gross income as adjusted income in a deliberate effort to inflate the liability. According to the restaurateur's representative, "The Service knew that the man was selling prepared meals. The Service knew that he had to buy food, but allowed no deduction for food, despite the fact that they had the records."

Guilty Until Proven Innocent

"Water" can be added to assessments in many ways, and not just through the use of BLS (Bureau of Labor Statistics) data and by revenue agents who refuse to acknowledge the obvious. In fact, we found that agency regulations can be read to encourage inflated assessments, and tools are provided so Service employees can make them. Just like Columbo and Joe Friday learned to follow their "hunches," agents and auditors are instructed to go beyond objective examination of tangible evidence to incorporate their powers of discernment. They're taught, as more than one employee explained, to examine the taxpayer as well as the return, to listen to their "inner feelings" and look for hints that might suggest the taxpayer is better off than his stated income indicates.

"The standard of living generally is an accurate barometer of a taxpayer's income," the Internal Revenue Manual explains. "*Since living costs are assumed to represent taxable income unless shown otherwise* [again the problem of proving a negative], in-depth examinations should include a computation of cost of living."

Is your lifestyle beyond your means? Be careful. Are you a value shopper? You better save your sales slips. Do Mom and Dad lavish you and the grandchildren with beautiful gifts, help with education costs, or pass on family heirlooms? You better ask them to include invoices and receipts. With the IRS, an extravagant or seemingly insupportable lifestyle could cost you dearly. According to instructions in the Internal Revenue Manual, "The agent should observe the neighborhood, house, furnishings, automobiles, etc. The quality of clothing worn by taxpayer and family, as well as their shopping places and methods, should be noted. Their travel, entertainment and recreation styles are good barometers. The schools attended by the children afford another guide."

Do you see the problem? Not only are you now being audited on your income, but on your neighbors' income as well. And your home—the home you were able to purchase only with the help of your parents—is being used to assign extra income to your liability, as are the Tommy Hilfiger shirts you bought your kids at the outlet mall and the trip you took to Disney World courtesy of the $2,500 credit limit on your new MasterCard. And why shouldn't the examiner consider these things? The higher the assessment, the brighter his or her future. That's why, according to the manual, "The observant agent" will be eager to "draw a very good picture of a taxpayer's income by evaluating the taxpayer's standard of living." Does the examiner have to verify that these items are actually an indication of your income? Of course not. "Some items will be estimations and not subject to verification," the manual offers.

On the other hand, if you don't want those items included as indicators of income, you had better be able to verify that they are not. The burden of proof is on you. The problem, of course, is that estimations are exactly that—a guess. And this begs the question: If the IRS is going to make a mistake, to whose benefit do you think it will be made?

We discovered that the answer has two parts. First, it is in the best interest of the agent and up-line managers to arrive at the highest tax liability possible. This helps them pad their statistics, meet their quotas, and achieve individual and group goals. One agent who spoke with me admitted that he did not know of an audit, conducted by him or any other examiner, that was not inflated. Second, employees of the IRS maintain that from the moment they join the agency, they are trained to incorporate a mentality that puts the taxpayer in the position of adversary. Some are even taught to see taxpayers as liars and cheaters, and this attitude, as one veteran employee admitted to me, is then fostered by management throughout the system. "The result," he said, is that the attitude "forces revenue agents to treat all taxpayers alike. They are not looking at a taxpayer's individual financial situation. Every revenue agent I deal with thinks that every taxpayer is hiding a small fortune. And it's ridiculous. It doesn't take a brain surgeon to see when a taxpayer is in financial hardship."

The confrontational relationship the IRS engenders against taxpayers, and the underlying assumption of guilt, was caught in the admonition of one commissioner who encouraged Service employees to use the discretion given them by the code's complex rules and regulations to find taxpayers who have "larceny in the heart," and it was confirmed by Shelley Davis, who reported that the "us against them mentality" is so common, even among senior-level administrators, that she "witnessed and experienced [it] firsthand for over seven years working at the IRS headquarters."

The adversarial relationship that the IRS brings to its interaction with the taxpayer exacerbates feelings of helplessness. Not only is the examiner driven by quotas and able to assign extra income to the taxpayer's liability. Not only are taxpayers forced to defend their innocence by proving a negative. But as they are forced into such a position, they quickly come to realize that they have fewer rights than a criminal.

Even a casual comparison between our criminal justice system and the process of examination and collection used by the Internal Revenue Service makes it painfully clear that hardened criminals have rights that innocent taxpayers can only dream of. Take for example the well-known Miranda rights that have been with us since 1967. You cannot watch a cop show without hearing them: "You have the right to remain silent. . . ." Most of us can recite them in our sleep. Yet, when a person is suspected of being a tax cheat, and even when the IRS gives him or her a summons to appear for an intensive question-and-answer period with an agent, they will not read anything like a Miranda warning. The taxpayer will be compelled to engage in a thorough examination process, disclosing potentially incriminating information, which will then be neatly bound up and given to the Criminal Investigation Division (CID) should the case be referred. It is only after the case has been turned over to the CID that there is any duty to mention rights, yet the Criminal Investigation Division can use *all* of the information gathered during examination.

Beyond giving would-be suspects "the right to remain silent," the foundation of our criminal justice system is that an individual is innocent until proven guilty, and that the burden of proof rests with the government. There is no room in a criminal trial for discernment, speculation, subjectivity, and estimations. Evidence must be tangible. The defendant has the opportunity to plea bargain, and if unable to afford an attorney the court will appoint a public defender. From investigation, to arrest, to indictment, and throughout the trial a criminal case must be advanced with great care taken to follow the most stringent procedures, and there are checks and balances along the way.

Journalist James Bovard points out that taxpayers have fewer protections than welfare recipients. Anyone receiving public assistance, for example, is "entitled to a fair hearing before the government can terminate their benefits; on the other hand, the IRS can impose a levy on an individual's bank account with no evidence of his wrongdoing [and no hearing at all]. In a welfare termination hearing, the welfare recipient is presumed deserving of continued government aid unless the government shows convincing evidence that the person should not be on the dole; in the U.S. Tax Court, a worker is generally presumed guilty of receiving any unreported income the IRS alleges he received."

According to Bovard, "Federal court decisions have often bent over backward to stress that citizens' rights are nearly null and void in conflicts with the IRS." Against a water-laden assessment, taxpayers have the burden to prove that they did not earn the extra income, despite the fact that the assessment is based on an examiner's estimations and subjective judgment. Attempts to appeal the assessment will be not only time-consuming but prohibitively expensive.

Evidently, the cost was too high for the Barlows. Friends of the family say Bill died trying to fight the harassment. The IRS sees it differently. The agency simply maintains that the Barlows were unable to present evidence to change the assessments its auditors made using Bureau of Labor Statistics data. Indeed, proving a negative is impossible. After Bill's death, and a battle that lasted more than two decades, the agency seized the family home and scheduled it for public auction.

Quotas, Goals, Statistics, and Damn Lies

> "The primary drive for the examination function is dollars recommended for assessment."
>
> Bruce A. Strauss
> Former division chief and
> 31-year veteran of the IRS

One of the more compelling moments that occurred in our first series of hearings came when I approached the subject of goals, quotas, and statistics with Acting Commissioner Michael Dolan. The Internal Revenue Service's highest ranking civil servant, Dolan had found himself in the uncomfortable position of playing the apologist for the agency more than once, and it was clear from the beginning of our oversight effort that his instincts were to defend the status quo and to hope that our investigation would end with as little damage or change to business-as-usual as possible.

The use of quotas and goals by America's tax collecting agency has led not only to unjust treatment for countless Americans, but anger and at times retaliation against its collectors. From the 1794 Whiskey Rebellion that found George Washington, then a sitting president, leading an armed militia into Pennsylvania to end the violence against "excisemen" who had been sent to the frontier to enforce a 25 percent levy on liquor, to the federal revenuers who went up against moonshiners in nineteenth-century Appalachia, to this very day, there has been a legitimate need to protect the safety of public servants sent to collect the taxes. On the other hand, the same history is replete with examples of how excisemen and revenuers abused their authority for personal gain and used excessive force—even deadly force—to frighten citizens into compliance. Whether it manifests itself in the bonuses and promotions we discovered that IRS employees were receiving for meeting statistical demands or as the commissions earned by early assessors and collectors, the quota system inevitably leads to abuse of taxpayers and corruption within the agency, so much so that, according to Shelley Davis, "only three years after the establishment of the Bureau of Internal Revenue, a dismayed Congress appointed a Special Revenue Commission charged with 'reforming' the scandal-ridden bureau."

History does, indeed, repeat itself, and here we were once again looking at similar charges concerning the use of goals and quotas—examining their awful consequences in the lives of honest taxpayers—yet we were being told by Dolan in his testimony that goals and quotas were not being used.

I asked him to explain a report our investigator had uncovered in the agency's San Francisco district office. According to the report, revenue agents and tax auditors were being judged by the amount of dollars they were assessing per hour. Overall, the report indicated that the office was in need of general improvement. In other words, higher assessments had to be levied on the returns audited. The goal was for revenue agents to bring in $1,000 an hour and for tax auditors to raise $1,012 an hour.

"I do not care how you dress that up," I said, showing Dolan the report. "That is setting a goal. If you give that to the employees, they are going to understand that they are obligated to meet those goals. There is no way, in my judgment, that you can explain away this kind of chart."

Looking uncomfortable, Dolan suggested that the report was simply a way for the San Francisco district to view the work in its inventory and to see how hours are being applied. Unfortunately, and the acting commissioner's protests to the contrary, every other agent, officer, and employee read the San Francisco report as I believe it was intended to be read.

Courageous Jennifer Long, the only current IRS agent who testified without hiding her identity, made it clear. She said the document simply "tells you what the dollar per hour is—the average dollar per hour on 1040 cases, or individual tax cases. It tells you what the average dollar per hour is on 1120 corporate cases. It is from the revenue agent's side, then it tells also what the tax examiner's 1040 individual dollar per hour is. It tells what the goal is and what the average collections were. The goal [for a revenue agent] is to collect $1,000 per hour."

"So is it fair to say," I asked, "that this is setting a goal as to how much revenue agents should assess?"

"We talk about this in our district," she answered, with what I found to be a startling admission. "And I certainly try to beat the goal. To me, that is the way to be considered a good performer or doing a good job."

Her remarks brought silence to the hearing room. Several of my colleagues shook their heads in disbelief. Here was a dedicated employee of the Internal Revenue Service fearlessly admitting that employees who wanted a future in the agency realized that in order to be promoted they not only needed to meet but beat assessment goals set for them by management. "Taxpayers' rights are being violated," Long confirmed. "Auditors and agents are afraid to turn in a case without an adjustment. It's terrifying. You feel pressure to exceed the goal or quota." As she spoke, I wondered what would be paramount in the mind of a tax examiner operating under this kind of pressure, the rights and welfare of the taxpayer or the examiner's future with the IRS.

Lawrence Lilly, a tax attorney and 28-year employee of the Internal Revenue Service, described how quotas, goals, and statistics undermine service and fairness. "What you're saying is, spend less time with each taxpayer, produce more dollars. That means that you have to look quicker at what the taxpayer has to offer. You may not have time to consider it fully." Along with Jennifer Long and every other agency employee who testified before our committee, Lilly admitted that an emphasis on quotas and statistics for employee evaluations puts pressure on IRS employees to artificially inflate taxpayer income and to focus on taxpayers whose cases will not take much time. One witness answered that if you look at how much money per hour is generated by revenue agents, then the first casualty you have in an environment with a quota system is taxpayer rights. "You should not," he concluded, "have an environment where you evaluate people based on how much money they rake in per hour."

But fair and courteous treatment of the taxpayer is only one of the casualties of a system driven by quotas. Perhaps even more egregious than rushing through an audit or targeting those most easily audited to boost an examiner's personal statistics is the practice of deliberately "adding water" to a taxpayer's income in order to assess more dollars per hour as the auditor.

There was universal agreement among the examiners and practitioners we interviewed and indisputable evidence in the cases we had examined that the emphasis on goals, quotas, and statistics for employee evaluations leads directly to artificially inflated assessments. This is done not only to provide the auditor with a higher dollar-per-hour average, but also to frighten the taxpayer and provide the IRS with leverage to negotiate a quick settlement.

According to one certified public accountant with over three decades of service as a revenue agent, a field audit group manager, and an audit branch chief, "The IRS Examination Division knowingly inflates taxpayers' proposed additional taxes when they perform an audit." Why? Because "all revenue agents know that they get a better evaluation if they have amassed a

high tax dollar per hour of audit time based on their cases."
He emphatically explained that this means that for "every hour
a revenue agent spends on a taxpayer's audit, the more additional tax dollars that agent must propose as a result of that
audit. It does not matter if the court or the Office of Appeals
determines later that the taxpayer owes no additional tax (which
is most often the case); what counts is how much tax was proposed when the case leaves the Examination Division."

The former employee, who now works representing taxpayers, said that on many occasions managers in the Examination Division do not want to determine the correct tax, and
they encourage their auditors to "seriously inflate" their numbers, without any basis in fact, to look more efficient statistically or to achieve a higher settlement in the end. Statistics
confirm his allegation. When $13.6 billion in assessments made
by auditors and examiners were contested by taxpayers, either
through administrative appeals or in tax court, it was found that
the taxpayers actually owed only $4.3 billion, less than a third
of the liability claimed by the agency's examination personnel.*

Using the case of a client as an example, the former Service employee related how attempts to appeal the inflated assessment were rebuffed, first by the group manager in charge,
and then by the branch chief. "It was clear that justice was not
going to be realized at the Examination Division level," he
explained. "I was actually told by the group manager overseeing the audit that my client's proposed tax bill contained a lot
of water. The group manager [perhaps as a threat, or in an effort to force a compromise] candidly informed me that she had
previously denied another taxpayer's request to go to appeals
because she believed the taxpayer wanted to see how much of
the proposed additional tax, or water, he could get reduced.

---

*Transactional Records Access Clearinghouse (TRAC), Syracuse University,
for fiscal year 1996 (the last year for which records are available).

The group manager had denied the taxpayer's appeal of what the Examination Division stated he owed, based on nothing more than her mood or whim!"

This practitioner knew better. He forced an appeal, but was disappointed when the Appeals Office, after identifying the auditor's attempt to inflate the assessment, sent the case back to the Examination Division with a list of corrections. Not surprisingly, the Examination Division refused to make the corrections or do any of the work recommended by Appeals, "as it would increase the time on the case and decrease the tax, thereby hurting the audit group's statistics."

Undeterred, the CPA forced the case back to Appeals, and the office finally ruled that the assessed tax, penalties, and interest totaling $850,000 that came out of the Examination Division contained roughly $740,000 in water. Final assessment was a little over $100,000.

"The problem at the IRS rests on the fact that certain employees are not honestly performing their jobs," this veteran employee explained in summary. "And no one is reviewing their performance. Group managers do not conduct competent case reviews. This is based on the simple fact that it is in the best interest of a group manager not to reduce the amount of a proposed tax because the manager's own performance evaluation is based on the strength of his or her group's production figures. The problems are caused by dishonest employees who do not adhere to the IRS' rules and regulations, or who take unfair advantage of taxpayers for their own personal or departmental statistical performance."

How Much Justice Can You Afford?

While this taxpayer's case had a fair ending, the client getting the inflated assessment reduced to its legitimate level on appeal, many cases do not end so favorably, the simple reason being that the average taxpayer is unable to afford the services of a practitioner—a tax attorney, CPA, or enrolled agent—as a guide through the labyrinth of regulations, procedures, and misinformation that comes with most attempts to navigate the agency. For example, had the practitioner in the case above not known how to force the case to an appeal, the group manager might have successfully precluded the process that eventually ruled that the assessment had been grossly inflated.

Even many taxpayers who can afford to hire professional help in the preparation of their returns are unable to pay the practitioner if they are placed into a lengthy audit and appeals process. However, the most outrageous accusation we investigated early on in our effort was that the Internal Revenue Service has a tendency to target lower-income Americans for audit.

According to statistics, from 1988 to 1995, civil audit rates of nonbusiness taxpayers with earned income over $100,000 declined by a factor of four, while the audit rate of taxpayers earning between $25,000 to $50,000 doubled. These statistics were first introduced to us by David Burnham, whose research group, Transactional Records Access Clearinghouse, is perhaps the most thorough resource for raw data related to IRS activities.

During the course of our hearings, Mr. Burnham asked rhetorically: "Why is the IRS auditing fewer and fewer wealthy people and more relatively less affluent?" The major reason, we discovered, is extremely troubling and brings us back to the dangerous consequences of using goals, quotas, and statistics: because they're easy. The fewer resources a taxpayer has to fight with, the more attractive he or she is to an auditor seeking to improve numbers. At the same time, the auditor, group manager, and division chief know that without the ability to hire a professional practitioner whose fees run anywhere from $50 to $500 an hour, the taxpayer will be more likely to accept the assessment, particularly if the IRS—like a car salesman—inflates the calculations and then pretends to lower them as a favor to the taxpayer if the taxpayer will sign an agreement without taking too much time to think about it.

"As of late, we seem to be auditing only poor people," explained revenue agent Jennifer Long. "Currently, in a typical case assigned for audit, there are no assets, no signs of wealth—no evidence that would support a suspicion of higher, unreported income. These individuals are already only one short step away from being on the street."

Another auditor from the Los Angeles District, having read newspaper reports that Acting Commissioner Dolan denied the targeting of lower-income Americans, contacted me personally to share several of the heartrending accounts in which she had personal involvement. "In this district, low income taxpayers *are* targeted," she reported. She went into detail concerning the characteristics her managers looked for when selecting their targets, sending auditors into the barrios because "they are very easy to audit." This is nothing new, she claimed. "The IRS has been pushing the same statistical goals since I hired on in 1991."

Auditors describe how they are forced to go to homes where families live without the basic necessities of life. "These aren't people who are hiding their wealth from us," one observed, explaining that she could not figure out why the cases were being assigned to her. "These people are living just above poverty, and here I am being forced to intrude on their life. They're scared to death, embarrassed that you have come into their apartment—sometimes a single room barely furnished—and challenged their integrity, their honesty. Their children look at you through frightened eyes."

"I used to be called on to audit people that would hire a large accounting firm or a well-known attorney to defend them," Jennifer Long testified. "That is the type of people I would deal with. But I don't see that anymore. I do not know what has happened to those people. It's like the IRS is afraid to audit people who can hire a big-name attorney or a big-name accountant to defend them."

Long believes that this trend discourages many of the agents with whom she works. Others agree with her that this is one of the most unpleasant aspects of an auditor's job. "I can be very tough on someone who is not following the tax law," she explained. "But to go out to somebody who is in their sixties, who has worked very hard all their life and they do not have air-conditioning, they are old . . . to just harass this person, and I am encouraged to harass them, I do not like it. I do not think it is right, I do not think it is ethical. But I am getting an enormous amount of pressure not to bring that case back in without making some kind of an adjustment."

While lower-income taxpayers may be easy marks when it comes to padding statistics, they are certainly not the only targets of unethical revenue agents and their managers. Middle- and even high-income taxpayers have their breaking point, and IRS employees bent on meeting a goal rather than following the law know just how far to push.

One CPA who has represented taxpayers for more than twenty years told me, "The first thing I ask my clients when we get word of an audit or challenge from the agency is, 'How much justice can you afford?'" He detailed how common practice in his profession is to go through two layers of bureaucracy before finding someone versed enough in the tax code to deal competently with complex issues. "It costs my clients a huge amount of money to go through each step," he said. "Managers and auditors know this. They know there will come a time when the client will have to say, 'Enough already, let's give them what they want. I can't afford to go on.'"

An agitating imbalance can exist when a tax practitioner sits across the table from a tax auditor, or even a more experienced revenue agent. Possessing a CPA, a law degree, an MBA, or a masters in taxation, the professional practitioner has trained well beyond college and graduate school to represent clients. To earn the right to practice before the Internal Revenue Service, he or she has been required to gain sufficient experience and pass a lengthy and extremely difficult exam, and as a professional, will be held accountable—even prosecuted or stripped of credentials—for offering bad advice or engaging in unethical behavior. The practitioner is being paid extremely well. Because of this, any meeting that is not productive is a frustrating waste of time, not to mention a considerable amount of money.

In an effort to control the final outcome of a taxpayer's case, the IRS can use this to its advantage. And it often does. Far too often, the tax auditor sitting on the other side of the table lacks the experience and expertise of the professional. To compensate, however, he or she possesses the authority and resources of the United States government. It's been pointed out that the IRS has the free and unlimited use of the biggest and most powerful law firm in the country—the United States Department of Justice—and there are few, if any, negative consequences to either agency or employees when mistakes are made.

On the other hand, each step the practitioner is forced to take on behalf of the taxpayer to move the case from the auditor, to the manager, to the branch chief, to appeals, or tax court makes justice financially prohibitive for many. Agency employees exercising bad judgment, inflating assessments, providing faulty information, or demonstrating a complete lack of knowledge pertaining to the tax code are not held accountable for their actions to the degree the practitioner is held accountable. "IRS employees have few cost considerations," says David Keating, former president of the National Taxpayers Union.

"They often fail to take into account how inconvenient or costly their demands on a taxpayer may be."

Often, it can be their ignorance of the law that proves most costly. "I actually had one examiner yell at me when I questioned the authority she was using to deny what was a legal and proper deduction that my client had taken," a practitioner explained. "But I was appalled when she pulled a section of the Internal Revenue Service Manual off a shelf and waved it at me as she screamed, 'If you want to go by the tax code, we'll go by the code.' All I could do was laugh. This woman didn't even know the difference between the tax code and the IRS manual.'"

Who was footing the bill for the examiner's ignorance? The client, of course. Unable to find redress at that level, the client was forced to pay the practitioner to go on to the next level, and then the next, painfully discovering that in a fight with the agency, costs escalate quickly. Eventually the tax professional found an appeals officer who resolved the matter in less than twenty minutes, but it was after a struggle that lasted the better part of a year and cost the honest taxpayer over $13,000 in professional fees. "I got justice," the practitioner concluded. "My client, of course, felt otherwise."

3

Collections

"Revenue Officers capitalize on the taxpayer's inherent fear of the IRS and the intimidation that they can inflict on taxpayers without any consequence for their improper enforcement. With management approval, revenue officers use enforcement to 'punish' taxpayers instead of trying to collect the most money for the government."

Witness Number One
IRS revenue officer with over
two decades of experience, sworn testimony
September 25, 1997

The examples of outrageous abuse uncovered in our investigation and hearings disclosed problems within the Internal Revenue Service that went far beyond what I had expected. From blue sky assessments to quotas and goals to the adversarial nature of the relationship between agency employees and the taxpayers, the mounting evidence made it clear that necessary changes to the way the Service carried out its mission were long overdue. Many of these problems were related to the examinations function—the dynamic that exists between taxpayers and auditors. And these were perhaps the most pervasive, as it is the Examination Division that touches the lives of most Americans. But, as we also discovered, examples of abuse and mismanagement were certainly not isolated to that one area. In my opinion, far more disturbing pathologies were uncovered in the agency's collections function.

Tom Savage, owner of TSA, a small contracting firm in Lewes, Delaware, is one who learned that taking on the IRS collectors—or revenue officers—is like using a squirt gun to defend against nuclear conflagration. His self-described horror story began after the Internal Revenue Service tried to collect delinquent employment taxes from a subcontractor who performed construction work for the company owned by him and his wife, Frances.

No prior relationship had existed between TSA and the subcontractor, an independently owned small business that had won a state government bid to participate in the construction of a women's correctional facility. Unable to post the bonding necessary to execute the project, the subcontractor approached Savage, who agreed to a one-project relationship that would allow the construction to go forward, with TSA sponsoring the necessary bond. It was a simple arrangement, benefiting both parties, but what Savage did not know, when he agreed to help, was that the subcontractor was engaged in a dispute with the IRS over unpaid employment taxes, and that it would not take long for the revenue officer in charge of collecting money from the subcontractor to stick the Savages with the huge liability.

While the subcontractor's tax troubles had long preceded the relationship with Savage and TSA, and despite the fact that Savage had a clean record with the agency, the revenue officer began to fabricate a complex professional association that would hold TSA liable for the delinquency. He dummied up a fictitious partnership between the subcontractor and TSA, assigned it a new Employment Identification Number, and sent a bill for roughly $177,000.

Savage and his tax counselor filed an immediate protest with the local appeals office, but before they received the opportunity to be heard—and before an assessment, or judgment, had been entered against either the phony partnership or Savage's company—the collections officer seized a large check that had been written to TSA, a check the small businessman depended on to pay his own bills. This was a clear violation of the tax code, which makes it unlawful for the Internal Revenue Service to seize taxpayer property or undertake any type of enforcement action until an assessment has been appropriately entered against a taxpayer.

Tom Savage and his attorneys were convinced that the violations of the law were so egregious that even a cursory overview would establish that he did not owe the money and that the agency's enforcement action was a flagrant violation of his rights. A letter from the U.S. Department of Justice addressed to the District Counsel of the Internal Revenue Service stated clearly that "after reviewing the complaint, the motion for summary judgment, your defense letter, and all the information forwarded by the revenue officer, we believe that the levy in question was wrongful."

A logical mind would conclude that such a strong opinion from the Justice Department would encourage the IRS to back away from what, by this time, had turned into rabid persecution of Savage and his wife. Here were government attorneys making it clear to the Service that the collections officer in charge of the case had violated the taxpayer's rights. Logic, however, is an early casualty when dealing with employees and managers whose first priority is not necessarily to do what's right, but rather what's expedient and beneficial to their own success. Within the quota-driven Collections Division, a resourceful revenue officer had seized $50,000 belonging to TSA, and the IRS was not about to give the money back.

Compounding its duplicity, the Internal Revenue Service never disclosed the Justice Department's letter to Savage or his attorneys. In fact, the opinion surfaced only during the course of our investigation, long after the agency determined to drag the small businessman through a prolonged and costly battle, perhaps anticipating that with limited resources pitted against the inexhaustible legal apparatus of the federal government, Savage would either fold or be forced out of business.

Beyond the money seized by the revenue officer, Tom Savage and his wife spent another $50,000 in legal fees. Unable to sleep, and with their energy concentrated on finding a semblance of justice from their government, they lost $600,000 in work that they had to decline due to lack of time and resources. Faced with a win-at-all-costs attitude on the part of the agency, Savage—without the knowledge that the Justice Department attorneys had advised the IRS that what it had done was illegal—made the decision to settle, allowing the Service to keep their money after a federal judge explained that to continue the battle in court would run into hundreds of thousands of dollars in legal costs. Tom and Frances Savage simply could not afford to continue. "As much as it offended my wife and me," Savage testified, "we chose to settle the case. We wanted to pursue it to the end, but to do so would have destroyed us."

Taxpayers' Rights at Risk

It would be comforting to believe that Tom Savage's nightmare, as well as the others I've documented so far, constitute rare exceptions—aberrant behavior by a few self-serving agency employees—but recent internal investigations by the Internal Revenue Service itself admit that far too many of the countless assessments, seizures, levies, and liens that the IRS executes each year are inappropriate and in open violation of the law. Mistakes and abuses within the system are not rare. The overemphasis on statistics encourages—and some revenue officers even say *forces*—employees to do whatever is necessary to keep their numbers up. Citing our September hearings as impetus, Commissioner Rossotti initiated a series of internal audits in the final months of 1997. What he and his agency discovered was that the IRS has created an environment driven by statistical accomplishments that places taxpayer rights at risk.

According to the internal review:

- The IRS' corporate performance measurement system, through a statistical ranking of the districts, encouraged the collection field function to emphasize enforcement results without corresponding emphasis on case quality; adherence to law, policy, and procedure; or taxpayer rights.
- References to enforcement statistics were contained in 130 of 340 group manager evaluations. The sampled data suggest that more than a third of all group managers throughout America are being judged by the number of cases their agents and officers close, as well as the amount of money that is collected through assessments, levies, liens, and seizures.
- Approximately one fourth of the revenue officers and group managers stated that they feel pressure to achieve enforcement goals and take enforcement actions, even as national and regional oversight of the use of enforcement statistics and goals is limited.

If quotas, goals, and statistics lead to abuse in the examination process—as demonstrated in the preceding chapter—they can be devastating in the collections function. Deeply troubled by the report's conclusion, Treasury Secretary Robert E. Rubin made it clear that the inappropriate use of enforcement statistics was putting taxpayers' rights in jeopardy in districts around the nation. Experiences of abuse like that which shattered the lives of Bruce and Shirley Barron, Bill and Beth Barlow, and Tom and Frances Savage were not confined to one region, nor were they isolated to a rogue group manager and the heartless agents who do his bidding.

In September of 1998, the Internal Revenue Service issued another stunning report. A Special Review Panel set up by Commissioner Rossotti to "objectively and independently review and assess" evidence "concerning allegations of misuse of enforcement statistics" reported widespread abuse in all twelve districts. Among its findings:

- There is an unbalanced focus on measuring performance by productivity. Statistical goals and expectations had become the primary means of measurement, and IRS procedures were not being followed.
- At national and regional levels—and throughout all districts—the Service had created an organizational environment driven by statistical accomplishments that placed taxpayer rights and a fair employee evaluation system at risk.
- In all twelve districts, the IRS did not properly exercise its seizure authority in 246 of 467 cases reviewed. Again, these seizures resulted in part from a desire to enhance statistical measures without a corresponding focus on the appropriateness of the actions taken and on adherence to policy and procedures.

- Concerning examinations, Commissioner Rossotti's panel found inappropriate use of examination statistics in all twelve districts reviewed, due in part to unclear and inconsistent guidance given to examination personnel.
- Examination Division's corporate measures focused primarily on enforcement statistics, which fostered improper personnel management and interaction with taxpayers in the regions and districts reviewed.
- There were no corporate measures that addressed case quality, treatment of taxpayers, and the proper amount of tax assessed. This led to an environment at the group manager and employee levels that put emphasis on revenue and other statistical goals.

These disclosures not only confirmed what our investigation had uncovered and the agency had initially denied, but they testified to the extraordinary leadership of Commissioner Rossotti, and the willingness of principled individuals inside the IRS to set things right. They also signaled the beginning of what I believe will be a new era within the Service—one of more honest assessment and greater openness. With the release of these reports, many within the ranks of senior management resigned; others were penalized. It was movement in the right direction. But any desire to celebrate them as successes was diminished by the facts that: (1) the disturbing conditions that the agency was finally acknowledging existed in complete disregard for the laws and regulations that were already on the books; (2) they were condoned by managers and executives who knew that they violated the law; (3) taxpayers who have been wrongfully persecuted—many of whom we will never know—were, and even remain, victims of a government that should be serving and protecting, rather than undermining and persecuting; and (4) these outrageous conditions were acknowledged by the Internal Revenue Service only after a congressional investigation, the outcry of an enraged public, the appointment of a new commissioner, and the willingness of employees to come forward. What price liberty!

It's in the Training

Being forced into the abyss by managers and responding with a whirlwind of seizures, liens, and levies is not only required to make a name inside the Collections Division, it has become so much a part of the institutional dynamic that it's sometimes necessary just to keep a job. I listened to one account after another of officers who were threatened, berated, demoted, and even forced to resign because they sought to collect revenue by working constructively with taxpayers rather than by using the more brutal enforcement tools mandated by their supervisors.

I was outraged by a videotape given to me following our first series of hearings. Shot on a home-style camcorder, it documents the training of a classroom full of collections officers in the Arkansas-Oklahoma District. The instructor, whose get-tough attitude is on display as he swaggers from one side of the room to the other, speaks in an affected drawl and uses military dialogue. From boasting about high statistics that he's forced his own employees to achieve to warning the revenue officers that their days are numbered if they don't increase their seizures, his high-handed, self-absorbed delivery offends common sensibilities. He calls his class "basic training, or collection boot camp." I'll call him Napoleon.

"Nothing has changed in our operation in 134 years," he begins, dismissing several congressional efforts—including the Taxpayer Bill of Rights and the Taxpayer Bill of Rights II—to give Americans increased protections against the tax collector. "Not one thing!" His gestures are wild. "If you have any problem with what you hear me say today," he warns, "you may be in the wrong line of work. If you can't do what you hear today, your mental or physical health is not worth letting this job eat away at you."

What exactly are his troops—in short sleeves and tight neckties—supposed to do? Their job, he tells them, is clearly defined. Once an assessment has been made, their responsibility is to use all weapons in their arsenal to transfer money from the taxpayer's pockets to the government's coffers in the quickest, most efficient way possible. The vast majority of collections officers are well-trained law enforcement personnel, handsomely rewarded to confront taxpayers and to seize their homes, cars, bank accounts, or any other assets that can be converted to cash. If IRS auditors are taught to see the taxpayer as a criminal, then to the collection officer the taxpayer is America's Most Wanted.

"Make them cry," Napoleon instructs his troops. "We don't give points around here for being good scouts. The word is enforce. If that's not tattooed on your forehead, or somewhere else," he laughs a sophomoric laugh, "then you need to get it. Enforcement. Seizure and sales. That's our mind-set. That's our collection perspective and attitude. You're not out there to take any prisoners. Prisoners are like an installment agreement. They have to be fed and clothed and housed. All that stuff. They're expensive. We're not here to do that. If you've got an assessment, enforce collection until they come to their knees."

From the beginning of his presentation, Napoleon threatens his troops that their jobs are on the line. It became clear to me, as I watched his bellicose presentation, that the same intimidation and anger he's unloading on them will likely be taken out on others once his troops hit the streets—like the child who beats the family dog after being disciplined by Mother. "We are under attack," he offers matter-of-factly. "People want to eliminate the field branches. They want to do away with your job."

He explains that of all the avenues the Internal Revenue Service uses to collect delinquent taxes—service center correspondence, the automated collection system, and the revenue officers—the most ineffective in terms of dollars collected are the collections officers. "They say we're producing the least and costing the most," he warns. "If you don't do anything more than what [the other collections functions] do—basically phone calls, send out a few letters, maybe really get mean once in a while . . . or maybe file a lien once in a while; if you extend deadlines and let [cases] play on forever; if you don't do any more than that, they don't need you. It's entirely possible we have hired the last revenue officer we're ever going to hire. . . . What the hell do they need you for?"

Napoleon appears to be above the law, unaffected by rules that govern other managers and employees. For example, IRS policy statement P-1-20 states: "Records of tax enforcement results shall not be used to evaluate enforcement officers or impose or suggest production quotas or goals." According to the manual, "This prohibition is necessary not only to protect the employees from quantitative goals, but also protect the taxpayers against possible inequities." Therefore, the regulation states, "forecasts and monitoring aspects of work planning and control programs shall not be used as quotas, allegations, or as specific amounts of work that must be completed."

All of this means nothing to Napoleon. He tells his troops: "Some of you folks came out during the days when we did not talk about the 'P' words—production and performance. [But they are] what we're here for. Some of us weren't smart enough to figure out how we could deliver what we were supposed to deliver when we couldn't talk about the numbers involved. The groups I was in, we were never smart enough to figure that one out. So we discontinued to talk about it. . . . Well, welcome back to the future, folks, because we're going to start talking about it now. We're talking about seizures, sales, nominees, alter-egos, transferees, fraud referrals—all the things we're supposed to do. . . . We should have been talking about them all along!"

He instructs his troops to set goals and use statistics to determine their performance. "Every fiscal year you need to decide what your group is going to do," he orders. "What you are going to deliver. What division expects your branch to do. What your group's cut is of that. How you are going to deliver, and by when—the deadline. What do we measure every year? Dollars collected. Returns secured." He shows the class a poster of a thermometer. Written on the poster and charted on the graph are numbers of seizures and other performance statistics. "Some of our group meetings are like blood baths," he brags. "If you're not carrying your part of the load, we're going to tell you about it. We are very blunt."

If this is basic training, as Napoleon insists, then we shouldn't be surprised when we hear revenue officers, many from the same district, who express outrage concerning how the "collection perspective and attitude" advocated by this instructor, and others like him, plays out in the lives of taxpayers. And we should be frightened to know that Napoleon continues to instruct, and his supervisor has been moved to national headquarters in Washington, D.C.

Larry Lakey, a revenue officer with over 15 years in the Service, testified that "the job of collecting tax and treating the public with congruency and fairness is being hampered with constant pressure to close more and more cases. We were told by our mid-level or branch chief manager that our performance rating for the year will be in direct relationship to the number of seizures that we make. We have been told by mid-level and upper management that if we don't do seizures of property we better look for another job. We are told to ignore the law and do what they say. We are encouraged to ignore any issues that might slow down the collection process."

According to Lakey, collection statistics of revenue officers are actually kept in secret computer files and used to determine the performance and value of agency employees. "I know that they exist," he testified. "What is forgotten in dealing with statistics is that statistics are people's lives."

Tom Savage, whose business was nearly ruined because a revenue officer in pursuit of statistical self-validation bent the rules to seize $50,000, shows how quotas and goals result in undeserved pain. Not only did he and his wife suffer during the months that they were treated unjustly, not only did they lose confidence in their government, but well into their seventies, the couple will not be able to retire as they had planned; they will have to work for years to make up for the damage done to them and their company. Others who have been chased by unyielding revenue officers, like Shirley Barron, live with the pain of knowing that rebuilding what has been destroyed will never again be possible. She is reminded daily of how rules twisted and broken can destroy families, futures, and lives.

Just a Number?

Every year, the Internal Revenue Service places 750,000 liens, makes 3.1 million levies, and executes over 10,000 seizures. While it's clear that the majority of these actions are taken correctly, carried out by officers who follow regulations and remain well within the law, the cases we reviewed show how the system easily breaks down, allowing overly aggressive or even reckless officers to abuse their powerful authority. Enforcement comes without warning; punitive actions are taken without giving taxpayers the chance to right alleged wrongs. The case of Bruce and Shirley Barron—as well as many other cases we listened to—not only exemplifies the proclivity of some collections officers, encouraged by their managers, to use seizures to boost performance ratings, it also demonstrates the near-absolute power these men and women have over the lives of taxpayers.

With authority unparalleled in any other federal agency, an IRS collections officer could take a taxpayer's home with one signature from the district director. According to Robert Schriebman, tax attorney and author of ten books on practicing before the Internal Revenue Service, "a revenue officer legally doing his or her job of collecting the taxes cannot be stopped by anyone in this country, including the U.S. Supreme Court. However, it's just about as difficult to stop one who is discharging his or her duties illegally." The danger when the laws, regulations, and established procedures are not followed is that the sheer power possessed by collections officers allows them to destroy livelihoods and security with impunity, or, as Schriebman put it, "with all the tact and diplomacy of Pearl Harbor."

"Most collections officers are honorable and empathetic," Schriebman told me. "The problem comes when you run into the occasional officer who is hard-hearted and for the most part too young to have experienced many of life's tragedies."

To make his point, Schriebman cited the case of David, a California man in his thirties who suffers from crippling arthritis. A struggling small businessman, who had to close his doors after health problems forced him onto crutches, David failed to pay federal employment and withholding taxes for three years. Until that time, he had been in compliance, but medical costs and an increasing inability to work began to put a strain on his finances. In 1990, he went out of business and was unable to work. A year later, David married Susan, a teacher in the Los Angeles School District, and she took over sole support of the family on an income of less than $40,000 a year. David had no personal earnings after 1989.

Not long after the marriage, David was informed by the IRS that the agency intended to collect on the taxes between 1987 and 1990, despite the fact that he had had no reportable income for two years. They charged that he owed over $112,000, of which $46,000 was interest and penalties. David tried to explain that he was not working and that the only assets he owned consisted of a couple of junkyard cars and motorcycles. His only possession of any value was a fifteen-year-old GMC pick-up truck that had been specially equipped to compensate for his handicap.

David approached the IRS to make an offer-in-compromise. The agency did not respond. Rather, in late August 1994, the collections officer, accompanied by a local law enforcement official, entered his property without his consent and took the truck from his driveway. Two days later, David filed an application for a Taxpayer Assistance Order to stop the sale of the vehicle on the grounds that it had little or no value, and that the seizure of the vehicle would constitute an extreme hardship. His pleas were ignored. The truck was sold at public auction. It went for $900.

One month later, the IRS returned and attempted to garnish Susan's wages. Schriebman, however, was able to stop the action. "While there is no excuse for an individual to avoid taxes if he legitimately owes them and has the ability to pay," Schriebman explained, "the IRS has long-established avenues for dealing with people who cannot fully pay." The first avenue is a hardship suspension. If you can show the IRS that you're either financially, physically, or mentally unable to pay, the agency is *required* to suspend collection. The second avenue is an installment payment arrangement. The third is an offer-in-compromise. If the agency agrees to accept the amount offered, it will release all tax liens and wipe the slate clean in the interest of giving you a fresh start.

Problems arise when collections officers violate these established procedures—because of ignorance, laziness, open hostility, or the influence of perverse incentives—and refuse to work with the taxpayer. In David and Susan's case the IRS should have followed the first avenue and suspended collection activities. Instead, their lawyer believes, "they got a mean-spirited collector who was hell-bent on hurting them. And if a revenue officer wants to hurt you he can hurt you."

Without oversight and an undeviating administration of laws and regulations to protect the taxpayer, if the desire of a collections officer is to create misery, the immured agency environment allows the officer to do it. Our investigation discovered weaknesses and inconsistencies within the tax code and the Internal Revenue Manual. The central problem is that both empower the agency to do whatever is necessary to collect revenue, but they fail to promote balance and discretion in how such overwhelming authority will be used.

"It's unbridled power," Schriebman told me. "A revenue officer can abuse the system at will, and the odds are staggering that his actions will be backed 100 percent by his immediate supervisor or manager. You have to go fairly high up the IRS chain of command to find the quality of mercy."

A Startling Confession

"The problem," one current division chief in Collections told me during a late-night telephone call, "is that you're not rewarded for mercy." His candor and willingness to talk about the influences in his own career were remarkable, though he asked not to be identified. "You're not rewarded for service. No matter what you say it always comes down to seizures and the amount of dollars collected. This is how you earn respect and get promoted, and you cannot change that culture." According to the division chief, there is "absolute competition" between group managers and branch managers, and they push their employees to perform, to "make more seizures than the next person, even if they violate taxpayers' rights."

"You don't care about customer service," he told me. "There are a lot of good people who do care and try to give taxpayers an opportunity, but even some of them eventually get caught up in their careers and succeeding. They do what they have to do to produce. They get caught up in all these measures and lose sight of providing service. The way things are today, you either play the game or you wash out."

To move up through the ranks, the division chief admitted that his early career was marked by an overwhelming desire to perform for his managers. "Not all revenue officers are this way," he said. "You have some who just want to get by, and you have some who go overboard in favoring taxpayers. But then you have 30 or 40 percent who are ambitious. They want to please the boss and they know what the boss wants— the boss doesn't even have to say it. They end up using whatever tools they're given under the law to seize assets, close cases, and collect dollars—even if what they're doing isn't fair.

"I came in altruistic. When I first starting working for the Service I was amazed that we could literally walk into businesses—go in private areas—and lock them up, seize them. I remember being troubled by that, but I was out of college and gung ho. I was going to do what my bosses told me was good. I perceived it and I did it. There was a cockiness to it. The revenue officers out there don't have the life experiences to understand what it takes to be a businessman, to provide livings for others. They don't understand the sacrifices and sleepless nights businessmen spend trying to meet payroll. The Service doesn't train them in this area. When I started, I hardly understood what a mortgage was and what it took to finance a car. I didn't understand the pain of trying to run a company. I didn't understand what equity in a business was. What I understood was make a seizure, score a point. That's what my manager wanted. That's what I did. And it still goes on."

The division chief admitted that "revenue officers are not taught to think about what they are doing in terms of justice. They don't think about what is in the best interest of the taxpayer." He told me that the road to success as a tax collector is marked by an evolutionary process that he saw in his own development and has witnessed countless times in the careers of other revenue officers. "At first you think about what is absolutely legal," he said. "You think, 'If it's legal I can do it.' And then pretty soon you are dragged into a condition where you go beyond the point of what is legal. To succeed you have to collect. You have to seize. You have to take enforcement action. So you do whatever is necessary."

As a division chief he has seen managers force their employees to go out of line to make seizures the revenue officers didn't feel were appropriate. "When I was coming up through the ranks I was very much enforcement-minded," he confessed. "I was the kind of revenue officer who made a lot of seizures. That's the reason I got to where I am. I think it was wrong. We need to take each case and look at it on its merits and not have some kind of goal to treat a taxpayer in a certain way.

"There are cases I seized that I regret doing. I think that we could have taken a more lenient attitude, given the taxpayers more time, been more understanding of their condition and how they got into the financial jam. But I was clearly feeling pressure from my manager."

"Have you ever forced your employees to take actions you felt were inappropriate?" I asked.

He admitted he had. "As a manager I can tell you that I did force my employees to go beyond," he said. "By the time

I was a division chief I had changed my attitude. I had turned things around. I told my folks we were going to make decisions based on the merits of the case and not the numbers. I had attained the position I wanted and was satisfied and felt I didn't have to play the game. Not anymore."

If the abuses that take place within Examinations are a meandering stream, we discovered that those emerging in Collections are Niagara Falls. For example, the levels of review in the Examination Division were highly structured, and the taxpayer had several occasions to present his or her position, but just the opposite was taking place within the Collections Division. A taxpayer, bullied by a collector, had no established chain of command to follow in an effort to seek redress. A complaint could either be lodged with the collector's immediate supervisor or the district chief of collection. During an enforced collection, with your life in crisis, there was little time between the point of seizure and the point at which you would never see your assets again. As the division chief made clear, it is often the supervisors who are more interested in scoring statistics, closing cases, and reducing backlogs than the revenue officers. In those circumstances, trying to appeal to a supervisor would be as fruitless and foolish as begging a bookie to forgive your crippling losses at the track. Yet there was no other place to resolve your case other than within the tilted system.

Once a seizure had taken place, the most you could expect was for the officer to hand you a couple of small pamphlets containing little information. Meanwhile, your assets were on their way to the auction block. Several practitioners, as well as IRS officers, told us of the shortcuts the agency used during enforced collection. For example, while a taxpayer must have at least 30 days' written notice before the IRS is allowed to legally seize assets, too many times these notices failed to materialize. Often they were sent to incorrect addresses. The argument, according to revenue officers, was that advance notification of a lien, levy, or seizure gave the taxpayer time to hide assets, change bank accounts, or put property in the name of a spouse, friend, or relative. And this made the revenue officer's job much more difficult. Never mind the fact that the tax collector could use a process they call the "whipsaw" and seize the assets from the individual to whom they had been conveyed.

Motivated by managers to reduce their assigned inventory, revenue officers' primary objective was to close cases as fast as they could. This allowed rogues to perpetrate extreme hardships on taxpayers, such as forcing them into bankruptcy because a bankruptcy filing closed the case. Another way to close a case was to have the taxpayer commit to an installment payment arrangement. Here, again, we found abuses, belligerent revenue officers requiring taxpayers to agree to extend the ten-year statute of limitations for collection far beyond a reasonable period in exchange for an installment payment plan.

Taxpayers were told that if they did not sign the extension they would not be given the payment arrangement, their wages would be garnished, and other assets, such as bank accounts, would be taken immediately. Still others were put into payment arrangements they could not possibly maintain while meeting their ongoing tax obligations. One practitioner suggested that this was done deliberately at times to place the taxpayer in an impossible position, forcing a default that in turn would trigger immediate collection.

Installment Plans

Even well-intentioned revenue officers placed taxpayers in jeopardy through unrealistic installment payment arrangements. Before these were offered, the IRS required that the taxpayer become and stay current in filing and payment of ongoing taxes.

If an installment arrangement was too burdensome, the taxpayer's cash flow went first to satisfying the payment arrangement, the end result being that the taxpayer was unable to remain current. The problem of installment arrangements was further exacerbated by the fact that even without adding water to a payment plan, the IRS manual, as we discovered, did not take a reasonable approach to a person's living expenses.

Prior to September 1995, the Service generally allowed a taxpayer "all reasonable living expenses." There were no definitive guidelines to provide for costs associated with food, clothing, education, charitable contributions, and shelter. These expenses were generally allowed in full, no questions asked.

This came to an abrupt end once the agency established a goal that delinquent taxes were required to be paid in full within three years. In order to achieve this strategic objective, arbitrary national and local living expenses were set. Charts were created to dictate how much income taxpayers would be allowed to keep to provide for themselves and family. For example, where I live in New Castle County, Delaware, a family under the 1998 annual guidelines, would be allowed only $928 a month for mortgage, property taxes, and utilities. For food, clothing, and personal care they would be allowed an additional $1,218. The IRS would take the rest of their income and apply it to a payment plan. Under the original 1995 guidelines, the IRS disallowed charitable giving such as church contributions, educational expenses, and credit card payments.

It's easy to see how this kind of arrangement is difficult for most people. For families with high mortgages, consumer debt, and children in college, it forced many productive taxpayers who might never think of filing for bankruptcy to seek its protection. Under Chapter 13 of the Bankruptcy Code, a debtor can take up to five years to pay off the IRS without accruing interest and without worry of continued IRS harassment. The same taxpayer who chose to deal with the agency without declaring bankruptcy would get only three years to pay, with interest compounding daily on the unpaid balance, and would continue to live under the watchful eye of the agency.

A $2,100-a-month living allowance would create a struggle for most medium-sized American families. Certainly, they would have to organize their finances. They may need to sell their home and stop paying for their children's college educations. No longer would the family be able to contribute to their church. The IRS manual does require the tax collector to give their delinquent taxpayers a year to get their financial house in order to comply with the installment arrangement guidelines. Most families would certainly need that and maybe even more time to make the necessary changes to be able to provide for themselves on a little over $2,000 a month.

Here again, however, we uncovered another problem: many collection officers did not give taxpayers the one-year grace period; they demanded immediate acceptance and adherence to the installment agreement. Practitioners as well as collectors told me that this was a pervasive practice. "I think this abuse occurs more out of ignorance than maliciousness," one advised. "The problem is that most revenue officers do not read the IRS manual. That's not their priority. Their priority is closing cases in a manner they perceive to be in their short-term best interest—liens, levies, and seizures."

Offers-in-Compromise

Another major area of abuse in the collections process involves the acceptance and execution of offers-in-compromise. When a taxpayer owes the Internal Revenue Service more than he or she can possibly pay, or when a taxpayer is disputing a liability such as a penalty assessment, the agency is supposed to take a business-like approach and "resolve these collections and liability issues through a compromise." According to the Internal

Revenue Manual, "the compromise process is available to provide delinquent taxpayers with a fresh start toward future compliance with tax laws." The manual states that in "cases where an Offer-in-Compromise appears to be a viable solution to a tax delinquency, the Service employee assigned the case will discuss the compromise alternative with the taxpayer and, when necessary, assist in preparing the required forms."

While this sounds workable in theory, we were told by taxpayers, practitioners, and revenue officers that in practice the IRS often set up roadblocks in the compromise process. This was done in several ways. By far the most pervasive was refusing to process offers because of minor technicalities such as finding fault with the application forms, at the same time returning the entire offer package to the taxpayer with the information that it was not acceptable without explaining why.

The second problem brought to our attention concerned collections officers who failed to cease collection activity when an offer-in-compromise was being considered. The manual states clearly that "collection activity will be withheld on any open accounts if it is determined that the offer merits consideration and there is no reason to believe that collection of the tax liability will be in jeopardy." According to practitioners, however, even after the IRS had agreed to consider the offer, some revenue officers continued to badger and threaten taxpayers with enforced collection, unless they entered into an installment payment arrangement.

Collections officers did this because of pressure from their supervisors to get as many concessions—as much money—from the taxpayer as possible to increase the overall collection portfolio of the group and improve the revenue officer's and the group manager's positions for advancement within the system. This strategy abused the taxpayer in a number of ways. For example, installment money paid by the taxpayer while the offer-in-compromise was being considered would be counted by the collections officer as a payment against interest and penalties rather than against the underlying tax liability. As a consequence, when the offer-in-compromise was finally accepted, there would be no credit for the payments made, the original amount owed would not have been reduced, and the taxpayer would still have to pay the full amount offered in the compromise.

It is not only the taxpayer but the government that is hurt from the agency's lack of aggressiveness in processing and accepting offers-in-compromise. According to testimony that we heard, the GAO estimated that approximately $214 billion was owed by taxpayers having delinquent accounts in 1996. If the truth were known it probably would be more than double that amount. Even assuming, however, that the $214 billion figure is correct, the Treasury is losing tens of thousands of dollars per second in uncollectible accounts because offers-in-compromise are not being accepted and statutes of limitation are expiring.

Those uncollected taxes that do not expire are also lost to the Treasury when a revenue officer refuses to work with the taxpayer toward a reasonable offer-in-compromise, because a taxpayer who is bankrupt or out of business has an economic impact on family, community, suppliers, and employees. According to Schriebman, "The biggest scandal in American taxation today is that the IRS is willing to force an otherwise productive taxpayer into bankruptcy rather than accept a fair offer-in-compromise."

Fear, Abuse, and Intimidation

Our investigation and hearings demonstrated how IRS revenue officers can intervene in just about anyone's life. Homes and property could be seized on the signature of a district director.

No court hearing. No notice. No due process. No opportunity to litigate the merits of the agency's claim. We listened to stories of how the Internal Revenue Service closed down businesses, taking away taxpayers' livelihoods merely by filing a few papers in federal court. The processes were carried out *ex parte*, the judge hearing only one side of the argument before signing the seizure order.

The question we had to ask as our investigation moved forward was: How important is it that the IRS maintain near absolute authority? Certainly, agents and officers needed adequate tools to enforce tax laws. But had that authority come at the expense of fairness? Most revenue officers are highly trained professionals. They're reasonable, courteous, and committed to following the rules. But we realized that when even an aggressive handful, seizing upon the tremendous authority granted them by Congress, stepped out of line they—like bad cops—had the power to destroy anyone who got in their way. They could commit perjury and get away with it. They could harass honest Americans and go on to promotion. They could intimidate, badger, and twist the rules to render the taxpayer helpless—in the process wrecking reputations, careers, credit, and economic security. We saw too many examples and examined too much evidence to pretend these things weren't happening.

Finally, the agency admitted it was going on. Revenue officers were able to go about their business with near carte blanche authority. Not only did they have the power to lien, levy, and seize, but they were also responsible for selling seized assets and posting the earnings to the taxpayer's bill. This, as we discovered, led to even further problems, accusations, and speculation. We heard from several collectors that they had first-hand knowledge of assets that were sold to agents' friends and family at prices far below market value. One revenue officer even told us that one scam he had encountered took place when the individuals who purchased assets at a price many times below their reasonable value turned around and sold them for a hefty profit and then divided the windfall with the collections officer. I maintain a healthy skepticism concerning many of the reports we received, as some of the IRS employees who related them refused, or were unable, to provide names, dates, and places.

Another officer—an employee with more than two decades in the agency—testified that recently a tax collector "planned an elaborate sale to dispose of certain assets seized from a taxpayer. Many of the IRS employees were invited to help in the effort. The group manager was also present. Even though the revenue officer failed to achieve the minimum bid, as required by law, before selling the assets, he went ahead and sold the property at a significant loss to the taxpayer. Property which had a minimum bid of $40,000 was sold for roughly $7,000."

What a devastating loss this was for the taxpayer, as precious assets were being disposed of for pennies on the dollar. Where were the checks and balances? Who was present to look out for the taxpayer's interests? Did anyone care? Or was the officer and even his manager simply looking to score another statistic? Mercy, compassion, the law, agency regulations, and even common sense appeared to vanish when some collections officers were in pursuit of self-interests. "My evaluations over the years have always been very high," one veteran tax collector testified. "I am considered to be one of the most effective collection officers in my district. However, I find it disturbing to learn that even though I collect more money, with a substantially high number of my cases paying in full, that I am now evaluated on my number of seizures rather than my overall effectiveness. The message we are receiving from upper management is let's take the action that will get us noticed. Don't worry about whether it's the right thing to do or not."

A revenue officer reported to us that her office had taken to disregarding policies that stood in the way of taking strong enforcement action. Others claimed to witness a sharp increase in threats and dirty tricks. Robert Schriebman told me that his office, in the year and a half leading up to our investigation, was bombarded by calls from other practitioners, especially younger ones, who needed assistance handling the mounting aggressiveness in collection activity. "A longtime colleague told me that he's stopped representing clients with collection problems because of the outrageous behavior of revenue agents," he said. "The stress on his heart and emotions was killing him."

This stress, I was told, was the direct result of frightening and intimidating tactics. Schriebman himself had been a target. On one occasion, he opened his mail to find a local news article reporting the story of a Sherman Oaks, California, tax mediator who had been arrested in an IRS raid. In the margin above the story, someone had typed: "You and your clients are next! If you don't think it can happen, call (name withheld) and numerous attorneys in Los Angeles. You are currently under investigation and I'm waiting for the day your name is in the paper."

Schriebman was not under investigation and according to his knowledge never had been. He reported the threat to the agency. An internal investigation traced the note to the typewriter that had been used. It belonged to a revenue officer. Both the carbon film typewriter ribbon cartridge and the correction ribbon showed that the threat had been composed on the machine. This was confirmed by the Forensic Science Laboratory of the Internal Security Division of the IRS in Washington, D.C. Despite the evidence, no one was charged, and the episode stands as another example of the cavalier attitude some IRS employees have regarding the use of the dangerous power they've been given.

4

The IRS vs. Small Business

"The attitude is 'big cases, big problems; little cases, little problems!' Quantity not quality is the message. . . . 'Mom and Pop' cases are easy 'hits' and can be opened and closed quickly to bolster numbers, rather than investing time in the large cases which take longer and require more resources."

Witness Number Six
criminal investigator
with twenty-five years
in the IRS Inspection Division

Early in our investigation, I noticed that the majority of the cases coming to our attention involved small businesses. This did not come as a surprise, as such entrepreneurial enterprises dominate our economy. There are well over 20 million small-business owners in America today, and 800,000 new businesses start up every year. Nine out of ten firms in this country have fewer than twenty employees, and nearly six out of ten Americans get their paychecks from small businesses. They contribute more than half of all the sales in the country and provide the lion's share of our economy's output.

In that they account for such a large percentage of America's business concerns, there's no question as to why small businesses attract so much attention from the Internal Revenue Service. Processing tens of millions of small business returns and ensuring compliance with so many employers, there is bound to be increased vigilance, random audits, daily collection efforts, and even mistakes, like that which surprised a couple in Vacaville, California. Ken and Judy Reed own a small antiques and furniture store. In early 1998, they anxiously awaited a $175 tax refund. The money was earmarked for a weekend vacation. When the envelope arrived from the IRS, Ken tore it open to find that instead of a refund the agency had sent him a bill for $300,000,082.17, despite the fact that Ken's total earnings for the tax year in question was less than $30,000. The IRS admitted the bill was a mistake, one of many that are bound to occur when processing 200 million tax returns a year, and the problem was quickly remedied. However, other interactions with small-business owners are not so innocent. There are conditions inherent with such enterprises that make them easy marks for auditors and collections officers who, for whatever reason, may want to engage in some mischief.

First, as one longtime practitioner told us, "Small businesses are targeted because the IRS perceives that they do not have the wherewithal to hire forceful representation." Bruce Strauss, who worked as a division chief in collections, explained that "the small businessman is at a disadvantage from the beginning. Working hand to mouth to survive, he cannot afford professional help." According to Strauss, the complexities of the tax law have turned him into a victim. "Quite often you find that small businesses don't know how to deal with their own books, let alone a complicated tax law. And a law that's hard to understand and ledgers that are not in satisfactory condition equal trouble."

Second, as we learned from one of the first letters we received—and as we have confirmed time and again throughout our investigation—there is an active effort underway within the Internal Revenue Service to have independent contractors identified as employees. The reason is easy to understand: employees who have taxes automatically withheld are more compliant taxpayers than independent contractors who must take the responsibility of filing their own returns. In fact, a full 95 percent of salaried employees comply with their tax obligations, not only because their taxes are withheld, but because accurate reporting mechanisms are in place that allow the IRS to better determine their income and liability. The more you move away from withholding and information reporting, the compliance rate drops.

The remedy, according to the IRS? Force small businesses and those who work for them into employer-employee relationships. Author James Bovard believes this is a misplaced emphasis that has resulted in "a massive campaign against the self-employed that seeks to force over half of America's independent contractors to abandon their own businesses." He writes that such an effort has resulted in a "campaign targeting small businesses with less than $3 million in assets—in most cases, businesses without in-house counsel that cannot afford a lengthy court fight against the agency."

How does the IRS determine when independent contractors should be classified as employees and go about having them classified as such? They conduct compliance checks, using what practitioners call the "Infamous 20 Factor Test," a list of questions that have been handed down from common law precedents going back almost 900 years. Even a Commissioner Advisory Groups established by the agency in 1990, claims the process is "confusing, complex, antiquated, and unfair." The agency looks at such things as whether the worker provides tools, whether the worker's services can be terminated at will, whether the employer has the right to control the worker, and whether there is workman's compensation.

A major problem in determining a laborer's status is that the common law tests, as the Treasury Department admits, lack the "precision and predictability" that are needed to "yield clear, consistent, or satisfactory answers." Moreover, the agency has often reached a foregone conclusion. Before the IRS employee even begins the test, the decision is usually made that the workers will be classified as employees. No matter what arguments are used, or how many of the 20 factors are in the employer's favor, the examiner will likely hold that the factors favoring the agency's position are more important.

James Bovard explains that "many IRS agents threaten exorbitant penalties to coerce businesses to sign agreements swearing never to use independent contractors again in return for a reduction or waiver of the penalties." He believes that the "IRS is capitalizing on the vagueness and inconsistencies in the current law in order to greatly increase its own power over small businesses."

"The fundamental issue is the drive to produce revenue," Bruce Strauss, the former Collection Division director, told me. "Turning an independent contractor into an employee is one sure way to raise revenue. It's got a long history. The IRS predetermines that all workers are employees." According to Strauss, he has never seen one case where workers were determined to be independent contractors by an IRS agent conducting a compliance check. "On the other hand," he said, "every case I've taken to appeals I've won." Strauss explained that another indicator that this hard-nosed approach is for little more than raising revenue is that in many cases where the workers are independent contractors, and have already filed and paid their taxes, the IRS again assessed taxes against the employer. "It's not supposed to happen," he said. "But again, it's another tactic to improve an individual agent's or group's performance by raising revenue on the back of small business."

Employment Taxes

A third disconcerting characteristic marking the relationship between small businesses and the Internal Revenue Service concerns the agency's response to a company's failure to stay current with and file employment taxes on time. Here, the best word used to describe the IRS' attitude is intolerant. As with Americans who fail to pay income tax, there is little, if any, excuse for a business owner to neglect this obligation. It is a trust, and a very important part of doing business, and in this sense the Internal Revenue Service views failure to comply as a form of theft.

The agency has an official policy of closing down small businesses that have repeated employment and withholding tax problems instead of working them out in a way that would allow the businesses to continue. The irony—as described in the preceding chapter—is that for an employer who has run into trouble with the IRS in the past, the inability to get and stay current can be caused partly by the agency. As one veteran of the Collections Division told our committee, "On more than one occasion, I have seen the IRS punish a taxpayer by not allowing reasonable, necessary living expenses, even current tax payments. Why? Because the revenue officer and the manager did not think the taxpayer obeyed their commands."

During the course of our investigation, we discovered that a revenue officer, driven by numbers, irritated by a taxpayer, or determined to close down a business, could place such a burden on the taxpayer to pay delinquent liabilities that it became impossible to make current payments. "They can be harsh and unrealistic," Strauss told me. "But my feeling is that it's done less out of malicious intent and more as part of a drive to raise revenue. Every day the agency deals with the same question: How do we put more money in the till?"

Businesses that fall behind in their obligations can be turned into real revenue generators for the Internal Revenue Service. Placed on installment plans that with penalties and interest require them to pay the agency well into the future, they are literally locked into a form of servitude. Such a burden, however, only tends to exacerbate problems. "Before long you're going to run into a quarter where you can't pay everything," Schriebman explained. "You might make a token payment. Pretty soon, you're making token payments on old quarters. You're unable to stay current. You're continually playing catch-up, trying to meet ongoing liabilities while paying heavy past assessments with their penalties and interest. It leads to disaster."

The IRS calls this pyramiding, and they have no compassion for it. There was a time when the agency would have tried to get that taxpayer back in the system and been more lenient about the older unpaid liabilities. But more recently, its goal, according to taxpayers and practitioners who testified before our committee, is to close down small businesses that are falling behind, no matter how many people are put out of work. The agency gets the assets. The collector gets the statistic. And the small businessman becomes an example to others who are frightened into compliance.

These tactics, combined with the complexity of the tax code, create an environment where many small businesses find it increasingly difficult to survive. The *Wall Street Journal* reports that some accountants "are charging as much as two percent of a small firm's revenue simply to prepare a tax return." A small businessman from Nebraska told Senator Bob Kerrey that his biggest problem in business today is not new accounts, it is not computers, it is not changing technology. "My biggest problem," he explained, "is dealing with the IRS. I spend countless hours on the phone trying to work out the problems associated with payments being credited to the wrong quarter. If we all must pay taxes, we should not have to hire someone just to tell us how." As a small-business owner he files fourteen times a year, observing that he has clients he doesn't talk to that often.

One tax examiner told me point-blank that she was taught to assume that all entrepreneurs were tax cheats. "We were encouraged very strongly to find that the business activities were not-for-profit or sham activities," she said. "We were taught to assume beforehand that all of the returns filed by small businesses had something wrong with them."

Another wrote that this attitude and the tools examiners and collections officers are given to go after small businessmen resulted in "the squashing of the entrepreneurial spirit." In 1992 the House Government Operations Committee issued a report stating that IRS activities present small-business taxpayers with a menu of problems and impossible policies that defy common sense. Six years later, I came to see firsthand that, if anything, the problem had only grown worse.

A heartbreaking story that recently came to my attention demonstrates how laws and policies can wrongfully conscript families to endless financial servitude. It involved a couple whose identity we will protect as they're trying to start life over in another part of the United States. For our purposes here, we'll call them the Westergards. Larry Westergard, a young father, had just graduated from a prestigious MBA program and taken his first real job with a computer firm on the west coast. With three small children, one of whom was suffering from brain cancer, Larry and his wife believed they were about to embark on building financial security. According to those who know him, he was a bright, well-educated, disciplined employee, who soon found himself promoted to a titled position within the company. Among his new responsibilities he was to sign checks for utilities, rent, supplies, and other day-to-day operational needs of the office where he worked. He was one of several who had signature authority at the bank, yet he had no authority or responsibility for payroll and tax obligations. This was reserved for the owners.

Trouble for the Westergards began when the company started to experience financial difficulties. Unknown to Larry, both president and shareholders had a prior history of tax problems, and several of the owners began to concentrate on building an operation in another state. They siphoned off cash and transferred inventory and corporate assets to the new site without Larry's knowledge, leaving him alone to manage his office on a budget they provided. Payroll checks and tax compliance were being taken care of out of state. At least this is what Larry was told.

His first awareness that there were problems with the Internal Revenue Service came when a collections officer dropped by the office. At the time, Larry was the senior ranking employee available to meet with the tax collector. The company's owners were now operating from the new office across state lines. The revenue officer informed Larry that the company had been delinquent in payroll and withholding taxes. He demanded immediate payment and threatened to close down the operation. When Larry contacted the owners, he was told that there must have been a mistake and that everything would be straightened out.

Fresh out of school, Larry Westergard had never experienced this type of a situation, and nothing would prepare him for the Kafkaesque experience to follow. Trusting his employers, he diligently pursued his job until the owners told him the company was folding and he would have to find employment elsewhere. Possessing a winning personality and excellent credentials, Larry soon landed a job in the aerospace industry. Once again his career began to thrive.

Then one morning Larry arrived at his new place of employment to find an IRS collections officer and a representative of the agency's Criminal Investigation Division waiting for him. They informed Larry that he was under suspicion of diverting corporate assets and other actions that frustrated the collection of employment and withholding taxes. They advised him to get a lawyer.

A few weeks later, Larry's attorney met with the revenue officer. It was a cordial meeting. The officer represented that they were looking at the owners, who had a history of tax evasion, and that they were going to prosecute them criminally. The agency employee told the attorney that Larry was not their primary target and that if he was cooperative they would recommend leniency for any liability he may have had in the matter.

Larry believed he had done nothing wrong and was willing to cooperate completely. When I met with Larry, he told me that he knew nothing about the payroll operation of the business. His focus, he said, was exclusively on the day-to-day business affairs of the local office, and he was doing everything in his power to keep it going with the capital the owners provided him each month. He made a full disclosure to the IRS, and, according to both him and his attorney, "they seemed quite pleased with the information."

Larry's attorney explained to him that under the provisions of the Internal Revenue Code, Section 6672(a), any person who is responsible for payroll tax compliance can be personally liable if he or she "willfully fails to collect and pay over" those taxes. In practice, Larry was not the individual within the corporation whose function it was to take care of payroll tax compliance. That duty remained with the owners, who had assured Larry that it was being taken care of. Given this, and the promise of leniency from the revenue officer, both Larry and his attorney felt that his exposure was "minimal at best."

The IRS felt otherwise. It was determined that since Larry's signature was on file at the bank, and as he had the power to sign checks to pay for the day-to-day operations of the California office, he was as much of a target for the penalty assessment as the owners of the company. "The offer of leniency went out the window just as soon as Larry had cooperated," said his attorney. At the age of 32, Larry Westergard and his family were handed an economic life sentence. He was assessed over $750,000 in trust-fund liability penalties and interest. "In almost thirty years of practice I have never seen anything more unjust and unfair," said his attorney. "It was brutal and deceptive."

Larry's attorney tried to show the IRS that such a monstrous assessment was unwarranted and could not be paid by this young family. It would ruin them. He told them about the struggle they were having with their infant daughter, about excessive medical bills, and the untold stress her condition was placing on Larry and his wife. He reminded the tax collector that he had promised to be lenient. Larry had cooperated fully. He and his wife attempted an offer-in-compromise that would be difficult for the family to pay, but at least it wouldn't be terminal. It was rejected out of hand. "At every turn, they were unreasonable," Larry's attorney told me. "I consider that case my biggest failure. The law is so loosely written that the IRS can do just about anything it wants with these young families." While today Larry's little daughter has recovered from her brush with cancer, the family's financial servitude to the IRS will never end.

Three years ago, a federal judge in New York felt the same sense of frustration that continues to haunt Larry's attorney. Judge Whitman Knapp heard a similar case in which a 28-year-old man, Nathan Unger, was held liable for $1,046,357 in taxes, penalties, and interest on unpaid withholding obligations. Unger and his attorneys showed that the young man, who was working as the chief financial officer for an advertising firm, repeatedly urged the company's president to pay the government, but on every occasion he was instructed to do otherwise.

Judge Knapp's hands were tied. He admitted that holding Nathan Unger responsible was unjust. The young man, according to the judge, was "essentially a cabin boy on a sinking ship." But the law dictated that Unger be held liable. Judge Knapp ruled on the side of the IRS, but then he gave the young man some advice that should trouble anyone who believes in the spirit and promise of America. He told the boy to leave the United States and try to start life all over again.

"Nathan Unger has been stripped of all his assets," the court noted, "and is faced with an undischargeable debt of more than $1,000,000. So far as we can determine, the only course open to him is to migrate to some more civilized country and try to start life all over again. It is difficult to understand how a rational government could so treat its own citizen. It certainly could not do so to a prisoner of war."

Some Call It Extortion

David Patnoe, a former revenue officer who now works as an enrolled agent—a taxpayer representative authorized to practice before the IRS—told me another story that further illustrates to what lengths tax collectors will go to find money. He was hired to assist in a matter involving the improper use of a levy. The IRS had issued the levy on a receivable owed to a small businessman—a sole proprietorship. According to Patnoe, the tax that the IRS was trying to collect on the levy was not owed by his client. It was in fact owed by a company that the small businessman had worked for at one time as an employee—a company in which Patnoe's client had had no ownership or interest.

The revenue officer, who at the time was acting as an on-the-job instructor for another agency employee, went to the client's business with seizure papers in hand. According to Patnoe, the client was given a choice: pay $7,000 or lose your livelihood. "Being faced with the seizure of his new business," Patnoe told me, the small businessman "became very afraid and paid $7,000 to forestall a seizure. He paid this despite the fact that he did not owe any tax.

"The IRS basically scared this person or extorted him into paying money that he didn't owe with the threat of seizing his business for the debt of the company he had at one time worked for." After the initial payment of $7,000 was made, the same revenue officer refused to leave the small businessman alone. She issued a another levy on a different account receivable— this time for $21,000.

"That money was going to be used to pay the client's payroll," Patnoe said. "The seizure of those funds would have effectively put the client out of business. The levy itself was an amazing flight of fancy by that revenue officer. Remember, there was no relationship or common ownership between these companies. The client simply had been an employee of the company that owed the tax. The IRS was well aware of these facts. Despite having the explanation laid out in black and white, the revenue officer would not release the levy or refund the $7,000 she had collected illegally by scaring the taxpayer when she first showed up at his door."

Patnoe explained that there are instances when a tax can be collected from someone other than the taxpayer. A third party can become liable if there was a transfer of assets for less than fair consideration, or if a party is holding property in their name simply to evade the seizure of those assets for taxes due. However, prior to collecting from a transferee, or a nominee, the IRS must go through a number of steps involving a group called Special Procedures Function and the office of the district counsel. "In this particular instance," he said, "none of this had been done. I informed the revenue officer that she had not taken any of the required steps and had acted without benefit of legal counsel. I added that her actions were not just abusive but blatantly illegal."

How did the revenue officer respond?

With a shrug and a single word: "And?"

"Only when she realized that we would make every effort possible to expose this action did she come back with a release of the levy," Patnoe said. "When you consider that this was an experienced revenue officer acting with her group manager's approval, not to mention also training other revenue officers, her actions were absolutely beyond comprehension. It is this type of behavior that is designed to intimidate and instill such fear that the IRS's actions can succeed without question."

Patnoe and every practitioner we interviewed made the same observation: If you go in to the IRS and you are not represented by a CPA, an enrolled agent, or an attorney, the agency can, and often will, use fear and intimidation to get its desired and predetermined result, because you are three things: alone, scared, and ignorant. And the IRS knows it. "It's like an immigrant being let off the boat in New York City," Schriebman said. "You don't know a soul. You don't know how the system works. You can't speak the language. You don't know where to start. You're a stranger in a strange land. And with the IRS, the natives are out to get you." Agency employees themselves admit that taxpayers are paying taxes they don't owe just to keep the IRS off their backs. "They don't say it with pride," Strauss clarified, "but they acknowledge it's a problem. Taxpayers will send payments they know aren't due because they fear the agency."

Given examples like these, is it any wonder that a 1990 survey by *People* magazine found that the most frightening words people could imagine hearing when they answered the phone were: "This is the IRS calling." According to another national survey conducted in March of 1997, more Americans say they would rather have root canal surgery than deal with the agency. Even Margaret Richardson, former head of the Internal Revenue Service, admitted to the attack of nerves she had the day she went to the family mailbox shortly after she was appointed as the agency's new commissioner. She took out an envelope with the IRS' logo emblazoned in the corner. "I had to stop and shake a minute before I opened the envelope," she said. When she opened it, Ms. Richardson found her paycheck.

Though the former commissioner's story is amusing in retrospect, for most Americans the experience of receiving a letter from the IRS does not have such a delightful ending. One lovely woman, who was drawn into a 17-year battle with the agency when it mistakenly confused her husband's small business income with that of another man, tearfully told me why she agreed to continue paying assessments that she knew she did not owe. "When you have someone come to you from the IRS and tell you they are going to take your home, your vehicles, whatever you own, close your business so you have no way of making a living, you do what they tell you to do," she said. "Over the years I worked with eighteen people, and I was harassed by every one of them."

"It's a classic situation," a practitioner aware of her case explained. "The agency forces people into compliance without following the manual and the guidelines. Threat and intimidation are as important to some agency employees as liens, levies, and seizures. I see that all the time." And once the IRS gets you to agree to an assessment it's almost impossible to get out of it. Even though the Taxpayer Bill of Rights II allows a taxpayer to petition the IRS for reduction in a monthly installment payment arrangement, taxpayers discover that when they file a petition for relief they don't get a response. "People come in and say, 'I've got a $5,000-a-month installment payment with the IRS and it's killing me. They wouldn't let me out without signing it. And now they won't give me any relief.'"

Why?

Because that's not the agency's focus. As we discovered, the IRS' interest is not in taking care of the taxpayer. It's on raising money any way it can.

Strauss said that another way the Internal Revenue Service uses intimidation is to coerce taxpayers into allowing an extension on the statute of limitations concerning their cases. Feeling inundated and unable to process their backlog, examiners and collectors will wait until the cases are at the point of expiring. At that time, they will pressure taxpayers to grant an extension to the statute. What they do, Strauss said, is "threaten the taxpayer to sign the waiver or risk enforcement action. That's abuse. It's inappropriate."

This kind of behavior by certain employees is part of an arrogance of power, an attitude of indifference that only contributes to the hostility between the agency and the taxpayer. It leads to anger, and, as one current agent told our committee, "in some instances instigates many of the threats, assaults, resistance to, and lack of cooperation experienced by IRS employees when dealing with the public. If police officers displayed this same attitude when interacting with the public, they would be fired! Why is it tolerated and encouraged by the IRS?"

One of the most distressing testimonies our committee heard came from a veteran employee who said he had "observed little or no accountability for misconduct, mistakes, and/or errors, whether innocent or intentional, and seldom—if ever—does the IRS or the responsible employee ever apologize to the taxpayer for the errors committed." This is callous behavior. It is counterproductive, dangerous, and all too prevalent when we keep in mind that the agency's own audit, released January 12, 1998, confirmed that a third of all revenue officers interviewed feel they are being pushed to use enforcement tools, including seizure authority, and that 34 percent of the seizure cases reviewed by IRS investigators did not meet agency procedural requirements and resulted in the mistreatment and abuse of taxpayers.

5

Management

"Pressure is coming from management. . . . Hostility in the workplace is becoming unbearable."

Larry Lakey
Nineteen-year revenue officer
Offer-in-compromise specialist

Following Congressman Douglas Barnard's hearings in the late 1980s, Commissioner Fred Goldberg called for a top-to-bottom review of the ethics and attitudes that defined the culture of the IRS. The Barnard hearings had exposed numerous shortcomings within the agency and led to a decline in morale. Goldberg's objective was to define the problems, work to improve them, and then burnish the Service's image publicly. "No agency of government," he said, "depends more on public confidence in its standards of ethics and integrity than does the Internal Revenue Service. That confidence is not incidental to accomplishing our mission, it is essential, for without it, the system of voluntary compliance cannot function."

Goldberg, a bright, articulate leader who understood the value of public relations and how it fit neatly into his desire to turn the agency around, contacted the Government Ethics Center at the prestigious Josephson Institute. He asked the institute to conduct the most intensive study ever into the manners and mores of the agency. Michael Josephson personally oversaw the project and worked with the commissioner to make sure that the study's findings accurately reflected reality within the massive organization. Their objective was to establish benchmarks that fairly represented the ethical profile of employees and managers. Using these benchmarks, Goldberg and Josephson planned on initiating a series of thorough training seminars to sensitize and educate. They believed that with a consistent effort it would be possible to change behavior.

What they did not count on was resistance from management. According to Michael Josephson, it appeared that from the very beginning the initiative ran into one obstacle after another from the career executives. "Commissioner Goldberg was determined that this is what we were going to do," Josephson told me. "But the deputy commissioner, who was like the agency's chief operating officer, was defensive, very suspicious."

With Goldberg firmly dedicated to the program, Josephson pushed ahead with an extensive survey that defined the values, opinions, and priorities of employees at every level of the agency. The effort of collecting and sorting the data took the better part of 1991 (managers' survey) and 1992 (employees' survey). "It had to be statistically valid if it was going to work," Josephson said. "We asked extremely hard questions and then we broke the data down by region and function."

The result was a 200-page report that provided an attitudinal portrait of the Internal Revenue Service, a report that moved beyond anecdotal evidence and succeeded in quantifying the problems that were plaguing the agency and making life difficult for taxpayers and employees. What was the IRS' initial reaction? Once again it was time to circle the wagons. "There was a huge 'kill-the-messenger' reaction to our work," Josephson explained. Immediately, the agency's career executives challenged the data, arguing that the report should be dismissed out of hand. Given some of Josephson's findings, their reaction was understandable. According to the report's summary, "The data reveal several 'trouble areas,' especially regarding unfair handling of taxpayers' complaints, deceiving taxpayers to coerce compliance, deceiving audit agencies, and political favoritism."

Josephson outlined the problems:

- *Unfairness*—30% of all IRS employees observed at least one instance of unfair or uncaring treatment of taxpayer complaints within the past year, while 13% observed such conduct at least three times.
- *Political Favoritism*—19% of IRS managers said they observed situations where taxpayers with political clout were given preferential treatment at least once in the past twelve months while 10% said they saw such conduct at least three times.
- *Deception*—15% of all employees observed instances of "lying to or misleading a taxpayer to coerce compliance." 7% said they had seen this at least three times, and 8% admitted they had personally deceived a taxpayer within the past year.
- *Deceiving Government Audit Agencies*—15% of the managers said they observed instances of lying, deception, or deliberate concealment regarding a government audit agency.

Goldberg and Josephson were undaunted by the criticism coming from upper-level managers and career executives. "I decided to meet it head on," Josephson told me. "I said bring your statisticians into the room. Let's sit down. We'll go over every question. We'll look at every answer." That's exactly what the IRS did, and according to Josephson it was not long before the careerists had to accept the report.

"The kinds of problems we discovered were not out of the norm for most other organizations," Josephson told me. "The problem is that with such absolute power, and with over 100,000 employees, there has to be a zero tolerance for the negative behavior our study documented. For example, 15 percent of all IRS employees claiming to have observed instances of taxpayer coercion translates into 15,300 individuals within the agency, and who knows how many taxpayers were involved outside."

An Obsession with Numbers

Shortly after confirming the data with the agency's top-level managers, Commissioner Goldberg called on all of his district directors to attend full-day training seminars. The first half of the day was spent going over the information contained in the report in an effort to quantify the problem; the second half of the day was used to work on solutions. A comprehensive plan was developed to improve conditions. Training films and workbooks were created to take the message of reform to every individual in the agency.

"The effort received terrific response from employees," Josephson said, explaining that there was a clear, overriding reason why the negative pathologies had emerged in the study: a numbers obsession. "Many forms of improper conduct revealed can be traced to an unusually high level of commitment to efficiency and productivity, which has translated into a seemingly compulsive numbers chase," Josephson reported. "Management, from the very top down, generates ambitious (sometimes overly ambitious) business plans with goals and objectives that place great pressure on subordinates to 'hit their numbers.' Consequently, most of the major problems involve coping mechanisms and survival strategies that have produced harmful management tactics and an unacceptable willingness to distort data and even lie to accomplish, or appear to accomplish, goals."

How does all of this translate into the lives of nonmanagerial employees? Josephson discovered an alarming breakdown in terms of internal trust and the "reliability of internal communications." Distrust and cynicism is found to an "unusually high degree" within the IRS, the report found. "In addition to the tendency to be obsessed with numerical goals," he concluded, "the culture seems to generate a management style that relies on implicit or explicit intimidation, which, whether real or imagined, produces justifications for dishonest and distrustful conduct by subordinates."

The consequence of this dishonesty is that within the agency productivity and quality goals are based on seriously inaccurate assumptions. Nevertheless, hard-pushed employees are required to meet them and managers are required to report them, even when most of those engaged in the process know it's a charade. "A substantial majority (61 percent) of all employees said that if all IRS employees were completely honest on all internal reports, standards of productivity would have to be adjusted downward," Josephson explained, describing how many "IRS employees are not convinced that top management is itself totally committed to doing the right thing, regardless of cost, or that their immediate superiors want them to put ethics over expediency."

Forcing subordinates to reach for numbers that most everyone agrees cannot be achieved, then pretending that they have been achieved, and finally adjusting them upward on an exaggerated new baseline must lead not only to internal dishonesty and never-ending frustration but to mistreatment of taxpayers. This numbers game is one of the reason why, as veteran collector Larry Lakey said, "The integrity of the Internal Revenue Service is more suspect by the employees than it is by either Congress or the public we service."

Testifying before Senator Don Nickles' field hearings held in Oklahoma City, Lakey described how managers treated one employee whose sense of propriety would not allow him to play the numbers game. "One of the finest employees that we've ever had," he said, "a 34-year veteran of the Internal Revenue Service, is now retired. His integrity is impeccable. His ethics are as unquestionable as his knowledge of the job. Now after all these years he has been pressured into retiring. He was treated like a criminal. This act of barbarity is unthinkable. But nonetheless his number of seizures was not at an acceptable level. After a lifetime of public service and at a time when he is most vulnerable, he was forced out of the workplace."

According to Josephson, the problem of internal dishonesty that his survey uncovered was "so serious" that he did not believe an ambitious training program would be sufficient to correct it. To succeed, he said, the agency would have to "convince its employees that it is willing to change entrenched traditions that have encouraged exaggerated reports and production levels." He warned that the only way to correct the dangerous trends would be a "comprehensive reevaluation of all quantitative criteria," and such a sea change would require an amnesty period to encourage and permit "managers and nonsupervisory personnel to restructure measurement and reporting practices without fear of punishment or negative performance reviews." He said that "unless the demands of present business plans are relaxed, honest and dedicated employees committed to improving the system may suffer the most because honest reporting will make them look unproductive."

This is what happened to Larry Lakey's colleague. And according to other agency employees with whom we spoke, the revenue officer forced into retirement was not alone. One auditor with five years of service inside the agency explained that the abuses she witnessed management engaging in were so egregious that she was willing to "crawl over ground glass" to tell me what she knew. "The IRS," she said, "is doing so many blatantly illegal things to both the public and the employees, and with such a sense of entitlement and complete freedom from consequences, that [managers] are incapable of correcting their own actions. They don't even seem to realize that what they are doing is wrong. It is so ingrained and built into the institutional culture that I doubt it can ever be separated."

Her account supported Josephson's finding that the root of the problem is management's fixation with unrealistic production goals and questionable quotas, objectives that are detrimental to taxpayers and employees alike. In a survey given to managers only, Josephson discovered that a third of them "*do not* believe that they are expected to do the right thing at the cost of expediency." Maintaining that agency executives often set a negative ethical example in their behavior, almost a quarter of the first-line supervisors polled by Josephson said that it is "sometimes proper to mislead or hold back relevant information from a taxpayer's representative regarding a matter in dispute." Twenty percent of all managers believed it is proper to use "tactics, including delay and the assertion of unsustainable positions, if it helps achieve just and proper results for the government." Only a third believed there is a moral obligation to be truthful, nondeceptive, and candid in relationships with the taxpayer.

Management's drive for numbers erodes fairness. One out of ten managers told Josephson that to do their jobs effectively and meet their responsibilities it was sometimes necessary to deceive outsiders. For employees, the results can be fatal. "When I was a union steward," one former employee told me, "I got a woman who was on the verge of a nervous breakdown. Like others, she had been destroyed by the stress. Three other employees were driven to commit suicide." She concluded that "before the public can feel any relief at all, the IRS needs to stop beating up their employees. Employees who are harassed and abused on a continual basis inevitably become demoralized and angry, and often respond to the public like attack dogs. The first step toward improving how taxpayers are treated is to improve how employees are treated."

The vicious cycle perpetuated by management is so simple to understand that one wonders why it has not been remedied. Artificially high numbers and a plethora of reports to measure compliance force supervisors, managers, and executives to push employees to the breaking point. To achieve the unattainable level of performance, employees must aggressively lean on taxpayers, lie about their statistics, or do a little of both. "It's smoke and mirrors," Josephson told me. "Managers can't be honest. They either continue to play the game or wind up looking incompetent."

Mona Meier, a current manager in the Collections Division with 20 years of experience, puts the abuse of taxpayers squarely on the shoulders of IRS executives. "Upper management determines the climate and policies for applying tactics and tax laws; therefore it is this level that [has] the greatest impact on the taxpaying public."

Field Office Performance Indicators

Another veteran employee concurs with Meier's assessment. Michael Ayala began his career with the Internal Revenue Service soon after he graduated from high school. Beginning in 1968 as a GS-2 clerk with a salary of $3,500 a year, Ayala eventually worked his way into management, becoming a top group performer within the Collections Division. He sees three specific areas where management adversely influences employees and taxpayers.

"First is the Field Office Performance Indicators (FOPI)," he told me. "Under this system, districts are rated one through thirty-three, depending on how much money they collected and how many cases they closed. You can imagine the message management may give their employees if they are ranked at the bottom. You can also imagine what offices ranked at the top did to get there. Look at what the Arkansas-Oklahoma District did to get ranked number three."

The Arkansas-Oklahoma scandal broke after our lead investigator, Eric Thorson, was contacted by several agency employees working within that district's Collections Division. After substantiating the reports and documenting the abuses, Eric, in an effort to shed light on what he believed was a crisis in immediate need of attention, shared the story with Michael Hirsh at *Newsweek*. Hirsh's conclusion, like Eric's, was that "victimization of taxpayers isn't just the isolated deviltry of a few agents. The IRS itself has become a rogue organization, wielding its awesome power under a cloak of secrecy."

In an October 13, 1997 cover story, Hirsh introduced America to Ronald "King" James, head of collections for the Arkansas-Oklahoma District. Hirsh described James as a prince of the church in the "spare, cloistered world of the Internal Revenue Service." He detailed how the Arkansas-Oklahoma District led the nation in property seizures that were eight times the national average per agent, and how James was richly rewarded for his efforts.

"James's team pushed for ever more property seizures from delinquent taxpayers," Hirsh reported, "even though the IRS manual says such moves should be a final resort, riding roughshod in some cases over their rights to appeal. They closed cases and sometimes slapped on levies and liens prematurely—which boosted the enforcement stats that the IRS rewards with cash awards for top officers."

James made it clear to his employees that their evaluations, promotions, and bonuses would be based on the number of seizures they made. He looked out for his favorite managers, some of whom, Hirsh wrote, "seemed to relish their power as much as he did." Hirsh reported how one of King James's foot soldiers was heard to exclaim, "Let's go rough up some taxpayers," as he left the office one day. The allegations against James encapsulated the abuses our investigation was documenting—wrongful enforcement procedures, unaccountable managers with near-absolute power to ravage employees, an informal policy of *omertà* that results in threats and retaliation against those courageous enough to come forward.

Michael Ayala, who worked for more than a decade as a manager in the Collections Division, agrees with Hirsh's assessment that "there's a widening gulf between the IRS's collection officers, who actually have to meet and work with troubled taxpayers, and an ever more remote and arrogant management. The latter sees the same taxpayers as ciphers and their assets as numbers to beef up their year-end reports—and to feed the insatiable demands of Washington for revenue and more efficiency."

According to Ayala, numbers come before ethics. "A year or two before the Arkansas-Oklahoma incident, managers in the New York office manipulated statistics to get cash awards," he told me. "I've recently reported another example to the commissioner where one district office improperly closed 83,621 cases. This was 99.44 percent of all the cases closed in such a manner in a fifteen-state area. What they did was pull inactive cases from the queue and say they were going to survey them, or close the cases without collection, because they had cursorily reviewed them and arbitrarily determined that there was no potential for them to pay."

How does one district closing over 83,000 cases stand up against others? According to Ayala, the fourteen other states in the Southeast Region closed only around 300 cases all together. "Closing these cases was done at a great cost to the government," Ayala told me. "Many may have had potential for collection. But in an effort to hit numbers the managers surveyed the cases at extensive financial cost to the public and to taxpayer fairness." The money lost by arbitrarily closing 83,000 cases puts pressure on the agency to make it up elsewhere. "There would be a tendency," Ayala said, "to be aggressive on other taxpayers to make up for all the surveyed cases and be ranked number one in dollars collected."

Though Field Office Performance Indicators were supposedly banished early on as a result of our investigation and hearings, Ayala believes it's a matter of semantics. "I've been around for thirty years," he told me. "Taking away FOPI doesn't mean anything in the IRS. They're still going to look at dollars collected and cases closed. While the rhetoric coming down is 'we're not going to rank,' the reality is that the districts are still going to have to explain the same things to the regional and national offices. They may not be published, and you may not have comparison and competition. But there will be measurements, and regional directors, district directors, and managers will know how they're doing and where they need to improve to stay competitive for promotions."

A Double Standard

The obsession with numbers is not the only cause of friction between IRS managers and their employees, and it is not the only dynamic that adversely affects the taxpayer. Michael Josephson had proven, with his 1992 survey, that while IRS managers at all levels have a "very high self-image" in terms of their own ethics, "a substantial proportion of middle- and first-level managers expressed a significant level of skepticism about the ethics and priorities of their superiors." Almost one in five middle- and first-level managers rated the ethics of top management as only fair or poor. Less than a third agreed with the statement: "IRS top management can be trusted to consistently do what is ethically right, regardless of cost." Almost one fifth "expressed strong cynicism" by saying that they "strongly disagreed" with the statement, and a quarter said that executives often set a negative ethical example in their behavior. Interestingly enough, one in ten executives agreed.

"Unfortunately, employees see it all far too often," Ayala told me. "There is a very clear and obvious double standard for high-level managers." High-level managers fall into the GS-15 and Senior Executive Service category. "There are tight and very regimented rules that govern the lives of employees and mid-level managers, but those at the top—those getting paid over $100,000—don't have to worry about abusing and misusing their authority. They're getting paid about as much as congressmen and senators, yet they have their positions for life. They don't have to worry about reelection or even about being held accountable for their actions."

What are some of the things Ayala has seen them do? "They create positions and fill them with friends and neighbors," he told me. "They take public funds and commit them to training seminars in exotic locations. These, then, turn into parties for executives who are being transferred or promoted. I've watched them spend tens and even hundreds of thousands of dollars to renovate their offices, while telling subordinates there's not enough money for necessities."

Another place where Ayala believes the Service suffers a glaring double standard is in the area of sexual harassment. "There is a lot of it going on by the senior executives," he told me. "One district director requested an employee in his office to perform oral sex. The employee reported the incident to Inspections, and they put a wire on her. They got it all on tape, and she waited for something to be done. Nothing happened, so two weeks later she filed assault charges with the local police department. The district director was arrested. The incident was reported in the papers. What infuriated me—and many others—is that the acting commissioner at the time sent a voice mail to all employees. He said please be considerate of the district director and his family. Please don't spread rumors to hurt the man. But he didn't say one thing about the lady—the employee and her family."

What happened to the district director? According to Ayala —and several others with whom I confirmed the story—he was moved to the national office, and because the transfer generated a cost-of-living increase he ended up getting a raise. "To anyone's knowledge, he wasn't reprimanded or held accountable for acts against one of his employees," Ayala told me. "The rumor is that a large dollar settlement was given to the lady, and she dropped the charges."

One IRS inspections employee, who is close to retirement and requested that his name not be used, confirmed Ayala's story regarding how the district director was handled. "The punishment was far too lenient for the crime," he said. "It was a case of executives looking out for executives." The sad irony is that while the district director was merely transferred to the national office to await retirement, he had only a short time earlier fired three subordinates: one for providing false information in a job application, another for missing a few meetings, and the last one for failing to observe designated duty hours.

This case, as well as others I reviewed, made it clear that on the rare occasion when an upper-level manager or executive is found to be engaging in improprieties, the executives have a tendency to keep each other out of serious trouble. "It's a golden handshake and a transfer," Josephson told me, explaining that his study confirmed feelings of a double standard. "There is widespread belief that executives get minor sanctions for actions that result in serious penalties for lower-level employees," Josephson said. "Even 34 percent of executives think this is not unusual, and 11 percent think it happens often." How do they protect themselves and each other? Promotional practices provide everything they need to keep themselves and subordinates in line. And this is the third point of friction that Ayala sees between management and employees.

"Management uses fear and intimidation," he told me. "That's why people are frightened to come forward; retaliation keeps them quiet. Why would you want to report on someone who carries your future in the palm of their hand?"

It appears that all tangible incentives within the Internal Revenue Service coincide with sustaining management and its objectives rather than questioning authority, even when authority is used to harm, distort, or impair. Josephson found that almost half of all managers "think that it is not unusual in the Service to see 'people who walk the line or set a bad ethical example' get promoted." Almost one in five first-level supervisors and middle managers said this "occurs often or very often."

"There seems to be a high degree of implicit or explicit intimidation, which, whether real or imagined, produces justifications for occasional deceit and the withholding of information known to be relevant," Josephson told me.

"This has a direct consequence in the lives of taxpayers," Ayala explained. "When taxpayer abuses continue to go on, who's willing to go forward to report them? People come forward and they are shot down. This has been allowed to carry on for years. What makes you think they are going to treat the public fairly when the people who come forward to report integrity violations are retaliated against? Who, within the IRS, is going to protect the taxpayer?"

Fifteen percent of the managers polled in Josephson's survey admitted that it was "common or customary" that those who make internal criticisms regarding unfair, illegal, or improper activities are punished. More than a third of the managers and a full quarter of the executives said that "it is common or customary for executives or senior managers to 'kill the messenger,' causing subordinates to distort, omit, or conceal negative facts or opinions."

Forcing subordinates to make such compromises to remain viable in their careers initiates a corrosive process in an environment that must be beyond reproach. Inaccurate benchmarks, a bounty on production, and a management that admits it is unwilling to receive bad news produces a system where employees have to begin wondering what place integrity and ethics have in the equation. The integrity of the organization must come into question. Employees must wonder how seriously management can be taking issues like internal fraud, taxpayer abuse, and harassment in the workplace if the vast majority of those who work for the IRS agree that candor is discouraged, negative information is concealed, and facts are tailored to please superiors.

"Once you start on the road of 'Whatever it takes to appear that the job is getting done,' you get into danger," Josephson told me. "Especially when you have the kind of power the IRS has. People are being forced to lie. You have your own people admitting they are committing fraud by cooking the numbers. This leads to decay and doubt in other areas. Without a greater degree of candor, much negative information, like hidden land mines, will be concealed for self-serving reasons, making it difficult if not impossible to deal with potential problems and make intelligent management decisions."

The pervasive "kill-the-messenger syndrome" was so widely acknowledged by IRS personnel that one out of three middle managers and 44 percent of first-level managers admitted to be willing to withhold information from superiors, and over half of the middle and first-level managers and about 39 percent of the executives do not consider it a serious ethical violation to be dishonest to a superior. One out of five middle- and first-level managers said that he or she had actually deceived a superior within the last year. Eleven percent of the executives admitted to such deception.

A Fallen Star

Michael Ayala learned the consequences that befall those who are bold enough to step forward. His stellar rise in the IRS appeared to come to an abrupt halt after he reported and tried to stop inappropriate behavior from taking place in the IRS' Southwest Regional Office where he worked. The event involved a manager's birthday party and a stripper named Miss Goodbody. Several colleagues and subordinates in Ayala's office approached him days before the party was to take place and complained that they believed the scheduled entertainment was demeaning, lewd, and against regulations in a government office during business hours.

Ayala did not believe upper management would approve the planned entertainment and was surprised to learn that the executive assistant to the district director had written a memo granting permission for Miss Goodbody to perform. Having recently been appointed an Equal Employment Opportunity (EEO) counselor, Ayala believed it was his duty to represent his colleagues' concerns to upper management.

Nothing was done to stop the event.

Not only did Miss Goodbody, dressed in a nurse uniform, show up to strip, but the party celebrated with a birthday cake depicting a nude female, complete with chocolate icing for pubic hair. Ayala and those who had voiced their protest stayed out of the conference room. "We could hear the laughter and the stripper's music," he recounted to me. "But the door was closed. It was extremely uncomfortable for us—in conflict with our sexual harassment policy that says sexually explicit or offensive objects are prohibited in the office."

To compound matters, Ayala's manager, who had been approached on a number of occasions and asked to cancel the event, brought his video camera from home to film Miss Goodbody's act. Her routine must have been appreciated because word about the mid-morning bash quickly spread to other regions, and within days the Georgia regional commissioner was feeling the heat. He wanted an immediate explanation. Ayala, who had met with his EEO supervisor on the regional level to discuss the concerns that had been expressed to him, mentioned that the show had been videotaped.

According to Ayala, with evidence available and his own manager identified as the trigger man on the camcorder, upper management scrambled to control the damage. Their decision was to initiate a series of rehabilitation and sensitivity training seminars to demonstrate that they understood the serious nature of their decision to allow the event to proceed, despite protests, and to hope that such a *mea culpa* would mitigate any formal sanction. The irony is that the very individual who approved Miss Goodbody's performance conducted the seminars, and those who had objected—including Ayala—were required to attend.

For a time the storm appeared to be over. But all was not well. Ayala had broken the code of silence, and it soon became apparent that, in reporting on the manager who had taped the stripper, he had all but eliminated any future chance of career advancement. At first when he questioned why he was being passed over for promotions, Ayala was told that those who had been promoted were "name selected," or that they had been asked for specifically by the divisions, regions, and districts where they would assume their new responsibilities. The excuse did not satisfy Ayala as he watched individuals with less tenure, experience, and education get promoted ahead of him, and it unraveled the day his name was requested for a position by the division chief in Nashville, Tennessee.

It was the opportunity he had been waiting for, and Ayala was confident that, with his former manager gone and his new manager supporting the promotion, it would be assured. He was wrong. The director and executive assistant who had originally approved Miss Goodbody denied the promotion. On what grounds? They wrote that Michael Ayala was "not aggressive or assertive enough," subjective words that are often used to spike a promotion when a legitimate reason does not exist. A year later, Ayala's name was requested again, this time for promotion to a position in the Birmingham, Alabama, office. Once more, he was denied.

Chutes and Ladders

"One of things that distressed me most when I was working as the historian at the IRS was to see how the agency treats employees like Michael Ayala," Shelley Davis told me. "Here were people who had devoted their lives—their hearts and souls and careers—to the IRS, then at the pinnacle of their careers, everything would come crashing down. It's like Chutes and Ladders. You have all these people starting at the bottom and clamoring for the top. There's not a lot of difference when they start, but when they step on the chute they slide down. They're confused. They don't know what to do, whether to sit tight or fight. Most just button up their lips and sit quietly at their desks. There's no predicting who's going to end up at the top and who is not."

According to Davis, one of the most glaring examples of the double standard that exists within the Internal Revenue Service is how differently from lower- and mid-level managers upper-level managers and executives are treated when they make a mistake. A serious infraction of the law will rarely make a dent in the career of an executive, while a simple misstep has the potential of becoming terminal for an employee of lesser rank. "It's absolute common knowledge," she told me. "Within the IRS, no one's surprised when an executive or a GS-15 is transferred to national headquarters after doing something that most people would look at as being egregious. And no one's surprised when a mid-level employee is demoted or fired for even a minor infraction."

Shelley Davis and others I spoke with believe the double standard is the product of a secretive and hand-picked clique of executives who not only control the lives of the rank and file by deciding who does and does not get promoted, but who control the IRS' information flow, its paper trail, and hence its history. "Executive misconduct is information that the IRS knows how to protect," she said. "It either doesn't exist 'officially' or they destroy it to protect each other.

"One of the strangest experiences I had as historian," she told me, "was when I walked into the Office of Executive Support." Davis, who had been a longtime historian for the Department of Defense and had top-secret clearances to work with the most sensitive national security documents, described the Office of Executive Support as being as secret as the "inner sanctum of the National Security Council." As she explained to me, the office not only helps in the selection of each new class of the Executive Development (XD) program, and runs the six-month school for the select few who are chosen each year, but it protects executives once they are anointed, virtually assuring that they will retire to a full pension following a successful career.

"Once you become an executive you are removed from the IRS in all ways," Davis said. "Any trials you run into, any mistakes you make, are funneled through the Office of Executive Support. It's their way of controlling all information pertaining to IRS executives. They look out for each other. They've selected each other to be a part of the exclusive group. Only they know what's really going on at that level. Their world is very secret. The Office of Executive Support is the most controlled environment in the entire national office."

It is also the most controlling. "To be promoted you must play the game," Davis explained. "You are chosen to be placed in the IRS' Executive Development program—the ultimate path to power inside the Service. Aspirations to be selected for XD keep many mid-level IRS employees on the straight and narrow for years."

Davis says that before an employee is selected for XD, he or she has been molded and proven by those who are already members of the elite corps. "Training begins when you are selected to become a staff assistant to an executive," she told me. "That is the internship. It's like being a personal aide to an officer in the military. You do everything from get your executive coffee to get him women. You're the bag holder. You learn the behavior patterns. You learn to mimic those above you."

Once you are a part of the executive cadre, your success is virtually guaranteed. To make her point, Shelley Davis told me about one executive who was caught for falsifying travel vouchers. "Since he was an IRS executive, the Office of Executive Support quietly removed him from his prestigious position and put him in a backroom job. While his new responsibilities amounted to a do-nothing, fade-into-the-wall existence, they allowed him to keep his salary and take complete retirement when he left the Service to join a big accounting firm."

It does not seem fair. Michael Ayala mentions that his manager used a video camera to record Miss Goodbody, and his own career comes to an end. (According to Ayala, at one point the agency actually sent him a notice of termination, but withdrew it when he told the district director that he had been contacted by CNN.) The executive that falsified his travel vouchers had his career salvaged by the mysterious machinations within the Office of Executive Support. "Look at what happened after the Barnard hearings," Shelley said, her voice animated by the irony. "Those congressional hearings in the late 1980s focused almost exclusively on ethical misconduct of IRS executives. Congressman Barnard documented dozens of cases of misconduct. He proved that abuses were going on everywhere. Only one manager was ever disciplined. He was suspended for five days without pay. If a regular employee had been caught doing the same things Congressman Barnard proved the executives were doing, he would have been fired."

Yvonne DesJardins, a chief in the Employee and Labor Relations Section of the Internal Revenue Service, described how the sequestered executive realm takes care of its own. For more than two years, DesJardins was responsible for handling reports of misconduct made against senior agency officials. The reports came into her office in the form of investigations, hotline complaints over the telephone, and written memoranda. She logged them into inventory, completed a case analysis, and participated in preparing and forwarding remedies and recommendations to the deputy commissioner.

"There were instances of serious misconduct which ultimately required disciplinary action against a senior official," DesJardins told our committee. "In some instances, actions were taken. However, in many instances they were not." In the cases where nothing was done, DesJardins said, "it appeared that those individuals were being protected by the organization by either being reassigned, with payment of relocation expenses, or kept on until they either retired or sufficient time had elapsed to make the matter moot."

DesJardins cited several examples to illustrate how pervasive the protection of senior employees is, and how the modus operandi was simply to spike the report of wrongdoing by keeping it in a drawer within the deputy commissioner's office without taking action, even after allegations were well documented by the Treasury's Office of Inspector General. This is how the executive who committed travel fraud was protected. Another case cited by DesJardins concerned an IRS official who had a reputation for "abusing and mistreating subordinates, regardless of where this person worked in the organization." Again, Treasury's Office of Inspector General looked into the charges and determined that evidence supported "serious disciplinary action." According to DesJardins, however, "the case remained in the deputy commissioner's office for well over one year with no action taken." A third case involving sexual harassment by a senior official came in with allegations substantiated and disciplinary action recommended, but according to DesJardins "it remained on the deputy commissioner's desk for over two years, at which time the executive retired and the case was closed. The disciplinary action was never issued to the executive."

These incidents were a few of many reported to our investigators and related to the committee during the course of our hearings. All told, they were numerous enough to give credence to DesJardins' claim that "senior-level officials [are] consistently protected by their fellow executives." Despite the fact that Treasury's Office of Inspector General finds wrongdoing and reports it back to IRS for action, it is extremely difficult for one executive to take action against another. "The executives of the IRS are close to each other, frequently socializing with each other, and often developing lifelong friendships," DesJardins testified. "I observed that in most instances warranting disciplinary action, more effort went into how to clear the person than into what needed to be done to ensure the misconduct did not recur. Exceptions were made and preferential treatment was granted."

Throughout our investigation, it was difficult enough to listen to the outrageous battering suffered by taxpayers and employees, but as I listened to Yvonne DesJardins document how senior-level employees were almost methodically protected by a system weighted heavily in their favor, my anger came close to the surface. "Do you mean tell me," I asked Ms. DesJardins, "that misconduct reports on senior IRS executives are being shelved at the deputy commissioner's level?"

Her simple answer: "Yes, sir."

"How often is this a practice?"

"My observation," she said, "was that in those instances where there was serious misconduct, which would support a disciplinary action against an individual, they tended to be shelved and no decisions were made in terms of recommendations of what actions would be taken."

"So it was not an exception, but more often a practice."

"Yes, sir," she answered softly, and it became clear to me that so finely tuned was the IRS' defensive mechanism, and so tightly knit and secretive was the cadre of executives running the agency, that they had managed to create a world where, as David Burnham correctly reported, they were "a law unto themselves," accountable to no one and feared by everyone.

"An Ethical Lobotomy"

"Disparate treatment is rampant in the Service," an official in the Treasury Department's Inspector General's office told me. "I see it all the time. The way the IRS metes out discipline varies immensely depending on a person's position and grade level. It's particularly noticeable at the management level. Often serious misconduct by a senior official goes unpunished or the individual or violator is given a minor discipline action such as an oral reprimand. However, employees at a lower level have the book thrown at them. It's because they don't have the powerful network available to the executives. Frequently the union in different parts of the country is not even supportive of the rank and file because the union officers are too tight with high-level managers."

There is a joke in the Internal Revenue Service that when an individual is selected for executive development, a mind-control device is placed in the brain that wipes out principled behavior. "We call it an ethical lobotomy." Davis laughed, explaining how she came to know so much about the powerful Office of Executive Support and the XD program. "I wanted to do a brief history of the office," she told me. "I wanted to leave a record of its past and write about what it does for the agency. That idea got shot down real quick," she said. "They don't want people to know what goes on inside. The bottom line is that the IRS is the best secret-keeping agency in our government today. They are better than the CIA, better than the FBI. The American people do not have a clue about how the Service goes about doing its job, and that is just how the agency wants it."

The Office of Executive Support—or "executive protectorate"—is so efficient that on occasion employees who write letters to complain about abuses by their managers find their correspondence being answered by the very individual whose misbehavior they are reporting. Even Internal Security and Internal Audits, which were supposed to provide protection for whistle-blowers, often bucked the charges being made back to the party charged. As journalist Michael Hirsh described, the convoluted system is "so twisted . . . and so top-heavy with managers protecting fiefdoms, that even longtime employees are not sure who's reporting to whom. 'Problem resolution' caseworkers assigned to look into complaints actually fall under the authority of the managers they're supposed to be looking at.

"Frontline agents despair over the way their many complaints [disappear] down a vast institutional memory hole, despite the supposedly careful self-policing procedures in place in Washington."

Internal Revenue Service inspections officers who testified before our committee explained how the self-policing procedures break down, and how the culture at 1111 Constitution Avenue not only interferes with the inspections process but is often turned by executives into a weapon to keep lower-placed employees in line. Prior to passage of the IRS Restructuring and Reform Act of 1998, reports of misbehavior and lawlessness inside the Internal Revenue Service were handled in one of two ways. If the allegation was made against an agency employee with a grade level of GS-14 or below, the agency took care of the complaint "in-house," through the Office of Inspections. This office was divided into Internal Security and Internal Audits. If the report of wrongdoing was leveled against a senior employee—GS-15 and above—it was directed to the Inspector General's Office of the United States Department of the Treasury.

Both avenues had serious shortcomings, ultimately allowing managers and executives to control and even terminate investigations and subsequent punishment of those they wanted to protect. According to the Treasury IG officer with whom I spoke, problems associated with the IRS Office of Inspections went far beyond coziness between investigators and managers. The line of authority within the agency was not conducive to fairness. "It's true that in the field the inspectors have close relationships with district directors and regional commissioners," she explained. "If you're an employee, how do you disclose wrongdoing when the people whose misdeeds you're reporting are having lunch with the people who are supposed to investigate them? But the problem is much larger than that. The chief inspector reports to the number-two executive in the Service, the deputy commissioner. The executives then decide what they want to do with the information.

"There is no outside policing agency or judicial system. In the end, even if the investigation has been thorough and fair, it's the executives who determine who gets punished. They can take care of their protégés and destroy those who challenge them. Employees know this. So do the investigators. Consequently, the employees are very careful about coming forward, and the inspections personnel are cautious about how aggressive they are in pursuit of their investigations. It can be very political."

When it comes to looking into reports of misbehavior by executives, the "good old boy" network makes it difficult to conduct investigations in the first place. "When we look at senior-level employees and executives, often we have to question their statements and affidavits," the IG investigator told me. "Our people often doubt the veracity of some of the statements executives make on behalf of others. The corporate culture within the IRS is that everyone has to get their stories together. You have to be a team player—carry each other's water. It's hard to break through the barrier they set up. Regional commissioners and district directors are considered to be 'gods within their territories.' They have their own little kingdoms and they have employees who do their will. In some places within the IRS it's like a dictatorial environment. It's difficult to discover the truth about the dictator. People around him are rewarded for their loyalty, but not far below the morale is terrible and ultimately the taxpayers and the American public suffer."

Cozy relationships, blind loyalty, and concern about career advancement were not the only factors that determined the focus and outcome of investigations inside the Service. There was also manipulation through the budget process. The Office of Inspections was directly controlled by the IRS. By controlling where the money goes, executives within the agency created what we were told are "subtle limits and boundaries" on who and what are investigated. "We are dependent upon the very people and agency we investigate for our budget resources, and every year have to go hat in hand to get money," the witness from within Inspections told the Finance Committee.

The political and economic control of those charged with policing the Internal Revenue Service did more than simply protect certain employees at the expense of others it turned the investigative process into a tool that was used to retaliate, intimidate, and harass. "I've seen many examples of how IRS management and executives use Internal Security as a tool to hammer employees who have made complaints or allegations against management," the Treasury IG officer told me. "Internal Security has been used by executives and senior managers against mid- and low-level managers to target them as well, to either force them out or to make their lives miserable. For some inspectors the power and authority they have goes to their head, and they're willing to play the game to further consolidate their power and ingratiate themselves with those who are in charge."

Who gets retaliated against? Employees like Michael Ayala, those who refuse to quietly accept the decisions of their managers, despite how errant those decisions might be. "Mike is a whistle-blower," a senior attorney inside the agency told me. "He's an extremely honorable man, but he made a bad decision even though it was the right thing to do. He called attention to something that was extremely offensive—something that had been condoned by management."

Ayala, a Vietnam Airborne Ranger who had overcome one obstacle after another as he worked his way from private to major—and then found similar success as he rose within the ranks of the Internal Revenue Service—came up against a final adversary he could not overcome. According to the senior IRS attorney, because Mike chose to blow the whistle, he has been demoted and moved out of his office. He has had to mortgage his home to pay his lawyers. His health is broken. His wife has suffered a heart attack. And within the agency it is near common knowledge that his career is over.

Observing the consequences suffered by Ayala and others, the Treasury IG investigator expressed her opinion clearly. "I would never recommend anyone inside the agency to be a whistle-blower. The distress and anxiety are not worth it. The retaliation is incredible. The degree to which a whistle-blower

has to go to protect himself, his name, and his job is just phe-
nomenal. The process is cumbersome and nearly impossible.
You stick your neck out. You're an open target during the whole
process. Often you are out there alone. The personal and professional anxiety you go through is not worth it. You may win
the battle, but you will lose the war."

Survey Feedback Action Reports

Following the Barnard hearings, federal lawmakers praised Fred
Goldberg's resolve to root out corruption and reprisal within
the Internal Revenue Service. A memorandum he sent out as
the hearings were drawing to a close stated that the Service
would advance a strategic initiative on ethics to assure that the
IRS maintains "the highest standards of integrity" and is fully
capable of "investigating itself and other Service employees,
including senior managers and executives." Goldberg promised to provide an "environment in which employees feel they
are safe from retaliation," one that would "hold senior managers and executives to the same high standards expected of the
rank and file."

The foundation of Commissioner Goldberg's plan would
be the Josephson study and an Action Plan to "provide a framework for integrating the broader lessons" that had been learned
through the painful congressional investigation and in their
ethics initiative "into our organizational culture." Goldberg
promised to share the results of their findings and the progress
of their plan with Congress, the Treasury Department, practitioner groups, and the public. It would be the beginning of a
new era of openness.

Unfortunately, that is not what happened.

"No institutional memory exists within the IRS," Michael
Josephson told me. A little over a year after promising a strate-

gic initiative on ethics, Fred Goldberg left the agency. "The next commissioner had some interest," Josephson said, explaining that it was rough going against the hard-line executives who still wanted to keep his study out of view. "In the IRS, there's a level that never changes. I tried to convince them that what we had discovered wasn't terrible if people looked at it honestly and in an effort to address the problems." Shirley Peterson was named to replace Goldberg. She remained for a year. Margaret Richardson became commissioner in 1993, and the Josephson study was all but lost. In fact, when I requested copies of the two-part report it took some time to find anyone who knew what it was. Then I received only half of it, with a vague excuse that the other part could not be found. (I finally chased it down through an alternate source.)

"Everything just kind of ended," Josephson explained. "Pretty soon no one returned telephone calls and it became clear that the new regime wasn't interested. It was like ethics were getting in the way." Part of the problem is that the Josephson Institute was an independent party, an outside organization that could not be controlled by forces within the agency that sought to limit access to information. While Goldberg had promised to share his findings with Congress and the public, others believed such a goodwill gesture would be foolish, that it would result in more ridicule and continued congressional oversight, and inhibit the agency's ability to collect taxes. Giving Congress and the public that kind of knowledge would empower them; openness would dispel fear and intimidation, emotions that many career executives still believe are necessary for the IRS to carry out its mission.

With the Josephson Institute out of the picture, cynicism among mid- and low-level employees increased. Those who had enthusiastically embraced the ethics initiative began to see it as a public relations ploy. The executives had to admit that the information was useful in helping them keep and control the temperature of the agency, but why did it have to be made public?

In 1993 the third floor of 1111 Constitution Avenue came up with a compromise. They called it the Survey Feedback Action (SFA) Process, a service-wide study similar to the Josephson project that would be conducted every two years to, as the initial report claimed, "create an honest dialogue" between managers and employees about "organizational performance and working conditions," and to "establish baseline measures and track progress." SFA questionnaires were sent out to almost 90,000 employees and managers. Well over 80,000 responded. This time, however, the results came with an ominous warning on the front page: "The information contained in these reports is to be treated confidentially and is to be used only by agency personnel in the course of official duties." Commissioner Goldberg's effort to bring *perestroika* to the Internal Revenue Service had ended in failure, and the results from the SFAs made it clear why—for the agency—that was probably a good thing.

The SFA reports demonstrated increasing despair concerning the pathologies Josephson had identified in his earlier data. For example, the 1995 SFA indicated that well over 50 percent of employees service-wide either disagreed or strongly disagreed with the statement that "management communicates honestly with employees." Only one in four believed such honesty existed. Of the managers and employees who participated in the survey, a full 54 percent said that there is distrust between their ranks. Almost 50 percent disagreed or strongly disagreed that "the same ethical standards are applied to all employees regardless of their position within the IRS." Only 41 percent believed that management maintains high ethical standards, almost one in three indicated that management does not, and 29 percent replied that they neither agreed nor disagreed.

When asked if there is adequate protection against reprisal for employees who report misconduct, 72 percent either disagreed, strongly disagreed, or did not care to comment. More than one in four indicated that they believe management fails to treat employees with respect. And 30 percent strongly disagreed that "disciplinary actions are applied fairly to employees."

While the IRS insists that the aggregate Survey Feedback Action report for 1997 is not available, copies of mean score comparisons were sent to regional, district, and branch offices to show local managers how attitudes in their respective areas stacked up against similar attitudes service-wide. Many employees shared these results with me, and the numbers demonstrated continued distrust, animosity, and suspicion regarding fairness, ethics, and cooperation between employees and their managers. "The two most interesting trends in the 1997 data," one region-level analyst confirmed, "are the continued decline almost across the board and the fact that far fewer employees responded to the '97 survey. That demonstrates an increase in cynicism. Agency personnel have given up on the promise of constructive change." His assessment confirmed what the IRS discovered in the '95 survey. When asked if they believed the results of the survey would be used constructively, one third of the 80,000 employees and managers who answered the question said no. Another 29 percent neither agreed nor disagreed.

6

Management's Impact
on Taxpayers

"IRS management today acts as though it does not work for the American people. They are not available. They are not accountable. They don't return calls. The standard line is that they are always in a meeting, and unless you have inside information as to how to get to these people, or unless you're a sophisticated practitioner, you will never reach them."

Robert Schriebman
Tax attorney and author
of twelve books on tax practice

One glaring omission in the 1997 Survey Feedback Action poll concerns questions related to the treatment of taxpayers. Except for vague inquiries like "management follows up on employee suggestions for improvements in products, services, and work process" (one in four employees disagreed), there seems to have been little emphasis on the customer. There are probably several reasons for this, but a look at the results of the '95 survey makes it clear that one reason must have been fear concerning what the employees had to say. For example, when asked in 1995 if there are effective, well-defined systems for linking customer feedback to those who can act on the information, almost half of the respondents said no. Twenty-two percent said yes. To the statement, "Customers have the opportunity to evaluate formally the quality of products and services provided by employees," 47 percent answered that they did not. Only 23 percent agreed. When asked if "Progress toward customer service goals is tracked, reported to relevant work groups, and used to plan for improvements," 41 percent said no, and only 26 percent felt that it was. From the earlier report we learn that well under half of all managers and employees believe that agency products, services, and work processes are designed to meet customer needs and expectations.

The 1995 Survey Feedback Action poll included the above questions in a category called "Customer Focus." No such category appears in 1997. Most of the questions focus on employee empowerment, relations between labor and management, quality of work life, and diversity in the workplace. It asks about discrimination (20 percent of the respondents claimed that they "personally experienced discrimination on the job in the last two years while employed at the IRS"), sexual harassment, and the effectiveness of the union. Meeting the needs of taxpayers was either immaterial to the survey or the agency knew better than to ask the questions. Employees who spoke with me believe it was the latter.

"I felt like Alice through the looking glass," Margaret, a recently retired auditor, told me, relating how harassment, intimidation, and coercion by frontline employees are, in her mind, most often reflections of the values and operating styles of up-line managers. "It took me months away from that job before I felt even remotely human again. My husband said it was like watching someone become deprogrammed. Most employees I knew felt that way."

While she claimed to feel uncomfortable carrying out the instructions she was given—and more than once threatened to file formal protests inside the taxpayers' case files—she told me that as far as she was concerned the current agency environment is so heavily weighted in favor of management that you either indulge their will or look for another job.

One example she shared with me involved a young woman who was seven and a half months into a problem pregnancy. Her doctor had confined her to bed. Her husband was stationed overseas in the military. She was alone for the delivery and, according to the former auditor, frightened about losing the baby. Having received a letter to call the local IRS office and set up an appointment for an audit, she complied. Her call was handled by Margaret.

"She simply needed her appointment deferred," Margaret told me. "This was December and a lot of the auditors had scheduled their holiday leave. In addition, other auditors had been pulled away to help train new hires." The group was down to seven working auditors out of a group of twelve, and had a case order more than double what was normal for a fully staffed audit group. "Appointments were already scheduled for six weeks ahead," Margaret explained. "So giving this woman what she wanted would have involved only an additional two-week delay."

Before she could confirm the appointment, however, Margaret had to check with her manager, something that is required before granting extensions. "I asked her permission to schedule the case ahead if we got a doctor's note. She refused. She said that pregnant women were always exaggerating and faking symptoms and that the taxpayer had to come in at the first possible opportunity."

Margaret questioned the decision, but the manager was firm. "I went to the taxpayer and tried to tell her as gently as possible that I couldn't do what she was asking," Margaret told me. "She got very upset and asked to speak to the manager." At first Margaret's manager refused to take the call. "I had to beg her," Margaret said. "I didn't want the taxpayer any more upset than she already was."

Angry that Margaret had insisted, the manager took the call, and according to the retired auditor, "she yelled at the taxpayer until I was cringing inside. Then she hung up on the woman and told me to prepare an examination report showing a deficiency and make sure the case was closed out as soon as possible."

Margaret asked her to reconsider, but the manager would not back down. "Again she directed me to send the taxpayer a report," Margaret said. "And I did what I was told. Thirty days later when the case purged out, I got it with a note from my manager telling me to close it that same day. I closed the case and felt horrible about the whole thing."

Margaret told me that the IRS is doing so many blatantly illegal things to both the public and the employees, and with such a sense of entitlement and complete freedom from consequences that they are incapable of correcting their own actions. They don't even seem to realize that what they are doing is wrong. "It is so ingrained and built into the institutional culture that I doubt it can ever be separated," she said. "They need oversight and they need accountability at the very least."

Lack of Training

While some experts cite arrogance, petty mean-spiritedness, and pressure from above to close cases as the cause for behavior like that witnessed by Margaret, Bruce Strauss, the former Collections Division chief, believes it also reflects a serious lack of training and people skills. A full 50 percent of employees and managers who participated in the '95 survey agreed that there is insufficient training to promote quality improvement. "You have to look at who is occupying these positions and what their backgrounds are," Strauss told me. "You have to ask who is getting promoted and why. Even at the highest levels and in some of the regional commissioner positions you'll find they have very little experience in applying tax law." This results in a natural and negative dynamic. Every employee is evaluated by a manager. If the manager has inappropriate goals and a wayward manner of operating, he or she promotes those employees that conform to them.

Former revenue officer David Patnoe sees the dynamic as a vicious cycle: managers, knowing little about what their employees are supposed to be doing, are evaluating them on how well they follow orders, close increasing numbers of cases, and collect more taxes. "Since these managers do not know enough about tax collection, they have a tendency to require [their employees] to take actions that might not be correct but which the managers feel would lead to a higher closing rate or higher dollar collection," he testified. "Sometimes the action might even be illegal but the managers did not know it, simply recognizing that a particular action resulted in more closures. The newer [employees] might not know a particular action is illegal because they haven't been around long enough, or are simply not sufficiently trained. [Those] who have been taking direction from these managers get promoted."

The agency's escalating tendency to place unskilled employees into management positions concerned Patnoe while he was working for the IRS. "I used to call these people the 'ninety-day wonders,'" he said, "ninety days being the span of time they spent doing revenue officer work between the two phases of revenue officer training classes." Patnoe testified that many times collectors who may have never actually knocked on a door, collected a tax, or worked with others in the process of collecting taxes were promoted to management positions simply because they were at the right grade level at the right time.

"I can't remember the number of times I heard, 'You don't have to know how to collect taxes to be a manager,'" he told our committee, "'you just have to know how to manage!'" Patnoe finds it amazing that individuals who do not know much about collection are put in charge of people who are sent out to collect. How, he asked, is the revenue officer supposed to depend on a supervisor for advice on difficult cases when the supervisor has never collected taxes?

According to Patnoe, this prevailing condition within the agency becomes frightening when you consider that these managers are required to review and approve the strident and near-unstoppable actions of revenue officers based on their own understanding of what actions are appropriate under the IRS policies, as well as the law. The consequence, he testified, is that "many of these managers are basing day-to-day decisions on whatever they determine important to their own supervisors in order to look good."

And what were these managers judged on? "Sheer numbers," he told us. "How many dollars collected or how many cases closed was—and is—the bottom line. Make no mistake about it, there are goals, quotas, that may be unstated but well known to the agent, that are driving . . . managers who are not thoroughly schooled in the collection of taxes but making decisions based on how they can get their numbers up."

Patnoe believes that as a result of this training and promotion practice, new revenue officers have become less and less effective, while many of the current managers do not know what the revenue officers are supposed to do. And among those who shared their insights with us, he was not alone.

Darren Larsen, another witness who testified before our committee, worked as an attorney in the agency's Office of Chief General Counsel for more than a decade. During that time, he dealt closely with all the different functions of the IRS: examination, collection, criminal investigation, and disclosure. According to his testimony, he was appalled by the lack of technical knowledge on the part of the frontline managers and the consequences it had on employees who interacted with taxpayers.

"I knew group managers who had the responsibility to review and sign off on administrative summonses who did not know the basic requirements for content of the summons or the rules for service," Larsen told our committee. "The less experienced revenue officers unfortunately learned from these managers and consequently made mistakes. I knew one manager who did not understand the distinction between a lien and a levy."

Larsen said he was also "dismayed at some of the 'on-the-job instructors' who were lacking in the legal fundamentals and passing on their incompetence to newer revenue officers." The cycle continues, he told our committee, and the quality of service rapidly declines.

"A Phalanx of Drones"

Another area of increasing concern is how managers can, and often do, avoid contact with taxpayers, leaving the difficult situations to their employees without giving them the requisite authority to remedy the dilemma. I was surprised by the strong reaction I received from practitioners when I asked about management's accessibility. There was almost universal agreement with Bob Schriebman's assessment that IRS management today "acts as though it does not work for the American people. They are not available. They are not accountable. They don't return calls." The standard line, according to Schriebman and others, is that "they are always in a meeting, and unless you have inside information as to how to get to these people, or unless you're a sophisticated practitioner, you will never find them. It's as if they have a phalanx of drones surrounding them," he said. "They're elusive from the top down."

The practitioners explained that most often the district director won't talk to a taxpayer or a taxpayer's attorney or CPA on a one-to-one basis. Rather, the practitioner must deal with the manager's subordinate. "You try to look up a manager's number in the telephone book—a division chief or director— you won't find it," Strauss told me. "Why not? Because they don't want to be accessible. Inaccessibility has been going on a for a number of years, and as they are more and more criticized there is a tendency to be more and more inaccessible.

"Look how foolish it's become," Strauss continued. "The IRS will tell you that one of their special initiatives is the problem-solving days the agency's holding around the country. That's good, but you have to ask what's going on here. We're saying that we have problems in the system that need a special day to solve—that our employees are not otherwise available to address your concerns? The whole concept is fundamentally ridiculous. Every day ought to be a problem-solving day. Managers should be accessible and ready to help taxpayers without having to make a big deal about it."

A career employee who became a top manager himself, Strauss admits to a significant compassion for the IRS employees and their thankless responsibility of ensuring that each citizen files and pays their fair share of taxes. "You're never going to make it a popular job," he said. "Nobody has ever liked bill collectors, but the Service can be professional, efficient, and understanding." The fact that it is not, he believes, is due to the ineffectiveness of the agency's top management. "Instead of assessing the current trends and taking appropriate steps to correct problems, management becomes aggressively defensive and goes into denial. They maintain that mistakes are rare and those mistakes that do gain notice are blown out of proportion, that they are statistically irrelevant due to the 200 million returns that are successfully processed each year," he said. "But based on my knowledge, such a statement would not be factual."

It's Not a Mistake Unless It's Discovered

With Shelley Davis' analogy of Chutes and Ladders fresh in our minds—how one mistake can terminate even the most promising climb through low- and mid-level management—it's easy to understand why the cultural proclivity inside the Internal Revenue Service is to dodge, deny, and bury mistakes, and why it's next to impossible to get anyone to accept responsibility. "There's no real leadership in the managerial and executive ranks," Davis told me. "Decisions are made by committee, so no one person has to take the fall for their outcome, and all executives have assistants who sign their correspondence, removing them from accountability."

The case of Michael Ayala and the stripper, Miss Goodbody, demonstrates how a well-used institutional redoubt of protection safeguards executives and upper-level managers from the adverse consequences of bad decisions, mismanagement, and even lawless behavior. Permission to let Miss Goodbody perform was granted not by the district director but by his executive assistant. The director remained one well-calculated step away from bad judgment—his career insulated from any adverse reaction to Miss Goodbody's performance. When news of the activity spread, and damage could no longer be contained, the assistant accepted full responsibility and organized the sensitivity training seminars as an act of contrition. What were the consequences to the assistant's career? There were none. She remained protected by her director, his clean record and upward mobility.

"What happened to Ayala is a clear example of why upper management and executives are surrounded by minions," Shelley Davis told me. "It's their way of avoiding responsibility. Lower-level folks have no such protection."

So, how do lower-level employees protect themselves?

"They admit nothing," Bruce Strauss said. "That's the rule inside the IRS. It's unfortunate, because you cannot have an organization with so much power unable to admit its mistakes and unwilling to make things right—to make the taxpayer whole." Just the number of times I heard the phrase "circle the wagons" made it clear that the lack of accountability and a desperate determination to avoid exposure of wrongdoing and subsequent criticism not only exists but is pervasive within the agency. And it has direct consequences in the lives of taxpayers.

I was told the sad story of one examiner who was given a file to work on that had been sitting for several months awaiting reassignment by the group's manager after the original auditor had gone on a detail to coach new employees. The case was very old at the time of reassignment and it took the examiner some time to locate the taxpayer.

"When the taxpayer was located," the examiner told me, "she was living with her parents in the Southeast. She had advanced ovarian cancer with an uncertain prognosis. She was undergoing chemotherapy and radiation treatments, which had weakened and sickened her to the point where she had to move back home to have her family care for her needs."

The taxpayer told the examiner that she had attempted to contact the IRS, trying to explain the changed circumstances in her life and asking that her case be transferred closer to the area where she was residing. Several letters to this effect were found in her file. Still, according to the examiner, "She had never received an answer." According to the employee, all requests to transfer files must go through the group manager, and in this case the manager had failed to respond, despite the fact that she had—the examiner believed—seen the many requests made by the taxpayer.

Upon discovering the contents of the file, and given the taxpayer's serious condition, the examiner approached her manager and asked that the case be transferred as the taxpayer had requested. "[My manager] refused," the examiner told me. "She said she did not want the receiving district to see how long the file had been sitting without her action." This presented a new set of problems, as the examiner had never conducted a correspondence audit, and the taxpayer's case was business related and included boxes of records that would need to be examined.

When the examiner called the taxpayer to explain her manager's decision, the taxpayer became upset. "She said it would be very hard for her to box up and ship the records," the examiner said. "The taxpayer explained that she couldn't lift the boxes anymore. She was in constant pain and couldn't drive. She wanted to have the audit done where she was living." The taxpayer asked to speak to the manager, who, according to the examiner, "spoke to her so roughly that [the taxpayer] was crying when the call was transferred back" to the examiner.

The taxpayer shipped the boxes over a long period of time and the examiner had to work the correspondence audit in between live audits. The manager would not block off appointments for the examiner to give her adequate time to work with the records and contact the taxpayer. "This added weeks to an already very old case and was an ordeal for the taxpayer," explained the examiner. "On more than one occasion the taxpayer told me that she did not know how much more abuse she could stand."

When the audit ended, and the report was sent to the taxpayer, it was signed and returned with a letter stating that the taxpayer was now terminal. She wished the IRS as much luck collecting the deficiency as the taxpayer had getting her audit done. She had no money, no assets, and no peace of mind. "She said the IRS had cost her the peace of mind she wished she could have had during the last few months of her life," the examiner told me. "I had to agree with her."

The taxpayer's pain and frustration were caused by the manager's refusal to acknowledge that she had kept the case much longer than she should have, that she had failed to respond to the taxpayer's correspondence, and that she was embarrassed to let another district know of her mistake. Beyond the rule of admitting nothing, low- and mid-level managers avoid being held accountable by stealing a page from the book of strategy used by their leaders in upper-management and the executive ranks; they, too, surround themselves with employees and assistants who are unwilling, for one reason or another, to report their misconduct. Far too many of the employees with whom I spoke commented not only about the necessity of cultivating a sense of allegiance—hitching their wagon to a rising star—but about how retaliation and intimidation are used at all levels to manage those who refuse to be "team players."

The agency-wide SFA (Survey Feedback Action) effort reported that only 28 percent of employees and managers feel there is adequate protection against reprisal for employees who report misconduct. Almost three out of four either disagreed or did not express an opinion. "Managers are insulated by silence," David Patnoe testified. "Upper-level management, in many cases, will never hear what happened." Indeed, the system is almost perfectly designed to contain bad news, with employees and taxpayers alike, frightened to come forward. So much power is concentrated in so few hands that a totalitarian-like dynamic emerges to keep the masses in line. Apparatchiks want to rise in the closed system, unmolested by threats and reprisals; the proletariat want to be left alone. "If you just had somebody harass you, take away half your life savings, but you still owed tax and it was still in the hands of that person, are you going to come forward knowing what that person just did and was capable of?" Patnoe asked our committee. "This fear by the taxpayers, some of it rightly earned because [the IRS has] done things that are outrageous, and some of it earned just by rumor, keeps the taxpayer silent." Patnoe told us that for every horror story that surfaces, there are hundreds that will never see the light of day.

Another reason taxpayers and frontline employees will not press a complaint was expressed by Jennifer Long, who said that they have come to realize that, even when mistakes are reported, there is a "total lack of response." According to Long, "No matter what proof you bring to them, no matter what you do, there is just no response. If they are forced into a situation where they have to answer for their mistake, I just cannot think of any other description but cowardly. I cannot understand it. They have more power than any other entity in our society. They have a fiduciary responsibility and a higher level of responsibility to admit and correct their mistakes in an honorable and professional way." But instead of openly addressing shortcomings, Long said, the learned reaction within the IRS is to try to "discredit and harm the unfortunate person who accidentally gets involved in one of their mistakes." That is, if they don't first bury them and then destroy records to make sure the mistakes can never be proven.

According to Patnoe's testimony, when lower-level managers find a mistake "they will do their best to sweep it under the carpet. They do not want to report it." If the mistake involves upper-level management and the executive corps, the IRS is known to completely shred incriminating records in open violation of United States Code, Chapter 101:

> Whoever willfully and unlawfully conceals, removes, mutilates, obliterates, or destroys, or attempts to do so, or with intent to do so takes and carries away any record, proceeding, map, book, paper, document or other thing . . . shall be fined not less than $2,000 or imprisoned not more than three years, or both. The same remedies apply to those who have custody of such materials and also holds that such individual be imprisoned for not more than three years, forfeit office, and be disqualified from holding any office under the United States.

"The cleanest way to protect yourself from your mistakes is to control your history," Shelley Davis told me. "And the IRS has it down to an art form." Davis believes that the Service considers itself to be above the laws that apply to the FBI, the CIA, the Department of Defense, and to every other department and agency of the federal establishment. "No other agency of our government could get away with erasing its past," she explained. "When you destroy your history, there is no way you can be held accountable. You can eliminate any potential smoking guns by trashing your records." In this way, it is conceivable that the Internal Revenue Service can do almost anything with impunity. And who is going to complain? "Why would any taxpayer ever question the one agency that can truly bite back?" Davis asked rhetorically. "Why would an employee complain when he knows that in doing so he's bringing his career to a premature end? Fear of suffering a personal attack from the IRS generally keeps most of us in line."

"Why won't the executives or upper-level managers protect the records?" I asked.

"Why would a manager or an executive complain when he knows that the ability to shred history actually benefits him?" Davis answered. "It ensures that he can never be held responsible for his actions. How can you prove any wrongdoing when the evidence is already destroyed? The IRS has learned that the privacy protections are its best weapon in its war against its 'customers.'"

The Pressure to Perform

Controlling history begins the moment the taxpayer faces the auditor. From that point on, the only material contained in the taxpayer's file as it moves forward is information that the IRS employee chooses to include. Auditors are not permitted to make photocopies of documents and other materials presented by the taxpayer. Instead, they are ordered to write up work papers based on the documentation. This results in the construction of history, allowing them not only to spin the evidence, but control it altogether. "Ordinarily, we describe what we see," one examiner told me. "But a bad auditor can omit or invent documentation to arrive at a conclusion that doesn't actually reflect the taxpayer's case. In this way, auditors literally hold the taxpayer's life in their hands."

With managers pressuring employees to assess and collect more dollars per hour, and with the managers themselves under pressure from above to hit statistics, it is easy to see how tempting it might be to misuse the tools employees have been given to meet the demands. "It's difficult for people to conceive how much power the IRS gives its employees," Margaret, the former auditor, told me. "In an office examination, if you think someone is hiding income you can get bank accounts with a summons. You can make people appear who don't want to appear before you. You can demand canceled checks. You can get credit reports. You can summons utility bills, phone bills, whatever you want as long as you get a manager to sign. And managers generally don't question you. If you don't like a taxpayer, for whatever reason, you can pull three years of tax returns and do an audit for every year."

There is even what IRS examiners call the "black half sheet," a form that allows them to refer a case to the Criminal Investigation Division. Generally, it is used to report suspicion of fraud, altered documents, or other serious crimes, but it can also be used for retaliation. Once a case is referred to CID and the service center, the taxpayer can expect to have his or her returns flagged for audit well into the future. Finally, auditors have tremendous latitude in the application of penalties.

"Auditors are encouraged to add penalties all over the place," Margaret explained. "Managers at no time are supposed to influence auditors, but they do. If an auditor flatly states, 'I'm not going to do that,' it's insubordination and the manager can get you fired."

To illustrate how the system can malfunction, Margaret told me about a case she was assigned to that had been sent to her audit group from Collections. "There was a particular revenue officer who would always refer cases for audit if he disliked the taxpayers," she said. " He would usually write up the case as suspicious, with fraud potential. He would also keep the collection code on the case, which would freeze it so that office exam could not close it or transfer it without his release. He was notorious for that, and most of the exam managers would not accept his cases."

A new manager had arrived in Margaret's exam group and, according to the auditor, "she needed some fraud cases for her performance appraisal so she took two cases from him on the same taxpayer."

She gave the assignment to Margaret, telling her that they were solid fraud cases. "I reviewed them and saw some questionable rental expenses," Margaret told me, "but nothing that looked like deliberate fraud and nothing to develop as fraud."

In the meantime, the taxpayer had moved to Las Vegas and asked to have his cases transferred there. "I took the cases to my manager for permission to transfer them," Margaret said. "I explained that there were no fraud issues. I went over the cases with her item by item. She agreed to transfer them, but then found out about the freeze code."

Margaret's manager approached the revenue officer. "He told her basically that if he said there was fraud it was going to be developed," Margaret said. "My manager came back to me and told me that I had to develop fraud. I again explained to her why I couldn't and asked to have the cases transferred to someone else. She told me no one else did fraud in our group and she really needed it and it would take care of the freeze code if I would just do it. Otherwise she could not close out the cases and they would age in the group for months.

"I told her I was sorry," Margaret said. "I couldn't develop fraud if it wasn't there. I handed the cases back. She went fuming off and slammed the door to her office."

The manager approached Margaret two more times that same day, pleading for her to develop a fraud case for the collections officer. Again, she explained how advancing the cases would help in her appraisal. "That was all I could take," Margaret said. "I approached the wife of the revenue officer's manager, who was a coworker and a friend. I explained what was going on. She spoke to her husband, and the next day he contacted my manager, apologized for the behavior of his revenue officer, explaining that he had not been aware of the revenue officer's actions on this case. He saw that the freeze code was taken off and asked my manager to come to him in the future with any problems she had with his group."

Instead of being relieved, Margaret's manager was furious. Developing fraud was not just an act of retaliation sought by the revenue officer, it would have helped the manager's career at the same time. "In the end, she succeeded in taking it out on the taxpayer," Margaret said. "She told me to close the cases on a report because she was not going to transfer them. I informed the taxpayer's representative, who called and harangued my manager, but in the end the cases were closed out unagreed and without being transferred."

In the months following, Margaret's manager continued to press the examiner with cases that she wanted to develop as fraud. Again, it was statistics driven. "I would review the cases and tell her when and why they didn't merit what she wanted," Margaret said. "On those occasions, she would simply take the cases to other auditors who she thought would be more responsive."

Employees of the IRS did not find the stories Margaret shared with me surprising. As I related them to others, they simply nodded, as if they were not out of the ordinary. They understood, as reflected in their answers to the agency-wide survey, that employees are not rewarded for providing high-quality products and services to customers. Advancement comes from hitting the goals that come down from upper-management. In the Examinations Division, that means dollars assessed per hour and the number of cases closed. In Collections, it means using the "full range of collection tools," a euphemism for seizures.

It All Comes Down from Above

I was disheartened when, only months after the agency's promise that statistics would no longer be used to influence employees, I received four current documents. The first came from the Southeast Region and clearly ranked districts within that region according to the number of seizures in 1997. It used qualitative terms to describe how well a district performed, and performance was based on how many seizures had been made. What I found most troubling is that the document also included the first three months of fiscal year 1998, again showing the districts within the region where they stood in relation to one another. From the same region came reports that during the first week of February 1998—four months after the IRS said it would no longer rank districts and divisions according to statistics—there was a meeting of branch chiefs that also involved executives from the national office. At that meeting, according to a supervisor who was in attendance, a report similar to the one shown to me was passed out, and the gathering was "told who was and who wasn't keeping their numbers up."

Witnesses told me that there were direct enforcement statistics presented in the meeting that compared the districts and divisions, including how their seizures for 1998 compared to the same period in 1997. If the statistics had gone down, a red negative was placed on the report. If they had gone up, it was indicated by a green positive. And all district directors and division chiefs who attended the meeting received the numbers. "There was no question about where they stood," a source explained. "And there was no question about what they were supposed to do."

One 25-year veteran of the Service with a decade of experience as a division chief who was in attendance at the meeting and requests not to be identified, explained the consequence such a meeting has in the lives of taxpayers. "I'll tell you what a division chief's going to do once he receives those numbers," he told me. "He is going to feel tremendous pressure to turn those red negatives into green pluses. He is going to go back and talk to his branch chiefs. The branch chiefs will have to respond. They'll put pressure on managers down line, knowing that if those red negatives don't become green pluses, their evaluations are going to be affected.

"It's absurd," he told me, "to think that upper-level management is going to use the statistics and that they are not going to affect the lower-level managers, collectors, and ultimately the taxpayer. It has to translate down. Lower-level will feel that they will have to improve those statistics. Branch chiefs, group managers, and revenue officers will have no alternative but to improve in dollars collected. They will have to reduce the number of cases they report as not collectable. They will have to reduce their overage—the number of cases over fifteen months old—many of them installment agreements. They will have to take action. That means increasing their number of seizures."

The other three documents that were sent to me came from the West Coast and contained ample evidence that, as with Collections, efforts are still underway within Examinations to keep statistics that allow managers to rank their employees. The reports sent to me concerned dollars per hour assessed by revenue agents at the division, branch, and group levels. Again, these comparisons continue to be made and disseminated while the national office insists that using statistics in this way has been banished from the Service. The three documents make it clear that the emphasis to assess more dollars per hour per revenue agent is prevalent not only at the regional level, but all the way down to the branch and group. Branch and group managers are shown how their employees stack up against others, and while the reports contain only raw data, those familiar with them told me that their existence sends a clear message that within the IRS it is still business as usual.

"The reports are generated so group managers will push their employees harder," I was told. "The continued consequence will be a drive to inflate assessments, target low-income and vulnerable taxpayers, and go after cases that will yield a return." In fact, one column of the multipage report reflects the percentage of returns that did not garner a higher assessment. "The objective," my source explained, "is to keep that percentage as low as you can."

While sincere efforts are being made by commissioner Rossotti and others within the Service to implement new congressional mandates, the division chief explained the current environment this way: "Right now the IRS is literally fighting the prohibition on using statistics. It runs contrary to the culture. Everyone inside the Service knows this, and they will not accept the change. Rather than do what Congress and the taxpayers want them to do, they are looking at the very letter of the law, as opposed to the spirit, to see how they can get around the current efforts to clean things up. But to get away from the old ways is going to require a big shake-up. It's going to require somebody to accept responsibility for what's happened to the Service and a consistent national initiative to break the culture and get rid of the people who are fostering it."

When Taxpayers Are Innocent

> "The IRS was really nasty to me. . . . I never cried so much. They threatened me and then they would put me on hold and give me to somebody else and then transfer me and put me on hold again. I was a Social Security number who they said owed a debt."
>
> Stephanie Toth
> Innocent spouse

Twenty-three-year-old Stephanie Toth thought her nightmare had come to an end the day she watched the sheriff march her husband from the courtroom. Skylee Kitzman, a Michigan logger and champion kick boxer, had been sentenced to thirteen years in prison for first-degree rape and six different counts of prostitution and pandering. His victim—with broken ribs, a scarred face, and a spirit numbed from five years of constant battering—had been his wife.

"I don't know how many times he threatened to kill me," Stephanie told me. "But he had a temper that when he said he was going to do something like that, you knew that he meant it, and you did what he said."

Fresh out of high school, Stephanie, a beautiful blonde with Nordic blue eyes, was introduced to 31-year-old Skylee by his brother Matt. "Skylee was a local celebrity," Stephanie explained. "He had won the Midwest championships. He was an expert in martial arts. And he had been on television. The first thing I noticed was that he had three cute little girls, and there was no mother around."

In the beginning, Stephanie stepped into the role as a friend. "I offered to help him do laundry and take care of the children. I helped around the house." Soon, they started dating. "We became engaged in March 1992, and I got pregnant with our son."

Stephanie remembers the early months of their relationship as being good, except for a series of court battles Skylee was going through with his ex-wife. "He didn't want to tell me about it," Stephanie told me. "He just said that she up and left, and he kept the girls." As time progressed, and Stephanie's pregnancy developed, the bully in Skylee began to manifest itself. "At first he cut off my ability to communicate with my family. He wouldn't let us get a telephone. He wouldn't let me have a driver's license. Every morning when he would leave for the woods to work, he made me come along and work with him."

In the early months, Stephanie enjoyed the time together, sitting in the summer woods and working beside her husband, but in the late months of her pregnancy—when rain and snow began to fall—she started to question his motivation for making her sit outside all day. "I was seven months pregnant," she said. "It was horrible, sitting, freezing, in the truck. I asked him why I had to go, and he finally admitted that he didn't trust me with his papers and his children."

According to Stephanie, at one point Skylee had been turned in for taking an improper picture of his little girl. "He worried that if I was alone in the house and had access to his belongings, I would find things that would get him into more trouble," she told me. "He was older and very violent. I was young, scared, and stupid."

In December of 1992, their son, Tyler, was born. Again, the relationship appeared to get better, and the couple married in July of the following year. But by October, Stephanie and Tyler were forced to check into a shelter for battered women, and the local court issued a restraining order against Skylee. "He was arrested a couple of times," Stephanie explained. "But the laws against domestic violence were really lean, and he had a way of getting out of everything. Even if he got pulled over and our car wasn't registered and he didn't have a license, he could talk his way out of a ticket."

In March 1994, Stephanie left the shelter and returned to her husband. "He threatened to kill my mother if I did not go back," she told me. "He said if I tried to leave him he would fight for custody of Tyler, and do to me what he had done to his first wife."

As they were now married, Stephanie believed that she had a legal responsibility to see that the couple filed their income taxes. She pleaded for Skylee to take care of it, but he indicated that he had never filed taxes and was not about to start. To protect herself, sometime after April 15, 1994, Stephanie gathered all the tax documents and business receipts she could find and filled out a 1040. "I didn't know what I was doing," she said. "But I felt I was doing the best I could. I thought that as long as I was making an honest effort with the IRS, that they wouldn't come back on us, and that I would be protected. I never believed that I was doing more harm than good. I didn't know how nasty they would be."

Shortly after Stephanie had filed the tax return, the IRS sent Skylee a letter telling him that it was in error. After reading the letter, Skylee beat Stephanie, leaving her with a black eye, broken ribs, and a bloody lip. "He took it out physically," she told me. "He said that if I didn't stay out of his finances, he would kill me. I was trapped. He was making $2,000 or $3,000 a week, but our electricity and water was being shut off. I would have to go to my grandma for help. She would give me gift certificates to K-mart so I could buy diapers for the baby. Both of us knew that if she gave me cash Skylee would spend it."

"Where did Skylee spend the money?" I asked Stephanie.

"He liked women," she said. "He would go to Hurley, Wisconsin—he would make me go with him—and he would visit one of five strip bars on the main road, and with me or without me, he would sit there and give them large tips, like the money was nothing, yet our kids were eating stale bread."

It was not enough that Skylee watched the strippers, but he soon forced Stephanie into what she embarrassingly called her "wonderful career as an exotic dancer."

"I told him I didn't want to do it," Stephanie said, her voice filled with emotion. "I cried, but he kept pressing me. I was tired of getting beaten up. I gave in, just as I did later when he forced me into prostitution. It was horrible, but I was trapped. I thought that the more money I made dancing the less he would make me prostitute myself. I couldn't stand it when he would take me into the bars and go over to guys and sell me. He didn't go into the bars as my husband. He pretended to be a customer, and tell guys how hot I was. Then he would tell me that a guy was a sure thing for $200, and that if

I didn't get him I wasn't coming home, he would kill me, or he would threaten the children."

Stephanie realized that Skylee was tormented by wild mood swings. His behavior was unpredictable. "If I didn't do what he said—if he didn't like the way I was dancing; if I wasn't smiling or if I was smiling too much—he would come up and bend my fingers until I cried, even in front of everyone. At first I thought it was the money, but it wasn't the money. It was him. Something inside of him."

By 1995, Stephanie had had enough. On September 20, Skylee brutally assaulted her in front of the children. In the corner of the room sat a laundry basket filled with clothes. Inside the basket was a child's tape recorder. As the assault continued, Stephanie managed to turn it on and record what I can only describe as the most harrowing, violent sounds I have ever heard. The next day, battered and emotionally numb, Stephanie opened her front door to find her grandmother.

"She said I didn't have to take it anymore," Stephanie remembered. "She said she would take me to the police department. It was there that I told them about the tape. They sent me to the hospital. As I was being examined, Skylee showed up and tried to take Tyler. I screamed to stop him, and he was arrested."

The police retrieved the tape, and it was eventually used as evidence in his conviction. Other explosive evidence included testimony from his first wife, who described how he had put her through a similar nightmare. Her fear, she expressed, was so profound that when she fled, she left the girls because she knew that if they were with her she would have to enroll them in school, and that would lead Skylee to their door.

With her husband sitting in jail, awaiting trial, Stephanie, for the first time in four years, felt safe. She told Tyler and the girls that Skylee wouldn't be released for a while. "They were happy," she said. "We ordered pizza and went out to the lake. There was a sense of relief that for forty-eight hours, at least, he was going to be gone."

The tape and the doctor's examination were enough for the state attorney to hold Skylee for trial. Forty-eight hours turned into a new week, and all appeared to be getting better, until Stephanie and Tyler returned home on a Tuesday afternoon to see a "fancy" car parked in front of their home. A well-dressed man got out and introduced himself as a revenue officer. He asked to speak with Skylee. Stephanie explained that her husband was sitting in the county jail, and she told him her story.

"He appeared to be satisfied," she said. "He was a nice man. He came into the house. He said he didn't think I would have a problem. I was still black and blue. He had to believe me. Besides that, he quickly saw that we had nothing to seize. I told him that I never had anything to do with our finances, Skylee wouldn't let me have money, and that I had just tried to do what was right when I filed the tax return. I said my only fault is that I had married him."

According to Stephanie, the revenue officer said that as long as she kept in contact with the agency and provided the information they needed, he believed that she would be fine. He left, and, in fact, Stephanie didn't hear anything from the IRS until well after her husband's trial and conviction.

"Skylee went to prison in June of 1995," she recounted. "Our divorce was final in August. The judge gave Skylee the obligation to pay the $10,000 that the IRS said we owed."

Stephanie went on with her life, continued to raise Tyler, found a new boyfriend, and took a job as a housekeeper in a nursing home. Then in 1997, when she prepared her taxes for 1996, she was delighted to discover that she was owed a $600 refund. "I promised Tyler that I would buy him a new bike," she said. "I had never before been able to do anything like that, and he had suffered a lot. This was my first real chance to do something special for him."

The refund never came.

Stephanie called to find out why, but was not given an answer until a letter arrived many months later stating that the IRS had taken the $600 refund and applied it to Skylee's $10,000 debt. "I sat down at the table and cried," Stephanie told me. "I called the IRS and asked how they could do this. Instead of answering, they put me from person to person. One lady came on and laughed at me. She said the divorce was a state ruling and the IRS is the federal government. I told her, 'This isn't funny. It's my life.' But she didn't care."

The Internal Revenue Service was going to hold Stephanie to what it calls the "joint and several liability standard." Under the standard, when a joint tax return is filed, the IRS holds each of the partners equally and individually responsible for paying the entire amount of the liability associated with the return. In this way, a non-working spouse, who may have nothing to do with the family finances, can be held liable for tax deficiencies assessed after the joint return is filed, even if the assessment is attributable to the income of the working spouse. The only way around this is for married couples to file separate tax returns, but this often results in a much higher liability.

Stephanie continued to call the IRS in an attempt to solve her case and claim the money. She tried to contact the one Service employee that had been kind to her, the revenue officer who had visited the house. Again, he was gracious enough to respond. "He told me to file for innocent spouse protection," Stephanie explained. "He said, 'Send everything you can and see where that goes, but don't mention my name because I'm not in any position to help you with this.'"

An Innocent Spouse Defined

Under the innocent spouse provisions then in place, an individual could receive relief from a tax assessment after a joint return had been filed, if it could be proven that:

- the innocent spouse had filed a joint return with the culpable spouse;
- the innocent spouse did not know and had no reason to know there was a substantial tax understatement; and,
- taking into account all the facts and circumstances, it was inequitable to hold the spouse liable for the additional tax attributable to the substantial understatement of the culpable spouse.

In addition, the spouse requesting relief must have met certain dollar thresholds that varied depending on the cause of the additional assessment:

- A tax liability resulting from an omission of gross income must have exceeded $500.
- A tax liability resulting from a deduction, credit, or condition that has no basis in fact or law must have exceeded $500 and also been in excess of certain income levels (10% of the innocent spouse's adjusted gross income for their preadjustment tax year if the taxpayer's income was less than or equal to $20,000; or 25% of the innocent spouse's income if the taxpayer's income was greater than $20,000). If the innocent spouse had remarried, the new spouse's income was included in this calculation whether or not they had filed a joint return. (United States General Accounting Office)

Though the rules were complex and extremely limiting, Stephanie did as she was instructed. "Several months later," she said, "I got a letter. It said my innocent spouse petition was denied. It said they had determined that I was solely responsible for the $10,000 because Skylee was in prison, without an income, and they threatened to garnish my wages and levy my bank accounts. They said if I got married they would take everything my fiancé had. All I could do was cry." In her mind, Stephanie's life had been destroyed, first by Skylee, then by the IRS.

"If I worked, they would take my money," she told me. "If I bought anything of value, they would seize it. The only choice I had left was to live on government assistance." Stephanie called attorneys and met with CPAs. They tried an offer-in-compromise, but she did not have sufficient money to pay what the IRS demanded. "Finally, my dad said why don't you try to write Senator Roth? I thought he was kidding. Who was I? When I told the CPA, she laughed at the idea. But my dad said, 'What's it going to cost you? Thirty-two cents.' I didn't know anything about politics. I really didn't care about politics, but I can't tell you how happy I was the day Eric Thorson called.

"Within days of talking to me, Mr. Thorson had my story on the cover of *USA Today*. By 11:00 A.M. that morning, a woman called from the IRS and said that she would be sending me my $600. She was a little irritated and said, 'If you have any problem with the IRS please would you call us first.' I told her I had tried. I asked her about my innocent spouse petition. She said they had to look into that further. A few weeks later I got a letter in the mail that said I wasn't being held accountable because it wasn't Skylee's intent to file taxes that year."

Stephanie cannot contain her excitement about how her case ended. "I finally won," she said. "It's behind me, now, and we set our wedding date. I get to learn how to live all over again." Unfortunately, for many other innocent taxpayers, their stories do not have such a happy ending.

"The IRS does everything it can to discourage auditors from determining innocent spouse," one examiner told me. "Management flat out tells you that an innocent spouse petition is a spurious claim and should not be determined unless the spouses were living separately. This is particularly true if the spouse seeking the relief has most of the assets." The examiner told me that on the occasions when she could not in good conscience deny an innocent spouse petition, her manager would take the case from her and reassign it to an auditor who would deny it. "The IRS would rather have the innocent spouse denied and force the spouse—in most cases a woman—into poverty, just for the sake of having another case closed," she said. "They are particularly unsympathetic to battered women. They simply do not accept that being beaten senseless on a regular basis affects your ability to deal with your husband's money and records."

"Why is the IRS so willing to place a woman into poverty or on welfare rather than help her remain economically viable?" I asked.

"Because after a divorce, the woman generally keeps the home and the old bank accounts. They have to get their own jobs and they are easier to locate than the husband who moves out, opens a new bank account, and sometimes relocates in a new state. In the IRS, they say, 'Go where the money is.' There is money—or equity—in the home. The wife now has to support her children. There will be money because she is working. And the wife is generally more vulnerable, less prepared to deal with the agency. She's an easier mark. Remember, it was the husband who was handling the finances and filling out the tax returns before the divorce. He has experience dealing with the IRS. His ex-wife doesn't."

Women for IRS Financial Equity

Elizabeth Cockrell, a witness who appeared before the Finance Committee to help us understand the dilemma suffered by innocent spouses, described the stark conditions these women face. Finding herself with a $650,000 tax liability left by a man she had been married to for two years, Elizabeth has battled the IRS for more than a decade and in the process founded Women for IRS Financial Equity (W.I.F.E.), an organization to increase awareness regarding the plight of these innocent spouses. "When letters started coming in from women all over America," Elizabeth told me, "I would go into my bedroom, read them, and cry for hours. These women were desperate, lonely, and frightened."

Like Elizabeth, most of those who contact W.I.F.E. are trying to raise children, struggling as single parents to maintain jobs, pay bills, rebuild lives, and do it all with the weight of the federal government squarely on their shoulders. "All they are guilty of is trusting their husbands and signing a joint tax return with him," Elizabeth told our committee. "Now, years later, they are suffering in great numbers." The General Accounting Office estimates that there are 75,000 to 80,000 instances per year of the IRS potentially pursuing the wrong spouse.

One elderly woman wrote W.I.F.E. to express her fear that she would soon be forced to eat dog food. Another, an accomplished pianist who had been abandoned by her husband, was forced to sell her home and piano to pay tax liabilities of which she had had no knowledge prior to being contacted by a revenue agent. She is now impoverished and living in subsidized housing in Florida. Many of the women who contacted Elizabeth were forced to sign returns at the hands of an abusive husband. Others reported that their signatures had been forged by their husbands or their husbands' secretaries.

"There are women whose husbands have bankrupted out of the tax liability, leaving their former wives stuck with the whole tax bill," Elizabeth said. "There are women who are on welfare, who are ashamed to be on public assistance, who want to work but are told by the IRS that if they go to work their pay will be garnished. One woman had to beg for money for diapers for her baby after her husband was long gone.

"How can a single mother raise emotionally healthy children when she herself is suffering, having had the IRS harass her for years with no end in sight? These women have the most important and critical job in the United States—raising the next generation. It is the children who are being hurt the most."

Elizabeth told our committee about the anger, depression, anxiety, and weight of helplessness that accompany being at the mercy of the IRS. An extremely attractive woman, with an infectious personality and successful career, she shared with me the toll that her ordeal with the IRS has taken in her private life. "Emotionally, it destroyed me until I came to the determination that I was either going to die or fight back," she said. "I can't describe the darkness. Every morning you wake up, wondering if that will be the day they take away your home, levy your paycheck, or freeze your bank account. Every night you go to bed and pray that the hopelessness and despair will go away, that you will be left alone to raise your children without the threat of not being able to provide for them. It is an overwhelming impediment to a happy and normal life. Your little children see you savaged and haggard, sometimes incapable of feeling joy. And each January you dream that the coming year might finally be the one that will bring closure to the nightmare you're being forced to live."

Most of the women who have contacted Elizabeth's organization have tried to work out their problems with the IRS. Many have written to the agency to provide their ex-husbands' addresses after the IRS claimed it had been unable to locate them. "These women begged the IRS to stop garnishing their own much-needed pay and to collect from their ex-spouses," Elizabeth said. "It wasn't as if their former husbands were difficult to find; the women were just easier marks."

The consequences felt by innocent spouses were vividly described in a letter Ann Kimbrough, a woman saddled with an IRS debt of over $100,000, wrote to Commissioner Rossotti. "I should be a negative statistic," her letter began. "I am black, a divorced mother of three children, including one with disabilities. According to the U.S. Census Bureau, I should be among those on welfare, especially considering that I have suffered incredible financial hardship and personal embarrassment from the IRS.

"Even though IRS revenue agents and a DeKalb County, Georgia, civil court agree with me that the tax liabilities during the few years that I filed a joint return were not attributed to my 'wrongdoing,' I am still being punished. Every attempt to resolve my situation has been rejected.

"Thanks to the IRS:

"Each year my overpayments are applied to my former spouse's account; each month I make payments to your agency on my former spouse's account; I filed bankruptcy in 1994; my blind and hearing-impaired son is without health insurance and health care; my retirement savings are depleted; my wages have been seized; I've nearly lost my home; I work up to three jobs to make ends meet; and the IRS has liens on my home. Each time I've sought better jobs with good wages, the IRS intensifies its demands. My home is again scheduled for foreclosure. And I now live with a negative credit rating."

Just how outrageous innocent spouse cases can become was described to our committee by Svetlana Pejanovic. Growing up in a little Bosnian town outside Sarajevo, Svetlana—the daughter of an economist—worked her way through the University of Belgrade, receiving her own degree in economics. In 1980, filled with great expectations, she came to the United States on a student exchange program.

"I was only twenty-three and spoke no English," she told me, describing how she quickly came to love everything American. She extended her stay and, when her papers were in order, eventually took a job in a small computer company. In time, she fell in love with the company's owner, and in March of 1982 the two were married. Now the wife of an American, Svetlana was introduced to the joint income tax return. "This type of tax did not exist in Yugoslavia," she told me. "But my husband asked me to sign it every year for the four years we were married."

Unfamiliar with the process, Svetlana trusted her husband and his word that he was taking care of their federal tax obligations. There were no indications that anything was out of order. In fact, it was not until years after their marriage ended that she was contacted by the agency and informed that, according to their records, she was in serious trouble.

"Following our separation, I did not receive any financial help," Svetlana told me. "I filed my own tax returns under the guidance of my former husband's accountant." Hard work and optimism allowed her to purchase a modest apartment in New York City and start life over. In her mind, America was, indeed, the land of promise.

Then she received a phone call.

"It came at the end of 1993," she said. "The IRS said I owed over $200,000 for back taxes from over a decade before when I was married to my husband." Svetlana was shocked. "I was totally honest with the IRS officer during this telephone call and provided both my home and work address. I stated to him that I owned the condominium in which I lived." She came to rue her mistake and naive honesty. "Immediately after this phone call a lien was placed on my home," she testified before our committee. "I called my former husband about all that had taken place and he assured me that he would take care of the problem. I still trusted him since he was the one who handled all our finances while we were married."

Three months after being assured by her ex-spouse that the problem would be resolved, Svetlana received what she described as the "most embarrassing call of her life" from her company's payroll department: her pay would be seized in two days unless she could make a deal with the IRS. "It was only after I informed my former husband of this latest problem that he confessed that he had, in fact, been receiving mail from the IRS," she told me. The notices from the IRS had been coming to him for years, addressed to both Svetlana and her husband.

According to Svetlana, she soon discovered that her former husband, the accountant they had both retained, and even others inside her former husband's company knew about the situation with the Internal Revenue Service. "They never told me," she said. "My former husband even admitted to me that he really did not think the IRS would ever go after me. He claimed he had no money for lawyers and that I was the stupid one for cooperating and being open and honest with the agency."

Sixteen years after her failed marriage, Svetlana was being haunted by the errors of a man who, by now, had learned to hide his assets. According to her, his home, automobiles, investments, and bank accounts were in the names of his current wife and children. And the IRS was unrelenting in its pursuit. Three weeks before appearing before our committee, the agency seized her checking account as well as her personal retirement.

"Is it my fault that my former husband was faster at disposing of his assets than the IRS was in collecting from him?" Svetlana asked. "Am I to continue to be the victim of the IRS' rage? My former husband is living in a home with his family and has an income. Why doesn't the IRS go after him for the taxes he owes? Are they coming after me because I can't fight?"

Svetlana contacted a lawyer, who advised her of limited options: (1) bankruptcy; (2) an offer in compromise; or (3) filing an innocent spouse petition. "He claimed bankruptcy was the easiest and cheapest way to resolve the problem," she said, explaining that she remained idealistic. "I responded, 'But I'm not guilty of anything!' I told him I would never declare bankruptcy—to do so was against my principles."

The attorney then suggested she should stop working until the matter had been resolved. "The lawyer charged me thousands of dollars and provided no solution," she told me. "Then I turned to an accountant who was a former IRS employee. For two years he argued with the IRS that I should be 'let off the hook' since I had never received, seen, or known about any IRS notices that had been sent to my former husband, and he insisted the statute of limitations had run out. Regrettably this argument went nowhere."

Friends and colleagues urged Svetlana not to fight the system. The attorney for the brokerage firm where she works even tried to persuade her from testifying before the Senate Finance Committee. "First my big boss told me, 'Svetlana, you don't fight the IRS. It's so powerful you don't mess with it.' Then, the biggest lawyer of my firm said, 'Do you really need to do this? We don't want the IRS to be after our firm.'"

But she was persistent. "I still don't believe they should be allowed to commit an injustice." Finally, an attorney informed her that her case was a classic example of innocent spouse. However, to prove it in court, she would have to put up the entire amount of money the IRS claimed she owed: by this time roughly $300,000.

This was impossible. "There is no way to defend yourself against the Internal Revenue Service," she told me several weeks after our hearing. "I have come to realize that I am no match, emotionally or financially, against their power. Like I told your committee, I left a communist country in Eastern Europe many years ago to study in the United States and enjoy, even for a short time, the freedoms democracy bestows on its citizens. Today, I am still thrilled to be able to live and work in this great nation. However, the actions of the IRS against me were not unlike actions that took place in my former communist homeland. Eighteen years after my arrival in this great country, I am on the verge of losing everything that I have worked for. My salary has been garnished, and the Internal Revenue Service has placed a lien on my property. One evening just last month, an IRS collections officer came to my home, unannounced, wanting to seize all of my personal belongings. The IRS is too powerful. It's responsible to no one. It does not care who it hurts, or how it gets its money."

Bad Law Administered Badly

Richard Beck, a professor at New York Law School and widely acknowledged as America's foremost expert on innocent spouse laws, described why women like Elizabeth Cockrell, Ann Kimbrough, Svetlana Pejanovic, and some 50,000 to 70,000 other women were having such a difficult time claiming protection under the Internal Revenue Service's innocent spouse provisions. "First," he says, "the IRS won't tell women about the election. Once they do, innocent spouse provides very little relief. The protections are much too narrow."

Professor Beck explained that if the tax liability assessed to a woman and her ex-husband was less than a certain number of dollars, or if the tax bill in case of deductions was less than a certain percentage of the woman's income, she did not qualify. "She's out," he said. "Period. It's only big tax bills that allow her to make an innocent spouse claim. And to figure out if the tax bill exceeds her income limits, sufficient enough to qualify her as an innocent spouse, the IRS will include her new husband's income in the equation." In other words, a woman struggling to unburden herself from an ex-husband's tax liability—should she remarry—indirectly shackles her new husband with the bill.

"As law, this is absurd and outrageous," Professor Beck told me. "Another absurdity is that no relief is available if the return is correctly filed. There has to be some kind of error or omission. If the ex-husband filled out the return correctly but failed to pay the bill, innocent spouse protection doesn't cover it."

Even when all the criteria are met—there was error, the wife did not know about it, the couple has divorced, the amount owed is sufficiently high to qualify, and her income is limited—there was still the burden of proof. "Even after meeting all the thresholds and proving that there is a mistake or wrong deduction and she can claim relief, the ex-wife then has to prove that she did not know and had no reason to know of the husband's understatement of tax. These rules are not spelled out, but the court cases have made this very hard to meet. The burden of proof is on the wife. She has to prove a negative.

"The courts have been very unfair," Professor Beck explained. "They have said that if the woman has a college education she should have enough knowledge to know whether or not her ex-husband filed their joint return correctly. This isn't justice, because when it comes to complicated tax law, most educated women have no more knowledge than a high schooler. Even an expert can't tell a legitimate deduction from an illegitimate tax shelter just by looking at the return. The point of a joint return is to make life easier for the couple and the government, but it often can—and does—result in a nightmare."

The reluctance of the IRS to allow an ex-wife to claim innocent spouse protection, the limitations and complexities of the provision, and the requirement to prove a negative were not the only problems we discovered confronting the tens of thousands of women carrying unjust IRS liabilities. Once again, there is the issue of cost. Very few women have the resources to fight. According to Professor Beck, "Unable to afford an attorney, the vast majority of women stuck in such a situation buckle under. The revenue agent bullies her into signing and she has no way of knowing what's happening. It shows the IRS' bad faith. They like to keep taxpayers in the dark. I think that some IRS agents are lazy. I'm being charitable. I think some like to use their power against defenseless women. I've seen many times when they go after a woman on public relief. I've asked them why. One IRS agent told me, 'Well she might get a job and have to pay it later.'"

Professor Beck believes that when it comes to the tax code, we have bad rules that are badly administered, and he lays much of the blame on Congress. "Capitol Hill has done everything possible to make couples file jointly. It's easier for the government when they do, so Congress makes the rates cheaper without disclosing the liabilities associated with joint filing." Then, the way the law was written, both spouses are held joint and severally liable; both are equally responsible for the entire debt, no matter who earned the income or committed the error or omission in filling out the tax returns.

Joint liability goes back to 1938, beginning with mistakes the Bureau of Internal Revenue made in the early '30s. One case, involving a Mr. and Mrs. Cole, stands out as the catalyst. In that case the agency assessed liability to the wrong spouse. The one who actually earned the income was protected when the statute of limitations expired. To compensate for their error, the Bureau invented a theory that both spouses should be held liable. In that way, the agency could go after either spouse and win. The new concept of joint and several liability went to tax court, and the agency prevailed. In 1935, it was appealed to the Ninth Circuit and the judge held for the taxpayer, despite the fact that the Bureau argued that it could not tell which spouse was responsible for which income on a joint return.

According to Professor Beck, the irony was that "at the same time the IRS was telling the judge that they could not tell whose income was whose, in a different area of the tax world they were insisting on new rules that would limit the amount of deductions for charitable contributions based on each individual's income on a joint return."

In the end, the Bureau of Internal Revenue lost the case and took its cause to Congress, insisting that joint liability was necessary in the code for administrative reasons. "That was wrong," Professor Beck told me. "And what Congress did for the IRS was much too broad."

There were three or four similar cases during the 1930s, and interestingly enough, not one case involved divorce. "I don't think it occurred to Congress that in time one spouse would use this like a weapon against another in divorce," Professor Beck said. "Following World War II, the IRS began to use it in divorces. The agency goes after the wife first because she's at the old address. If they think she can pay something they don't even bother looking for the husband. Suppose the husband is a millionaire but the wife has nothing, and the tax bill is a few thousand that they can get by garnishing her wages or seizing a bank account. They'll do it rather than chase down the husband.

"The way the IRS works it sets up a strange confrontation between ex–husbands and wives. Sometimes the ex–husband will actually appear at the trial as a witness for the government.

He's an interested witness, because if she pays he's off the hook. It's stretching things and certainly not in the spirit of the original intent. But today it has become a plague. No other country in the world does this. It is completely uncivilized to go after a woman for her ex-husband's debts. Yet the agency does, and these women suffer the consequences."

8

Criminal Investigations

"There is no hiding. If an unscrupulous special agent
wants to destroy you, he'll destroy you."

30-year special agent in the
Criminal Investigation Division

While each division within the IRS is important to the
agency's function of collecting and protecting the federal revenue, none has a history as colorful and heroic as that of
the Criminal Investigation Division (CID)—the roughly 3,400
men and women who are often referred to as the Giant Killers.
Their successes in collaring criminals and bringing down underworld empires include some of the most notorious names in
America: Al Capone, Irving "Waxey" Wexler, Huey Long, Jimmy
LaFontaine, the Gambino mob family, Dutch Shultz, the Big
Four bootlegging syndicate, Mickey Cohen, Lucky Luciano,
and even Joseph Nunan, a former commissioner of the Inter-

nal Revenue Service. It was the work of the CID that resulted in the convictions of those involved in the Teapot Dome scandal and led to the arrest of Bruno Richard Hauptmann in the Lindbergh kidnapping case.

Organized in 1919, in response to the Bureau's need to increase compliance and investigate charges of graft and corruption at a time when income tax revenues were exploding to meet the financial needs of America's involvement in World War I, the Criminal Investigation Division—then called the Special Intelligence Unit—consisted of six men, working under the direction of Elmer L. Irey, a 31-year-old former post office inspector.

Known for his integrity, Irey, more than any other individual in the CID's history, gave the division its identity and orientation. The duties of his highly qualified inspectors were to investigate and recommend prosecution of tax evaders, tax fraud conspirators, and Bureau personnel involved in collusion or other irregularities. They were also asked to check the backgrounds and assess the abilities of individuals seeking employment within the Service and those attorneys and accountants who were applying for permission to represent taxpayers before the Treasury Department.

With a certain understanding of the awesome power placed in the hands of his investigators, Irey constantly reminded them that the very nature of the investigative unit required them to operate with "tact, discretion, energy, and determination in no ordinary degree." The work of his group, he warned in 1936, "would invariably involve questions directly affecting the fate of human beings." Reputations are precious. "Injustice and irreparable injury to innocent suspects" could be the consequences of special agents who did not possess the qualities he required in his subordinates.

Intolerant of tax dodgers—especially those engaged in criminal conduct—Irey's indignation was fired by the inequities and increased burdens such individuals placed on honest Americans. He taught his men that cheaters were to be found in all walks of life and that nobody was above the law. But he warned that "in discovering the facts and weighing them, fairness and impartiality must govern every step."

Elmer Irey remained at the head of the unit until 1943, overseeing some of its most famous cases and turning his original band of six handpicked men into one of the finest law enforcement agencies in the world. "There was tremendous pride in the criminal investigations division," a special agent within CID told me, explaining how a cultural shift within the unit has, inside the last decade, led to frustration for some and early retirement for others. "Back then, you were among the elite— law enforcement officers who possessed the specialized financial knowledge and the analytical skills of an accountant. There was a high degree of professionalism among agents and a well-defined mission for the division."

By the 1960s, Attorney General Robert Kennedy was gratefully acknowledging the unit for the successes he was achieving in his fight against organized crime. In this effort, the intelligence division, Kennedy said, was effectively "carrying the brunt" of the work, and he was not alone in his praise of the operation. Other federal enforcement agencies were coming to depend on the highly trained special agents and their honed professional talent. The consequence was not only an increase in convictions against racketeers, mob families, and white-collar criminals, but that interdepartmental cooperation and joint training exercises began to take an increasingly firmer hold on the IRS division. This was a boon for traditional law enforcement agencies, which had come to realize that it was sometimes easier and cleaner to bring down sophisticated criminals with the pen rather than the sword. But stretching the mission and solidarity of the elite IRS warriors began to take its toll.

Within a few years, the unit was, as one special agent described it to me, a "bureaucratic stepchild in search of an identity." Indeed, by 1970, these highly trained tax-fraud specialists were being detailed aboard commercial aircraft as sky marshals in an attempt to combat the threat of hijackers. At the same time, the Bank Secrecy Act, enacted in an effort to investigate and prosecute illegal money laundering, forced others to move away from criminal tax investigations to aggressively pursue the war on narcotics trafficking. In 1978, amid growing concern that the organization was losing its focus, the Special Intelligence Unit was renamed the Criminal Investigation Division.

"The mission of the CID was not so much tax enforcement as it was whatever the attorney general's priorities were," explained another agent with over two decades in the division. "Organized crime was first. Much of CID's resources went there. Later drugs, commodities, and health-care fraud. The Criminal Investigation Division began to move away from its mission—even housed away from the IRS—and it became hard for special agents to determine who was really in charge. Within the division, people may be in your employ but not under your control."

Many inside the organization told me how the continued convergence with other law enforcement agencies has resulted in a more bellicose CID, one where the agents are growing increasingly more fond of the aggressive tactics and tools used by FBI, DEA, and ATF agents. While in the days of Eliot Ness and his Untouchables, the Bureau of Internal Revenue detailee was the task force's mild-mannered intellectual, the agents coming into today's CID are more commonly described as cowboys. "The new agents want to kick down doors and bust crack dealers," I was told by a special agent with thirty years inside the division. "Today our people are training on obstacle courses, wearing fatigues, and learning SWAT techniques. They're trying to emulate the other law enforcement agencies. But that's not our mission. We're financial investigators, not street cops."

The Jewish Mother

Is this new attitude within the culture of the Criminal Investigation Division having a dangerous impact on innocent taxpayers? The answer, as we uncovered in our investigation, is a resounding "Yes." A case in point is that of small businessman John Colaprete, owner of the Jewish Mother, a trendy little restaurant in Virginia Beach, Virginia.

While John and his family were gathered at church to celebrate his son's first Holy Communion, dozens of armed agents with drug-sniffing dogs burst into his two restaurants, demanding that the breakfast patrons place their forks and knives on the tables and leave the premises immediately. At that same moment, another twenty CID agents broke down the front door of his home—tearing it off its hinges—while across town dozens of other agents raided the home of his restaurant manager, pulling him from the shower at gunpoint.

"They forcibly restrained my manager while he attempted to call an attorney," John testified to our committee. "His teenaged son was knocked to the floor." According to John, his manager's daughter, 14 years old at the time, had several friends over for a slumber party the night before. "These young girls had to get dressed under the watchful eyes of male agents, despite the presence of female agents," John testified. "The IRS agent stood in the doorway to the bedroom, gun drawn, refusing these young girls even a semblance of privacy."

What crimes had John Colaprete and his manager committed?

They had fired a bookkeeper who had embezzled an estimated $40,000 from their businesses. "She went to prison for her crimes," John said, "but not before turning my life and the lives of countless others upside down."

In March of 1994, John and his partner discovered a significant shortfall in their restaurant accounts. They confronted the bookkeeper, who eventually broke down and admitted to her scheme. She promised to reimburse the business. But John, finding that this was not an isolated crime, reported her to the police. Then, in retaliation, the former employee sought out the Internal Revenue Service, telling them "a fantastic tale of money laundering, gunrunning, and drug dealing" by John and his partner.

"Little did I know that the IRS would spend less than forty-eight hours investigating my bookkeeper's allegations before conducting raids on my businesses, my home, and the home of my manager," John testified. "Little did I know that the government that I had so proudly served as a captain in the Marine Corps would accept these allegations to be true, despite the alarming lack of substantiation, probable cause, or proof of any sort whatsoever. Little did I know that the IRS, when faced with the outrageous claim that I had thousands of pounds of cocaine stored like cordwood in my office, would subscribe to a policy of guilty until proven innocent."

The IRS impounded personal and financial records belonging to John and his manager, their cash registers, computers, and other personal property. His life had suddenly come to a standstill, and searching for answers, he found nothing. "All I was met with was, 'No comment, Mr. Colaprete,' at every turn," he told us. "Freedom of Information requests were ignored, ostensibly due to a backlog of such requests and despite legally mandated time limits on such requests."

Even the media, which had been aware of the raids in the beginning, were denied information concerning IRS motives and evidence. "Two newspapers in Virginia Beach made repeated requests under the Freedom of Information Act," John testified, "only to have the Justice Department thumb its nose at those requests." When one investigative journalist began to get to the bottom of things, he drew the ire of the IRS. According to John, the reporter had an opportunity to interview a special agent, but during that interview the CID agent interrupted the reporter's inquiries with a demand for his Social Security number.

"Within the year, the reporter was notified that the IRS wanted to audit his return," John said. "But when a local publication reported this, the audit was abruptly canceled. An IRS agent stated at the time that the agency does not retaliate against citizens through the use of audits, but the facts would seem to indicate otherwise."

What was the effect of all this on John and his family?

"I suffered a deep depression that lasted a year," he testified. "I was immobilized. I could not get out of bed some days. My neighbors shunned me. My wife, who is an artist, has not been able to pick up a paintbrush in four years.

"My children were taunted at school and told that their father was a gangster and a drug dealer. I raised my children with a zero tolerance for dishonesty, and now they must hear allegations that I am a major drug dealer and a tax cheat?"

However, according to John, compared to the suffering of his manager, he got off easy: "He has suffered severe depression, sought counseling from his pastor, literally has been shunned by friends and acquaintances, and has yet to get his life back in order. He has been ruined financially and emotionally, with little or no hope of ever getting his life back to where it was prior to these raids."

And what about the bookkeeper?

"She was kept in protective custody by the IRS in a motel up to the time of the raids," John told us. "It is almost unimaginable that there could be such a level of incompetence at the IRS, that they would not only take the word of this woman and begin any sort of investigation, but they would shield her from the authorities who were trying to arrest her. The IRS even allowed her to leave the jurisdiction of Virginia to go to North Carolina, where she was only later sent to jail for embezzling from three other employers in that state."

According to John, "The woman whom the IRS was protecting and on whom they had relied had already been convicted numerous times of embezzling and stealing. In fact, the outstanding criminal charge pending against her at the time she approached the IRS was for a crime involving lying and stealing." Yet the special agent she contacted within the Criminal Investigation Division made the determination to proceed, despite the fact that the FBI—when approached for their assistance—declined to cooperate.

A recently retired FBI agent swore in a deposition that he had advised the Internal Revenue Service to be skeptical about the bookkeeper's claims. "The FBI specifically declined to become involved," John said. "In the words of one of its agents, the whole story sounded like a B movie"—a movie that certainly had no happy ending for anyone, not even the IRS.

After four months of searching through the files and personal belongings confiscated from John and his manager, the agency realized that it had no case. The bookkeeper was simply trying to avoid prosecution by resorting to one of the oldest schemes in the book: saving herself by offering to turn in the big-time crooks. "In the face of [the bookkeeper's criminal record] how could anyone, let alone supposedly trained, professional inspectors with the IRS, accept at face value what the woman was saying?" John asks today. "Based on her word, [the IRS] not only commenced an investigation but completely shut down a business and turned the lives of innocent people upside down less than 48 hours after first meeting this woman."

Five months after the morning raid, John Colaprete's lawyers were contacted by the U.S. Attorney, who explained that no evidence had been found of criminal activity. A few days later, a rental truck pulled up in front of John's restaurant and dumped the confiscated belongings in a pile for John and his manager to sort through. "I never received an apology," John said, describing how the ordeal killed one of his businesses. "I just couldn't keep the other restaurant together," he said. "When you have a business that is out there in the community like a restaurant, you do not recover from an armed intervention such as this. This is four years later and we have not recovered."

What remains is fear and the nagging question of how such an injustice could occur in America. "I used to believe that such things could only happen in a communist-bloc country or police state," John testified. "I do not believe that any more. For every taxpayer like me, those who have survived armed assaults on our businesses and our homes, there are perhaps several thousands of taxpayers who, in fear, lick their wounds, tally their losses, and consider themselves lucky that the IRS has finally left them alone, their innocence notwithstanding.

"It's frightening that such a woman could have conned the IRS into believing that her employer, despite all appearances to the contrary, was a high-level gangster, and then shield her from the law in the belief that she would lead them to a bigger fish like me," John said, asking, "Is there such a competitive atmosphere within the IRS, such a need to add another feather in their cap, that they would ignore not only basic investigative techniques but the obvious flaws in this woman's character and simply accept her at face value?"

I asked the same question to a 15-year veteran of the Criminal Investigation Division, a woman who had spent many years as a group manager. Her answer is that, yes, the same statistic-driven atmosphere that exists elsewhere in the agency is alive and well in CID, and, yes, there are a few bad apples, as there are in any organization, but their reckless behavior is exacerbated by the fact that many managers, in her words, "are incompetent," and the culture of secrecy provides them the shelter they need to get away with their wretched activities.

"For the most part," she told me, "there are checks and balances in the system. Evidence like that presented by Colaprete's bookkeeper needs to be corroborated. Requests for search warrants need to be signed off by supervisors, and then the warrants need to be issued by a magistrate." Though claiming never to have witnessed such a miscarriage of justice herself, the former group manager, who has since returned to the field as a special agent, is concerned that such things can happen. "To my dismay," she told me, "there has been an evolution in the direction of more aggressive agents—agents who are coming in who don't have proper training but are still given the power, all the enforcement tools, and a culture that will protect them when they make outrageous mistakes and even break the law."

There are several reasons why overly eager, poorly trained, or even vindictive agents within the Criminal Investigation Division would be interested to jump on a taxpayer like John Colaprete. First, a significant portion of the division's budget is tied directly to Organized Crime and Drug Enforcement Task Force work. Many agents are told by managers that their very salaries are dependent on finding and bringing down the kinds of individuals John's bookkeeper portrayed to the agency—money-laundering drug-dealing gunrunners. "There is tremendous pressure to work those kinds of cases," one special agent told me. "The Treasury budget gets extra money appropriated for that cause."

A second reason why some within the agency would be interested in the Colaprete case is the belief that notoriety increases compliance. When the names of well-known local businessmen appear in the media as targets of the IRS, according to this theory, other businessmen ante up their own tax liabilities without a fuss.

To Frame a Congressman

"District directors want a criminal fraud program," Tommy Henderson, a 30-year veteran of CID, explained to me. "They want high compliance rates and believe that the more criminal cases that are pursued the higher the compliance in the district will be as people are frightened." He described several occasions when he witnessed, firsthand, how colleagues framed elected officials and other distinguished members of the community in an effort to gain publicity and score points within the system. Our investigation discovered that among some of the nationally recognized names targeted by special agents inside CID were Congressman James H. Quillen and former Senate Majority Leader and White House Chief of Staff Howard Baker.

Quillen and Baker were falsely accused by a senior special agent of taking between $300,000 and $400,000 a month in illegal bribes over a seven-year period from a well-known national company. The agent alleged that, in return, the two legislators were pushing laws favorable to the corporation. According to Henderson, the special agent's group manager, the man sent his accusations on to the U.S. Attorney's office, as well as the FBI, without having the case reviewed by the proper authorities within the agency. "As a senior IRS special agent, he was attempting to establish a grand jury investigation without authorization," Henderson testified. "Early on in my career, I had seen special agents destroy the lives of honest taxpayers simply to make or redeem a career for themselves," Henderson told me privately. "When I realized what was happening to Congressman Quillen and Senator Baker, I said, 'Not on my watch.'" To verify his agent's case, Henderson assigned another senior agent to double-check the information being provided to the U.S. Attorney. "It was bogus," Henderson told me. "I brought the investigation to a standstill."

What happened then disturbs him to this day. "The agent was out of control," Henderson explained. "He was dangerous. I recommended to the assistant chief that we take his gun and credentials and place him on leave until he could receive professional help." The assistant chief took Henderson's request up the line of command, then returned with orders that Henderson was to "say and do nothing." The response was the result of a direct conflict of interest.

According to Henderson, the senior special agent was one of the district chief's hard-core drinking buddies, a fact he had discovered the first time he met the chief. "Shortly after being selected as the acting group manager, I arrived to start my new job late in the evening," Henderson testified before our committee. "At the same time the agents and district chief were having a party at a local hotel. My initial conversation with the chief occurred in his hotel room with him so intoxicated he could not stand."

Henderson testified that he soon learned the chief had a habit of showing up at outlying posts of duty with a trunk full of liquor in his government-issued automobile. "He would then insist that the agents and managers join him in his motel room, where significant amounts of alcohol were consumed. The gathering would then adjourn to a local bar." The bar, according to Tommy Henderson, had to have facilities to serve food, so the agents could justify driving their government cars to that location. "The eating, drinking, dancing, and whatever would continue until late evening," Henderson said. "I found that some of my agents on several occasions were so drunk that they could not find their government cars."

This lifestyle, according to Henderson, led to corrupt practices throughout the district. "We had agents trying to sell case reports to the Mafia," he told me privately. "Other agents were involved in selling cocaine. You had to look very carefully at those around you because you didn't know who to trust and who not to trust."

Clearly the relationship between the district chief and the senior agent who had attempted to frame Congressman Quillen and Senator Baker took precedent over doing what was right. Despite the special agent's history of alcohol abuse, gambling problems, and alleged violations of disclosure laws concerning, among other things, the case he was fabricating against Quillen and Baker, he was protected. The district chief and his deputy unleashed their wrath on Tommy Henderson. "I was called to the chief's office and accused of numerous things," he testified. "I was told that the entire group had lost faith in my management and wanted me removed. I realized that the chief and assistant chief were going to cover up the agent's activities. I was angry and hurt by management's lack of ethics and support, and I resigned from the position of group manager."

What happened to the special agent? He was eventually fired, though not because of the vacuous cases he was building against prominent politicians. Rather, because he was arrested—found by the local sheriff to be in possession of cocaine, scales, and other drug paraphernalia—and, according to Henderson, "being public knowledge, it was impossible to cover it up."

"I Can Make You or Break You"

If Tommy Henderson's story seems difficult to believe, let me add that it was corroborated in public testimony and private conversations with several other special agents. One called what she witnessed a "conspiracy," testifying that "rather than risking embarrassment by prosecuting allegations of sexual harassment, alcoholism, drugs, and fraud" that had been committed by the special agent and "repressed" by IRS officials, the district chief "pressured Tommy Henderson into resigning from management." Following Henderson's resignation, the witness testified, he was "subjected to a campaign of ostracism, harassment, and retaliation intended to force him out of his job."

Testimony from another special agent who worked in Henderson's group confirmed that the agent fabricating the case against Quillen and Baker was "well known for his repeated outbursts disclosing protected tax and grand jury information [including sensitive information about the senator and congressman] in local bars" yet "he was never once reprimanded by management for this outrageous and clearly career-ending behavior."

According to the witness, the renegade special agent had been assigned as her mentor, often requesting her to perform activities clearly beyond official duties. "Among these," she testified, "were demands for sexual favors," followed by the warning, "You know, I can make you or break you."

"I feared him because of his constant sexual harassment," she told me. "I did not know at the time that I was not alone in this fear. I later learned that he had attempted to rape another female agent just a few years prior to my arrival at the agency." In this incident, as with the others, managers looked the other way.

The criminal conduct of this special agent and the inability—or unwillingness—of management to take action, or at least precautions to protect other employees and taxpayers, demonstrate how even a few employees dangerously out of control can destroy taxpayers as well as their colleagues. CID special agents are series 1811 federal law enforcement officers, licensed to carry firearms. They can solicit bank accounts, credit histories, even private medical and educational records. With the signature of a supervisor and a magistrate they can search and seize property, conduct raids on homes and businesses, and, in the process, forever sully the names of honest taxpayers. Oftentimes, friends, family, and employers are told that a taxpayer is under investigation before the taxpayer knows.

"If an unscrupulous special agent wants to destroy you, he'll destroy you," the 30-year employee of the Criminal Investigation Division told me. "And there's no accountability. In fact, even if you're innocent, and he gets your name in the paper—and you're a prominent businessman, politician, actor, or whatever—he'll score points with the district director, who, again, believes that fear increases compliance."

Targeting Middle- and Lower-Income Taxpayers

"Beyond bad management," I was told by a former division chief, "the Criminal Investigation Division is plagued by a lack of continuity in its responsibilities. They're a group of cowboys looking for a mission. And you can get into a lot of mischief that way. The problems really began about eight years ago, and they have grown steadily worse."

High-profile taxpayers like John Colaprete, Howard Baker, and Jim Quillen are not the only people who have to worry about overly aggressive CID agents. "No one's immune, especially not the little guy," the former division chief explained. "And things don't seem to be getting any better. There's still the problem with statistics and goals, even after Congress passed the IRS Restructuring and Reform Act of 1998. In fact, I was talking to a regional commissioner just the other day— a friend of mine. I asked him what he was up to. He said that he was part of a working group that was convened to establish statistics and goals for the future. No matter what Congress does, the agency's culture always comes back to goals, statistics, and quotas. They drive the Service, and bad managers drive their employees to achieve them in whatever way they can."

This dynamic, it was explained to me, is what leads to middle- and lower-income taxpayers getting caught in the CID's line of fire. "The Criminal Investigation Division applies scant control over the special agents," Barbara Latham, a 17-year employee of the division, testified. As pressure builds within a district to refer fraud cases to the Criminal Investigation Division—as a result of the district director's desire to increase compliance through fear—often managers will prevail upon their special agents to pursue taxpayers who are the easiest to target, those without the sophistication or resources to fight back. "The special agents focus their investigations on smaller businessmen with smaller tax liabilities because they require less work than investigations involving larger tax deficits or serious criminal offenses," Latham explained.

The consequences were made clear by Tommy Henderson: "Middle- and lower-class people get caught in the net," he told me. "Special agents end up being forced to pursue fraud and evasion charges that should never be touched, going after taxpayers who wind up under criminal investigation and should not be under criminal investigation."

"That's the biggest problem in the CID," another group manager added. "Statistical motivations override the merits of a case. It's my biggest concern. We'll turn an ordinary taxpayer's life upside down for five or six harrowing weeks, just to hit our statistics. There was a change for a few weeks," she confessed, "while the Senate hearings were under way, but then when the stories in the media died down it was back to business as usual."

I had been pleased that the day before the Senate Finance Committee held its hearings to examine the Criminal Investigation Division, the agency unveiled a detailed seven-point plan to improve the division. Among other things, the April 27, 1998, plan called for a "centralized disciplinary process for CID managers and employees," as well as "institutionalized oversight" of the division and "a new complaint system."

According to those with whom I spoke inside the Criminal Investigation Division, not one of them had been given any training concerning the seven-point plan. A few even confessed they had not heard of it. Instead, what they eventually received was a detailed explanation of what upper-level managers inside the division did for six months prior to our hearings to spin the news and diminish the impact of our hearings. According to a lengthy article in the Spring 1998 issue of *CI Digest*, the assessment of the division's top man, Assistant Commissioner Ted F. Brown, and his cadre of upper-level managers was that after taking a hard look at "our organization to see if we did have any holes that could be tightened up, we could not come up with any changes."

I could not help but wonder if the assistant commissioner of the Criminal Investigation Division and his most senior managers were unaware of the myriad problems that were readily being shared with our investigators. If indeed, they believed that nothing needed to be done to "tighten up" the organiza-

tion, why, then, did they release the seven-point plan for improvement the day before the hearings? Was the agency sincere
in its objective to change? Or was the seven-point plan simply
a preemptive move to lessen the influence the agency knew our
hearings would have, once the horror stories we had uncovered were disclosed? Something Assistant Commissioner Brown
wrote to his service-wide employees suggests the latter, and it
explains why the changes within the division that the group
manager shared with me lasted for only a few weeks.

Detailing to his subordinates the machinations that he and
his senior managers went through to control what they knew
would be tremendous fallout from the congressional hearings—
six months of feeding "good news stories" to the media; advanced press briefings; a staff of eight to ten people working
full-time at national headquarters, gathering data to rebut Senate witnesses; a full-scale study to compare the Criminal Investigation Division to the FBI, Customs, the ATF, and the Secret
Service in the specific areas of using confidential informants,
search warrants, and undercover operations—Assistant Commissioner Brown admits that one request made by the Treasury Department was to take guns away from the special agents
(one of whom had actually used his weapon to kill a California
motorist in a traffic altercation). Brown and his senior managers refused, but he writes, "Knowing that we were going to be
under the microscope for the immediate future," the decision
was to "make the changes in the search warrant procedures
[increasing the number of signatures an agent needed before
executing a warrant] in the interim to demonstrate our concerns for doing the right thing." Then in his very next sentence
he makes the chilling disclosure that "the change in search
warrant procedures were P—political and P—public perception." Evidently, they were never intended to last, and, as I have

been lately informed, the CID has now returned to its old way of doing business.

"The sad part is that we have everything we ever dreamed of," one veteran CID special agent told me, "government-issued cars, guns, premium pay, the best retirement—but we have the worst management you can imagine. They set out to destroy your hearings. Rather than change what's wrong, they want to control public perception and try to discredit anyone who's brave enough to tell the truth."

The special agents who talked with us made it clear that, as with the other divisions within the IRS, bad management and the pursuit of statistics have become so ingrained that they hesitate to believe that conditions can be improved. "Bad managers hire other bad managers," one confided to me. "They expect them to be loyal to them, not to the law or the Constitution. And the taxpayer gets stuck in the numbers game, as we're forced to divert our attention away from the biggest and best cases to work itty-bitty cases that don't amount to much."

Tagalong Cases and Exaggerated Numbers

Another way the Criminal Investigation Division works the numbers is by participating in what special agents call "tag-along" cases—DEA drug busts, FBI kidnapping cases, ATF raids on illegal gunrunners—cases where the primary concern is not a tax violation, but where the CID agent can tack a tax violation on top of the principal criminal offenses. "As part of a guilty plea, they make the offender plead to one count of income tax evasion," I was told. "Then they work out the plea agreement: ten years for cocaine and we get a statistic. It's a total waste of our time and expertise, but we have GS-14 managers in Criminal Investigation who have only worked tagalongs. They've never worked real tax cases. They wouldn't know how, and as managers they're teaching their employees to do the same. Chasing statistics is creating these kinds of monsters."

Such quick-hit cases are partially responsible for two other serious problems that our investigation encountered in the agency's Criminal Investigation Division. Author David Burnham and Susan B. Long, professor of Quantitative Methods with the School of Management at Syracuse University, are codirectors of Transactional Records Access Clearinghouse (TRAC), a data-gathering, data-research, and data-distribution organization at Syracuse. Together they have demonstrated that CID has a "systematic inability to keep track of the work of its 3,352 criminal investigators," and that the division inexplicably enforces the nation's tax laws in an "erratic way."

For almost a decade, TRAC has used the Freedom of Information Act to gather information, including data tapes from the executive office of the U.S. Attorney. These tapes contain a thorough record of investigative agency criminal referrals recommended for prosecution. And what they have discovered is troubling. Not only is there wide disagreement between Justice Department data concerning criminal cases referred by the IRS, with the latter claiming 50 percent more prosecutions, 70 percent more convictions, and twice as many individuals sent to prison, but a wide disparity exists between regions concerning how the laws are executed.

While some variation is expected and considered normal in how other federal agencies apply the law, Burnham testified that TRAC's data demonstrate that when it comes to CID information "the variations that emerge . . . go way beyond such natural-occurring outcomes." For example, over the last five years the per capita number of IRS convictions in Memphis, Tennessee, in Ashville, North Carolina, in Charleston, West

Virginia, and Mobile, Alabama, are at least twice as high as convictions in important financial and business centers, including Boston and Los Angeles.

"Two questions present themselves about the erratic enforcement patterns of the CID," Burnham told us. "First, mindful of the constitutional mandate that government must work under to assure the American people equal protection under the law, is the IRS treating similarly situated citizens in similar ways? Second, at a time of scarce government resources, is the IRS effectively targeting its criminal enforcement activities in the areas and against the individuals and organizations where they are most needed?"

The evidence suggests otherwise, and, as noted earlier, several CID agents agree. "Each district director and CID chief appears to operate his own little kingdom and, in some instances, with little regard for the law or for government rules and regulations," Tom Henderson testified. "Management then uses the unlimited resources of the federal government, that is, taxpayer funds, to cover up its acts and to destroy its opponents, whether they be employees or taxpayers."

With this state of affairs, it is not surprising that the Criminal Investigation Division finds it difficult, if not impossible, to accurately monitor the work of its employees. Likewise, it is clear why wide discrepancies exist concerning how the laws are executed from region to region throughout the United States, and how taxpayers can be treated unfairly.

Burnham and Long believe evidence indicates that the IRS is engaged in an "active public information campaign intended to substantially exaggerate" its effectiveness. "Put directly," Professor Long said, "the IRS has been hyping its numbers." And both are concerned that the agency, for years, has refused to do anything about the problem. "They exaggerate to get increased funding," Burnham told me, "to scare people, and to make themselves look good." According to the author of *A Law Unto Itself: Power, Politics and the IRS,* it's difficult to know all the reasons why the agency's numbers are so far off, but part of the explanation is that the Criminal Investigation Division double-counts. Under pressure to perform (recall Michael Josephson's evidence that quota-driven managers, snagged in a prevaricated Catch-22, are forced continuously to cook the numbers to achieve inflated goals based on inflated benchmarks) a pattern develops where CID agents working with the FBI, the DEA, or another federal law enforcement agency will count cases as their own, despite the fact that the cases have been assigned to the other agency.

Burnham told me that it's certainly not the first time he's seen the IRS fudge numbers. In the 1980s, the IRS, in search of increased funding and more enforcement authority, claimed a substantial increase in noncompliance. In other words, the Service insisted that more and more Americans were failing to pay the taxman. Statistics used by the agency were based on the Taxpayer Compliance Measurement Program (TCMP), a huge number of random audits that were then used to project statistics for the entire nation. "They were taking these surveys and making claims that were accepted by the General Accounting Office, the Executive Branch, Congress, and the media," Burnham told me. "Congress passed a bunch of new penalties as a result. The agency was given more tools to collect taxes." Then, according to Burnham, Susan Long discovered a problem: the IRS had not adjusted for the increase in the number of taxpayers over the years, nor had the agency factored in a margin of error. "When Sue adjusted for inflation—the increase in taxpayers—and factored in a margin of error," Burnham told me, "there was no increase in noncompliance. It was about the same. I have to believe that they knew what they were doing, though I never got anyone to admit it."

9

Congressional Accountability

"Congress wrote the tax laws, created the IRS, and funds the agency. So who's ultimately responsible for how it works?"

David Keating
National Taxpayers Union

It would be both disingenuous and grossly unjust to lay blame for the abuses we've documented, and those we continue to document, exclusively at the feet of the Internal Revenue Service. Under the Constitution, it is Congress and not the Department of Treasury or the IRS, that has the power to lay and collect taxes. Used properly, and monitored vigilantly, that power allows government to effectively meet the demands and requirements of the American people, promoting economic stability, individual and collective security, educational opportunities, and a vast infrastructure necessary for transportation, communication, and commerce. It allows us to accomplish together what would be impossible if we were acting on our own. However, the power to lay and collect taxes is a sacred trust, one that must be understood and carefully administered by Congress, as well as by the departments and agencies Congress calls upon to carry out this duty. Few things are as important to individual well-being as the ability to earn and use resources in a way that best meets one's needs, and the needs of one's family. Government's authority to extract from our wallet the money we have earned—to deprive us and our families of its immediate benefit—if exercised unwisely, can quickly become, as John Marshall observed, "the power to destroy."

A government ever stretching to grab another dollar from the taxpayer, with a legislature unwilling, or unable, to bring it under control, not only threatens to slow down economic growth, by draining resources from the vital and most productive private sector, but it risks impoverishing individuals, robbing overburdened parents of precious time that could be spent with children, and crushing personal incentive. A small businessman struggling to provide employment to others, when overwhelmed by excessive taxation, an aggressive IRS, and complex laws and federal regulations, can find it much easier to downsize—lay off employees to lessen financial, regulatory, and managerial burdens—or go to work for someone else. This, of course, is counterproductive to promoting an environment marked by job creation and economic security, a responsibility that is among the most fundamental of a good and competent government. Yet trends over the last fifty years are clear: tax burdens increase, federal regulations grow, laws become ever more Byzantine in their complexity, and departments and agencies charged with administering those laws inflate both in size and influence.

There are many reasons why the reach of government continues to grow. Once federal programs and subsidies are created, their termination becomes next to impossible. Challenging demographic changes—population growth, the aging of America, and increasing illegitimate birth rates among single teenagers and unwed couples who are ill-prepared economically to take care of their children—demand ever-increasing resources. Military and foreign policy demands at home and abroad; upward trends in the social pathologies of crime, drug, and alcohol abuse; divorce; and parental neglect: these demand time, money, and attention, as does our aging infrastructure—highways, bridges, airports, and waterways, as well as computer and other communications systems.

Government programs to meet these challenges can always be made more efficient and cost-effective. This has been an objective of mine for many years. But even at their most efficient, such programs and the increasing burden they place on taxpayers will continue to grow, until there is strong enough consensus within Congress and the Executive Branch to radically restructure the way the federal government addresses these needs. Without such a consensus, we can only expect business as usual—intriguing, and sometimes even covert, attempts to fund the programs to address these upward-spiraling trends without appearing to be overtly shackling Americans with higher taxes. This is where Congress has been responsible not only for the increasing complexity of the tax code but for pushing the Internal Revenue Service to become more aggressive.

As the need for federal revenue grows, congressmen and -women—well aware of the aversion Americans have toward tax hikes—look for hidden ways within the code to fund their programs. Often, these increases are buried deep inside complex provisions that are beyond the understanding of any but the most well-studied tax experts. And even they have problems.

For eight years, *Money* magazine has sent financial data of a hypothetical family to 60 tax professionals, asking them to prepare the family's tax return. In 1997, of the 46 professionals who completed the assignment and returned their work, "no two came up with the same bottom line." It was the seventh time in the history of the test that complexity within the code stumped the experts to the extent that every outcome was different, despite the fact that each professional was working with the exact same data. "What was especially surprising this time around was how widespread the results were," *Money* reported. The professionals' answers ranged from a tax liability of $34,240 to $68,912—a chasm of 101 percent. According to *Money,* "That means our fictional family could have underpaid their tax by nearly $3,000 or paid nearly double what they owed."

This complexity is caused not only by congressional attempts to bury revenue raisers deep within the code, but also by the ideological differences between political parties. Every tax bill, whether an increase or cut, is the culmination of strident debate and Gordian compromise. This can lead to mind-numbing complexity as the different politicians, with their different philosophies, fight for a bill that represents their respective agendas. To pass the bill, the competing political factions split the differences and come up with Frankenstein, leaving taxpayers with the impossible task of sorting it all out. The philosophies of these congressmen are supported by countless special-interest groups and corporate concerns that employ more than 70,000 lobbyists in and around Washington.

The inevitable result of congressmen working with special-interest groups to pass favorable legislation is continued complexity in the code, as special breaks and even outright government funding are given to one and paid for by increasing or extending tax obligations on another. These preferences and "pay fors" have to be written into law. Someone has to cover their cost, and unless Congress is willing to pass overt tax increases, they are funded by intricate adjustments within the code that ratchet a tax up here and delay the phasing out of a tax cut there. In this way, the law is always and forever changing, requiring taxpayers to either blunder their way through the labyrinth or hire a professional—as *Money* points out—to blunder through for them.

In thirteen years, Congress has passed almost eighty bills that have made changes in the tax code. In the Taxpayer Relief Act of 1997, Congress added 285 new sections to the code and amended another 824. Since then, another 9 bills that included tax provisions have been passed into law, and today the code stands at 5.5 million words, requiring some 17,000 pages.

Complexity is not the only avenue Congress utilized to increase federal revenue without drawing undue attention from the electorate. For decades, it relied on deficit spending. Then, in the 1980s, as the deficit became a hot political issue itself, Congress began to pass legislation that strengthened the scope and authority of the Internal Revenue Service. The intent was to raise revenue through a crackdown on enforcement, and enforcement could be ever more severe because complexity had turned the code into a minefield. Penalties were increased. New tools were given to promote compliance. Auditors and examiners were instructed that they could find mistakes in 99.9 percent of filed returns. This led to a revenue windfall through penalty and interest payments as congressional pressure was placed on the commissioners and upper-level managers to collect more and more money. This strategy coming down from Capitol Hill pandered to the worst instincts of agency personnel, giving them the green light to use even callous methods to meet congressional mandates.

A Serious Lack of Oversight

At the same time, Congress neglected its responsibility to provide any meaningful oversight. Small hearings were held from time to time, when reports surfaced of taxpayer returns being dumped in trash bins at the Philadelphia Service Center, or when special agents within the Criminal Investigation Division raided and ruined the reputation of one clothing company in an effort to benefit another clothing company. This lack of oversight was due not only to the desire of previous Congresses to use the IRS in a way to raise revenue without directly raising taxes but—as several of my colleagues suggested—it was the result of intimidation, the concern that the agency, as it had been known to do, might wreck the political fortunes of the senator or congressman who probed too deeply into its activities. When Senator David Pryor fought for the first Taxpayers Bill of Rights in 1987, he discovered that concerns about agency retaliation made potential cosponsors of his bill hesitant to join the cause. According to Senator Pryor, it was not until he had a large enough group of senators committed privately that anyone would speak out for the legislation publicly. It was an issue of safety in numbers.

"It's been worse than a hands-off attitude," David Keating told me. "Up until now, it's been an issue of fear." Keating believes the Senate Finance Committee hearings were "a major turning point in IRS history," a moment "when the people in charge of the agency showed that they were not afraid to take a close critical look at how it conducts its business."

Any agency given the immense power that Congress has bestowed upon the Internal Revenue Service must be monitored closely, from within and without. The agency itself must be subject to formal checks and balances to assure that the vast authority it's been given is not used to abuse, harm, or destroy. Congress must be as vigilant in its oversight responsibilities as the Senate and House Intelligence Committees are when it comes to the operation and management of America's covert defense and intelligence-gathering entities. These requirements become particularly important when the authority granted by Congress is accompanied by privacy laws that at best can be used to cloud evidence and intimidate witnesses of mismanagement and abuse, and, at worst, can be used to altogether bury them. By strengthening Section 6103—laws prohibiting the disclosure of taxpayer information—in response to accusations that the Nixon administration was looking at the tax returns of individuals on the infamous "enemies list," Congress inadvertently handed the IRS a trump card, one that could be played at almost any time to keep Capitol Hill from getting information necessary to investigate wrongdoing within the Service.

Terrified of violating disclosure laws, agency employees are hesitant to report even the most egregious activities they may have witnessed. If they approach management about their concerns, they are often warned that taking the information any further will be a 6103 violation, punishable by termination of employment and possibly imprisonment. Stories abound of agency employees attempting to contact Congress, or testify before a congressional committee, who are visited by attorneys from the IRS Disclosure Litigation Office just hours prior to their Capitol Hill appointment. Ominous warnings are given concerning the consequences that will befall the employee who follows through with the commitment to testify. This, in fact, presented such a problem at the Barnard hearings in 1989, with witnesses canceling at the last minute, that I decided in our investigation and subsequent hearings that we would keep the witness list private, as well as the contents of their testimony. While that decision angered some senior executives within the agency, and even a few of my colleagues on the Finance Committee, it gave the employees who contacted our investigators and testified before our committee the confidence to speak openly, and, in the end, not one IRS witness backed out.

We discovered that Congress needed to find ways to make it easier for whistle-blowers to come forward effectively, legitimately, and without fear of retaliation. Despite the fact that I asked senior IRS managers who testified before our committee to guarantee that there would be no retribution taken against those courageous employees who testified, I have been deeply disturbed to hear from several that they are being hounded by their superiors. One witness from Examinations called to tell me how her performance ratings, always good and superior prior to the hearings, have since her testimony been nothing but failing grades, despite the fact that she consistently continues to get taxpayers and their representatives to agree to her auditing adjustments. "Since my testimony," she told me, "my manager scrutinizes every case I turn in. My evaluations have all been failures. They have even interfered in my work with a taxpayer. After the taxpayer and I had come to an agreement on an adjustment, management said they were going to give the case to another auditor. They're trying to build a case against me, to get rid of me. The taxpayer got a lawyer involved and they threatened to fight, so my manager backed down."

"Has anything changed in the quality of your work since you testified?" I asked.

"Nothing's wrong with my work," she said, her voice dampened by frustration and anger. "If I can get CPAs and lawyers to agree to my audits and adjustments—if I can get the taxpayer to agree and pay the assessments—then the work is good. For fifteen years I had fully successful evaluations. After I testified I got my first failing evaluation, and it seems like every time I go another step it ups the ante. Once I contacted people outside the agency things started falling apart for me."

In the days that followed this conversation—and in our ongoing effort to see that our witnesses are not harassed or retaliated against for their cooperation with our committee—I confirmed the auditor's information with two other employees in her group, as well as with her union representative. Each concurred that her work is excellent, she is well liked among her colleagues, but that they are threatened by management if they are caught talking to her. "She's paying a stiff price for cooperating with Congress," one told me, adding the people in this auditor's group have been called into the group manager's office and told, "You better side with the Service against her if you know what's good for you."

When an agency has the power to destroy the lives of taxpayers and even its own employees, Congress must have sure and workable methods of providing protection for those who break *omertà* and share information necessary for appropriate oversight and reform. At the same time, we must clarify the privacy laws, assuring that they are used to protect the taxpayer—as they were originally intended—and not renegade employees, managers, and executives inside the agency. Both of these conditions are necessary if we are going to effectively change the culture within the IRS.

Then, Congress must be willing to conduct oversight. Intimidation and fear aside, a forum must exist on Capitol Hill for open discussion of the abuses and problems that surface within the agency. Both the Senate Finance and House Ways and Means Committees have the authority to conduct full-scale investigations; each respective chairman has the power to examine all information necessary for a thorough review. This trusted authority, however, must be used in a systematic way. Throughout the course of our investigation and hearings, the Internal Revenue Service issued one unilateral policy change after another, as well as several studies confirming the evidence of taxpayer mistreatment that we were uncovering and reporting to the public.

There were changes in the intrusive operating procedures used by revenue collectors and criminal investigators. More than a dozen senior-level managers were reprimanded for serious violations of laws and policies. Others left the Service. Auditors and examiners were more carefully monitored and less driven to make assessments based on quotas, goals, and statistics. "There was real improvement for the taxpayer," one senior employee told me. "We were instructed to be a lot more prudent," added another. But both admitted that things are now slipping back, despite the fact that Congress overwhelmingly passed the IRS Restructuring and Reform Act of 1998.

In one of our many private meetings, Commissioner Rossotti told me that changing the culture of the agency would take ten years, a professional generation within the life of an average thirty-year career. I agree with him, but also know that without serious and consistent congressional oversight of the Internal Revenue Service, there will be no improvement, given any length of time. "We learned of the agency's quota system back in the 1980s and we outlawed it," observed Senator Charles Grassley, a leader in the restructuring effort. "Suddenly, we find an unofficial backdoor quota system still in place. It seems like you put out a brush fire here and it pops up someplace else." Oversight of the IRS is a step-by-step process, a long-term commitment. In its absence, management, pushed by Congress to collect revenue and increase taxpayer compliance, as well as assure fairness and a service-oriented environment, will focus on one mandate at the risk of violating another.

"We clearly are compelled to use the enforcement tools that you have given us," Michael Dolan told our committee. "The question is, are those tools used as you want them to be used? Are they used with the sensitivity and with the care and precision the Congress authorizes to use them? I think there have been some very valid questions raised in the course of the many people you've heard from about whether in each and every case they are."

Dolan admitted that the careless or overly aggressive use of enforcement tools was a problem requiring monitoring "certainly in the context of the IRS' overall responsibility." Unfortunately, the culture within the Internal Revenue Service does not lend itself to scrutiny. As illustrated in preceding chapters, whether it be bucking against Internal Inspections, the Treasury Department Inspector General, or Congress, there is an active effort to hide information, destroy records, suppress testimony, and counter oversight initiatives by declaring them to be inspired by ulterior motives. This is particularly the case when Congress is involved. The agency, according to journalist James Bovard, shows open disdain for congressional oversight, with three out of four IRS managers believing that they are entitled to deceive or lie while testifying before Congress. Citing a 1991 survey of agency executives and managers, Bovard reported that only 47 percent of the managers feel the need to be "completely honest" when testifying before a congressional committee, and the number drops to 24 percent when appearing before what they perceive to be a committee chaired by "a critical or headline-seeking chairman."

Congress Steps Up to the Challenge

Great events in life are seldom spontaneous. Rather, they are the culmination of careful planning, the consolidation of a collective vision, and many smaller endeavors undertaken by individuals who, while successfully laying the foundation for magnificent accomplishment, may not even be acknowledged for the marvelous work they performed. The Internal Revenue Service Restructuring and Reform Act of 1998, and the hearings that served as its most immediate catalyst, were no exceptions. During my tenure on Capitol Hill, congressmen, senators, and their sub-committees have held hearings focusing on one aspect or another of the IRS. In the last decade, two Taxpayer Bill of Rights have been signed into law. In the 1980s, Doug Barnard's House Committee on Government Operations took an in-depth look at problems existing in the quality of IRS correspondence with taxpayers, and then turned its attention to senior-level employee misconduct and mismanagement. In the 1990s, Congress examined the plight of taxpayer browsing, which is when IRS employees look up the returns of friends, family, neighbors, former lovers, prospective partners, even famous actors and athletes.

These efforts raised the consciousness of America—the awareness that all was not well inside an organization whose congressionally granted power allowed it to invade the lives of ordinary Americans. Yet there had been no effort to make wholesale reforms within the Internal Revenue Service in nearly half a century. This began to change in the summer of 1996, with the establishment of an eighteen-member bipartisan commission, made up of legislators, businessmen, government officials, and taxpayer advocates. Chaired by Senator Bob Kerrey and Congressman Rob Portman, the National Commission on Restructuring the Internal Revenue Service embarked on a year-long study to determine how the agency could be made more efficient, modern, and responsive. One of its most newsworthy concerns focused on the IRS' antiquated and deteriorating technology, and the fact that the agency had all but squandered over four billion dollars that Congress had appropriated to prepare its computer system for the twenty-first century.

However, according to several who served on the National Commission, including its cochairmen, without authority under

Section 6103 to thoroughly investigate allegations of taxpayer abuse, employee mistreatment, and case management, there were serious limitations to how effective the commission could be in determining the full scope of changes necessary for reform. Despite the restrictions, the commission's work and the recommendations proposed in its 1997 report, *A Vision for a New IRS*, led the way for the Finance Committee investigation and provided a detailed blueprint for the Restructuring and Reform Act of 1998.

Among the commission's recommendations:

- Congressional oversight of the IRS should be restructured and coordinated through a new entity that provides members and staff with sufficient information to make informed decisions regarding tax administration and policy.
- Overall responsibility for executive branch governance of the IRS should be placed with a new Board of Directors, accountable to the president and the American people, to provide the expertise and continuity to ensure that the IRS achieves its mission.
- The Commissioner of Internal Revenue should be appointed for a five-year term and should be given greater flexibility in hiring, firing, and salary decisions.
- The IRS should receive stable funding for the next three years so that its leaders can undertake the proper planning to rebuild its foundation.
- The IRS must address training, operations, technology, culture, and taxpayer education.
- The IRS must update its technology and treat taxpayer information as a strategic asset to improve its customer service and compliance functions.

- The IRS must develop a strategic marketing plan within the next ten years to make paperless filing the preferred and most convenient means of submitting returns for the vast majority of taxpayers.
- Additional steps should be taken to improve taxpayers' ability to recover damages for wrongful actions by the agency, and significant efforts should be made to protect taxpayers from unnecessary disputes with the IRS before they occur.
- Simplification of the tax law is necessary to reduce taxpayer burden and facilitate improved tax administration.

These were sound proposals. Historically, they represented some of the most far-reaching recommendations ever for changing the Internal Revenue Service. But I was concerned that they did not go far enough. Even before the commission released its report, Eric Thorson, our chief investigator, was sharing many of the horror stories I've documented in the preceding pages, and I realized that while operational changes were necessary, while technology needed to be improved and oversight needed to be strengthened, genuine attitudinal changes—a cultural shift—would be required if we were to realize permanent improvement in the way the agency interacts with the taxpayer and treats its employees. I also realized that the evidence we were gathering would, more than anything else, galvanize public attention and serve as the driving force for reform.

What troubled me was the way in which the agency, driven by quotas and aggressive managers, could use inflated examination assessments and brutal enforcement tools to strip individuals and families of money, property, and livelihoods. I was angered by the countless stories I heard about innocent spouses who were vulnerable under the law and hunted down by relentless revenue officers, despite the fact that they had little or no knowledge of the income tax problems caused by their former husbands and were responsible for limited, if any, of the income reported on the tax returns in question. I was upset that thousands of Americans were being designated "illegal tax protesters" and robbed of basic civil rights without their knowledge, and often for causes that were arbitrary and even groundless. I worried about the reputations of honest businessmen and -women that were run down by criminal investigators looking for ink on the assumption that such news stories increased taxpayer compliance. I felt it unfair that when taxpayers were abused by the agency, federal law generally prevented the courts from allowing them to enforce their rights. And I was frustrated by the fact that in everything our investigation was disclosing—in one heartrending story after another—the perpetrators of even the most outrageous abuses were going unpunished and even being promoted, and that often our requests for information concerning them, even with authority under Section 6103, were needlessly delayed by the agency, or altogether unanswered.

David Keating, who served as a member of the National Commission on Restructuring the IRS, was correct in his assessment: while the commission's recommendations were an improvement in the area of taxpayer rights, they were not as bold as they needed to be. "The commission made many sensible recommendations to improve the IRS," he told me, following the release of the report. "The problem was that it glossed over many other important issues." The composition of the commission made it difficult to collectively advocate many changes that were important for serious restructuring of the agency. "One of the things I faced inside the commission was that there was too much concern for how to make the IRS run smoothly—better software and better training," David said. "There wasn't much recognition among the commission members that serious cultural flaws existed in how the IRS went about the auditing and collection processes. And there was nothing in the commission recommendations about protecting taxpayers and employees or disciplining IRS personnel who failed to follow the law."

Something Good Made Better

Concerns about the way the IRS affects the lives of individuals became the focus of our Finance Committee efforts. Uninfluenced by the agency advocates, union representatives, and others whose work on the commission to protect territory and maintain the status quo diluted some of the stronger and more important initiatives necessary to change the agency, our investigators pressed forward. Concerned employees willingly cooperated. Taxpayers shared their despairing stories. Practitioners offered professional insight concerning how the system could be strengthened from the lowest levels of the agency to the office of the commissioner. Our investigators, and professional staff members on the Finance Committee, made certain that the evidence being gathered was corroborated by two or three witnesses and vetted against taxpayer files.

By the time the hearings arrived, we expected criticism—and, indeed, many within the Internal Revenue Service were working day and night to derail our efforts—but we also knew we were prepared. The heroic men and women who came forward left little doubt concerning the problems plaguing the agency and the abusive manner in which they were manifesting themselves in the lives of innocent taxpayers. Their courage and testimonies resonated with the American people. Operational shortcomings needed to be addressed, yes, but down where the agency touched the lives of average men and women—where it influenced the welfare of families and the future of small businesses—where innocent spouses were being forced onto welfare, where children were suffering from deprivation because revenue collectors found it easier to track down their mothers rather than the fathers who abandoned them, the very culture of the agency was rotting from the inside out.

The opening day of our hearings, I studied the faces of my colleagues as we heard from our first panel of taxpayers, some whose lives had been destroyed. Katherine Hicks, a wife and mother from California, was reduced to living with her daughter in a rented room after the IRS failed to send her a bill for an out-of-court settlement she had entered with the agency a decade earlier. Because of a delinquent tax debt owed by her former husband, Mrs. Hicks agreed to pay an assessment, but then the IRS failed to follow up with the bill she had been instructed to wait for—despite her repeated attempts to contact the agency and pay the settlement. As a consequence of the agency's inability to track Mrs. Hicks' account, and the lack of communication between IRS personnel, she was subjected to tax liens against her home and levies against her new husband's wages. In an effort to protect her new husband, Katherine declared bankruptcy, had him file for divorce, and came within seconds of ending her life.

Another witness, Monsignor Lawrence Ballweg, described the frustration of being unable to get a copy of his tax information within a reasonable time so that he could respond to the IRS allegation that he owed the agency thousands of dollars. It was a simple request—the type of request that could have been handled within minutes by a major credit card company—yet before his ordeal was over, and the Monsignor demonstrated that the agency was in error concerning the alleged liability, he had been subjected to harassment, abuse, and incompetence by nameless employees operating in a world where holding them accountable was impossible and the taxpayers were prevented from following up on their cases with the same individual. We listened to Nancy Jacobs tearfully share her story concerning the IRS' inability to comprehend the elementary fact that her husband, an optometrist, had been mistakenly assigned an employer identification number belonging to someone else. Instead of working with the couple to straighten out what was nothing more than a clerical error, the agency forced them into an 18-year ordeal, subjecting the family to liens, interest, and penalties for taxes that were actually owed by another.

There were common themes in all three of these cases: the inability of the IRS to perform a basic administrative task; the unwillingness of agency personnel to approach problems from the taxpayer's perspective, with an eye to resolving them; the inefficiency and frustration of never being able to contact, or get answers from, the same agency employee spoken to previously; and the lack of will by the agency itself to correct these problems before they were elevated to national attention. These shortcomings were then compounded by a horrible parade of unfounded accusations, gross threats, and heavy-handed enforcement tools used against the taxpayers, all of whom were innocent.

By the time our first panel of witnesses had finished their testimonies, Daniel Patrick Moynihan, our committee's ranking minority member and perhaps the most eloquent member of the Senate, expressed the feelings of many of us. Calling for accountability, he wanted to know what disciplinary measures were taken against those employees who so willfully violated the rights of these taxpayers. "We are deeply in your debt," he told the witnesses. "You have had some awful experiences. I hope it makes a difference to you that you are being heard in the Senate Finance Committee. We have learned a lot."

These witnesses were followed by others who shared many of the stories documented in these pages, and we quickly discovered that not only was the Finance Committee listening, but Americans everywhere were expressing their outrage, sharing their own stories, and demanding change. The White House, which was attempting to short-circuit strong agency reforms by advancing a bill that was even weaker than the one proposed by the National Commission, quickly reversed itself, throwing its weight behind the commission's proposal, fearful that as our hearings progressed real restructuring of the agency would become inevitable, something that administration representatives—particularly inside the Treasury Department and the Internal Revenue Service—did not want.

The original restructuring and reform bill, based on the commission's proposal, had been drafted and introduced in the House of Representatives less than five months after the commission had issued its report. On November, 5, 1997, it passed the House and sparked an active campaign by the White House and its allies on Capitol Hill to push for passage in the Senate. "Certainly the bill, even with its shortcomings, would be better than nothing," went the arguments, but I did not want to see a small step taken by Congress when I knew that events were coming together in such a way that we could restructure and reform the agency from the ground up. Only a few times in history had conditions been so ripe for change.

With support from the Senate leadership, and a strong vote of confidence from the majority of members on the Finance Committee, we pressed forward with our agenda. I went to the floor of the Senate day after day to answer the proponents of the weaker bill who were urging an immediate vote, while Eric Thorson and his investigators continued to meet with taxpayers and agency employees. And by our second round of hearings, in the spring of 1998, there was no question that much stronger restructuring and reform legislation would pass, receiving bipartisan support and even a nod from the White House.

"The Finance Committee hearings proved without doubt that the IRS needed more than just an internal reorganization," David Keating told me. "The hearings silenced opponents in the administration, and they emboldened us to go further in reforming the agency and giving taxpayers more protections. After the Senate Finance Committee let taxpayers and agency employees tell their stories, even the most ardent pro-tax members of Congress wouldn't dare go back home and try to say that there weren't serious problems inside the IRS."

The New Law

With information still pouring in from our investigation, the Finance Committee, during January and February 1998, held extensive hearings focused on restructuring alone. The committee staff began to put together a much more comprehensive bill than that passed by the House, and by the end of March, voting 20 to 0 in favor of the stronger measures, Finance sent the Internal Revenue Service Restructuring and Reform Act of 1998 to the full Senate, where it was also unanimously approved. So extensive were our reforms that Secretary Rubin and Commissioner Rossotti warned that many of the provisions could not be fully incorporated into agency policies and procedures until the year 2000.

Among the measures required by the new legislation, we gave the commissioner the authority to overhaul the governance and structure of the IRS. One of the many positive developments resulting from our oversight was that the president, for the first time in the Service's history, appointed not a tax professional but a well-qualified and proven manager to head the organization. Historically, the commissioner had been more concerned about tax law than the administration of the agency. As a result, the deputy commissioner carried the major responsibility of running day-to-day operations. This not only had the effect of insulating the commissioner, disengaging him from ongoing managerial concerns and effective interaction with employees and taxpayers, but it allowed the deputy commissioner to consolidate power independent of the commissioner's authority.

Charles Rossotti was exactly what the agency needed. Proven as a successful businessman, he had founded American Management Systems—an independent computer and consulting firm—with only a handful of employees in 1970. By the time he was nominated by Bill Clinton, on July 31, 1997, Rossotti had built his small firm into an international company with over 7,000 employees and revenues in excess of $800 million. As I said during his confirmation hearing before the Finance Committee, Rossotti's past demonstrated that he was "in touch with the needs, concerns, and risk-taking mind-set of entrepreneurs." It was my hope that his service in the IRS would be characterized by his unorthodox résumé, that he would buck tradition, take on the status quo, and run counter to the culture that had taken root within the bureaucracy of 1111 Constitution Avenue. The IRS, I said, "needs a leader who is willing to question and investigate, a leader who is able to see the agency in terms of its responsibility to government and its need to serve the taxpayer."

I can say without condition that despite these high expectations, Commissioner Rossotti has not disappointed me. He has taken responsibility for an organization that many believed was ungovernable. Within months of his confirmation, he brought his blueprint for operational change into my office. I was taken immediately by the fact that his plan reinvented the agency's structure; at its heart were two objectives: taxpayer service and agency accountability. His plan was to replace the Internal Revenue Service's antiquated structure, one based on an industrial-age grid of regional, district, and branch offices—each fiefdom operated by a complex hierarchy of directors, deputy directors, chiefs, assistant chiefs, managers, counselors, advocates, auditors, examiners, collectors, and special agents. For many taxpayers, the system was beyond their ability to comprehend, and there was no consolidated program in place to efficiently meet their unique needs. For example, an individual looking for help to file a 1040EZ form had to go through almost the same machinations as a small businessman who had more complex tax concerns.

"We must fundamentally change the way we think about our agency," Commissioner Rossotti told our committee. "We must become fundamentally committed to customer service. We must shift our focus, as many large companies have done in the last ten years, from expecting our customers to figure out how to navigate our system and our process, to thinking about everything we do from the taxpayers' point of view. That means we must find ways to gain a better understanding of the taxpayers' problems and how we can help them meet their obligations under the tax laws."

To accomplish this, Commissioner Rossotti's plan structured the agency around a set of operating units, each created and trained to serve a particular group of taxpayers. "Just as companies develop very specific marketing programs to reach customers with different needs," the commissioner explained, "we can help taxpayers far more effectively by tailoring our publications, communications, and assistance programs for taxpayers with particular needs."

This change, Commissioner Rossotti said, would be the cornerstone of a new service-oriented and more productive IRS.

To achieve it, he needed the authority to revamp the structure, as well as the ability to make personnel decisions, hiring those whose talents were needed to run the agency as he envisioned it, giving them a competitive salary to come to work—as he had—out of the lucrative private sector. He also needed the authority to fire those who abused the system or the taxpayer, or failed to respond to the changes he had in mind. Our legislation provided the commissioner with these tools.

Stronger Oversight

At the same time, the Restructuring and Reform Act established more independent oversight of the IRS, creating a nine-member board within the Treasury Department. As a summary of the bill prepared by the Joint Committee on Taxation reported, this new Internal Revenue Service Oversight Board will monitor the IRS in its "administration, management, conduct, direction, and supervision of the execution and application of the internal revenue laws." The board will consist of six members from the private sector, the Commissioner of Internal Revenue, the Secretary of the Treasury (or the deputy secretary), and an employee representative. Under the law, the board will have the authority to influence the appointment and removal of commissioners, as well as top-level officers, and it will work to ensure that the organization and operation of the agency is carried out as Congress intends.

Another measure to strengthen oversight includes strengthening the Office of the Taxpayer Advocate—making the advocate more independent and responsive to taxpayer dilemmas. Under the new law, the IRS Taxpayer Advocate is renamed the National Taxpayer Advocate. The individual is appointed by the Secretary of the Treasury, and, unlike in the past, the new National Taxpayer Advocate cannot have served as an officer or employee of the IRS for two years prior to appointment. He or she must also agree not to accept employment with the agency for at least five years after leaving it. This will minimize, and possibly even eliminate, some of the conflict-of-interest charges we uncovered, and it will embolden the new advocate to forcefully represent the taxpayer, as he or she will no longer be selected from within IRS management, only to return to IRS management after serving in the advocate's office. Under the new law, the National Taxpayer Advocate and all local advocates will be independent from the IRS examinations, collections, and appeals functions.

Taking efforts to strengthen oversight even further, the Restructuring and Reform Act eliminates the IRS Office of the Chief Inspector and, in its place, creates a Treasury Inspector General for Tax Administration. No longer will serious inspection efforts be handled within the agency, providing IRS management the ability to control their findings, influence their reports, and simply place recommendations for disciplinary measures in a desk drawer to protect employees who have broken the law, violated policies, or trampled on the rights of taxpayers. The new Treasury Inspector General for Tax Administration, and his or her staff, will report to the Secretary of the Treasury, with certain additional reporting to the IRS Oversight Board and to Congress. For example, the IRS will provide an annual report to Congress on allegations of employee misconduct. And the agency is now required to keep records of taxpayer complaints made against IRS employees on an individual employee basis.

To ensure that the agency properly archives and disposes of its records, instead of using disclosure laws to hide and even destroy material that should be preserved, the new law provides an exception to the disclosure rules to require the agency to provide records to the National Archives and Records Administration. We protect taxpayer privacy by applying to the officers and personnel of the National Archives the laws prohibiting disclosure that currently cover the Internal Revenue Service, though we need not be reminded that National Archives already manages America's most sensitive, secret, and valuable documents. This measure, combined with others, will help in the oversight effort, as the agency's culture comes to embrace the fact that personnel within the IRS can no longer escape their mistakes by destroying their history.

To protect whistle-blowers and other agency employees courageous enough to report unethical, inappropriate, and illegal activities—including incidents of taxpayer abuse and mistreatment—the new law allows them to communicate their information to the chairman of the Senate Finance Committee, the House Ways and Means Committee, or the Joint Committee on Taxation without running the risk of a 6103 disclosure violation. No longer can the agency use the threat of privacy laws to hinder employees from protecting the integrity of the Service and cooperating with congressional oversight efforts. Concerning ongoing oversight by Congress, the bill requires at least one annual review by a joint congressional committee. This review will look into the progress of the IRS in meeting its objectives under the new strategic and business plans. It will follow up on the progress of the IRS in its efforts to improve taxpayer service and compliance. And it will monitor the agency's progress concerning technology modernization.

Taxpayer Protections in Collections

Of all that the Internal Revenue Service Restructuring and Reform Act of 1998 accomplishes, the area that gives me greatest satisfaction concerns increased taxpayer protections and rights. The bill shifts the burden of proof in court proceedings from the taxpayer to the agency, if the taxpayer acts reasonably. Taxpayers may claim civil damages up to $1 million for recklessness or intentional wrongdoing by the IRS. The bill also allows taxpayers to recover up to $100,000 for employee negligence, and it increases the amount the IRS will reimburse taxpayers who prevail in their court proceedings, boosting the hourly cap on attorneys' fees and expanding the circumstances under which attorneys' fees and administrative costs may be awarded. To help taxpayers keep litigation costs down, we also liberalized the small-case procedure in tax court by bumping the threshold from $10,000 to $50,000. This will make a less cumbersome and more informal court hearing available to thousands who are now forced to abide by IRS administrative decisions or incur the costs of hiring professional representation.

The Internal Revenue Service Restructuring and Reform Act of 1998 contains many strong due process protections for taxpayers who are caught in audit or collections activity. These range from the simple, like requiring all manually generated correspondence received by a taxpayer to have the name, telephone number, and identification number of an IRS employee the taxpayer may contact, to the more complex, like changing the procedures by which the agency executes liens, levies, and seizures. It prohibits the designation and use of the term "illegal tax protester" and requires that any such designations now existing on the IRS master file, or anywhere else, must be removed.

Under the new law, the IRS is required to notify a taxpayer within five days that a lien has been filed against his or her property. The taxpayer then has 30 days to request a hearing with an agency appeals officer (made more independent under the new law) who has had no prior involvement with the taxpayer's case. Concerning the execution of a levy, the agency will now be required to inform the taxpayer of such an action by personal delivery or through registered or certified mail, and—as with notification of a lien—the taxpayer has 30 days to request a hearing. Once the taxpayer has requested a hearing, the agency cannot proceed with seizure activity until after the hearing has been held, and a taxpayer who does not like the hearing's outcome may take the case to tax court. These measures will go a long way toward protecting Americans from many of the experiences our investigation uncovered, where taxpayer property was seized without warning or under false pretenses.

The new legislation requires revenue officers to follow an established approval process before a lien, levy, or seizure is executed, and no seizure of a dwelling that is the principal residence of the taxpayer is allowed without prior judicial approval. The affected parties must be given notice of the judicial hearing, and at that hearing the agency must demonstrate that laws and administrative procedures have been strictly followed, that the liability is owed, and that there is no reasonable alternative for the collection of the taxpayer's debt.

If a taxpayer's liability is $5,000 or less, the agency is prohibited from seizing any nonrental real property used as a residence by the taxpayer or other individuals. When the liability exceeds $5,000, the agency must explore all other payment options before seizing a taxpayer's business assets or principal residence. The bill also increases the amount of personal property that is exempt from levy. Cases of jeopardy assessment and levies, or a termination assessment, require revenue officers to receive prior approval, after careful review, from the agency's chief counsel's office. Seized property cannot be sold for less than the minimum bid price, and the agency must provide a thorough accounting of such sales to the taxpayer, as well as a receipt for the amount credited against the taxpayer's liability.

The Internal Revenue Service Restructuring and Reform Act of 1998 also disallows agreements to extend the statute of limitations on collection activity, unless the taxpayer has agreed to an installment arrangement. As our investigation discovered, agents often coerce taxpayers into signing extensions within days before the statute of limitations is set to run out. In this way, they keep taxpayers vulnerable well beyond the date their cases are set to expire.

Taxpayer Protections During Audits

In examinations, the Internal Revenue Service can no longer use financial status or economic reality audits to assign income to taxpayers, unless the agency has a reasonable indication that unreported income exists. The Service must also disclose the criteria and procedures for selecting taxpayers for examination and provide taxpayers with detailed instructions concerning the entire process from examination through collection, including assistance available from the Taxpayer Advocate. One important step toward providing more help to taxpayers is a provision in the bill to establish clinics for low-income taxpayers and those for whom English is a second language.

When a tax deficiency is established during the examination process, the agency is now required to include with the deficiency notice the date determined by the IRS as the last day on which the taxpayer may file a petition in the tax court. Under prior law, taxpayers were left with the confusing task of trying to determine on their own the deadline for filing a tax court petition. The new law also extends the attorney-client privilege of confidentiality that in the past has existed only between taxpayers and their lawyers. Now taxpayers receive protections with any practitioner authorized to practice before the IRS, including accountants and enrolled agents. At the same time, the IRS must inform taxpayers of their rights to have professional representation, and when the taxpayer elects such representation, the agency cannot proceed to interview the taxpayer without this representative being present, unless the taxpayer agrees otherwise.

The new law also gives taxpayers more protection against IRS personnel who try to contact friends, neighbors, employers, or any other third party in an effort to obtain information, embarrass, or harass the taxpayer. On those occasions when IRS auditors, examiners, and revenue officers attempt to contact individuals other than the taxpayer in the process of an audit or collection, under the new law the taxpayer will have to be notified. If, in the process of investigating a taxpayer, the agency issues a summons to an individual other than the taxpayer, the taxpayer will have the opportunity to quash the summons by appealing to the U.S. District Court.

Offers-in-Compromise and Installment Agreements

To help a taxpayer meet a liability when he or she is financially unable to pay the entire amount, the new law requires the IRS to liberalize its acceptance of offers-in-compromise. It also expands the authority of the agency to accept such offers and helps those entering an offer-in-compromise by requiring the agency to establish schedules of national and local living allowances that will provide adequate living expenses for them and their families. Additionally, the new law requires the IRS to consider the unique circumstances of a taxpayer's case before determining whether or not the established schedules are appropriate and will adequately provide for the needs of the taxpayer and the family. Once a taxpayer has made an offer-in-compromise, the IRS may not collect a tax liability by levy until 30 days after the offer has been rejected by the agency and the taxpayer elects not to appeal. Likewise, a levy may not be executed during an appeal of a rejected offer-in-compromise, or while an installment agreement is pending.

The new law also guarantees taxpayers the opportunity to enter into an installment agreement if their liability is less than $10,000 (excluding penalties and interest). To qualify for a guaranteed installment agreement, the taxpayer must show that for the past five years he or she has not failed to file or to pay income taxes. Additionally, the taxpayer must submit financial statements demonstrating the inability to pay the taxes in full and agree to continue to comply with the tax laws and terms of the agreement. Under this provision, the installment agreement must be completed within three years, and the IRS is required to provide the taxpayer with an annual statement of the initial balance owed, the payments made during the year, and the remaining balance.

Innocent Spouse Revisited

Some of the most far-reaching protections under the new law provide relief to innocent spouses—in most cases women who, after divorce, are left vulnerable due to tax problems created by their ex-spouses. The testimony we heard from these women was profoundly moving. I vividly recall the gentle face of Josephine Berman, a New Jersey homemaker who innocently signed her name to joint tax returns over thirty years ago. Like many full-time wives and mothers, Mrs. Berman had tended to the home and children while her husband provided an income and cared for the family finances. Despite the fact that she had no earnings of her own, she signed the joint returns, taking advantage of the designation created by Congress to make filing seasons easier on the IRS by encouraging Americans to file jointly. Since signing those returns, Mrs. Berman testified that she has been "continually harassed, threatened, and intimidated into signing waivers of the statute of limitations." And she has had her entire retirement nest egg seized by the Internal Revenue Service.

What had Mrs. Berman done to warrant this abuse? Nothing. Her husband had simply claimed deductions for legal expenses he had incurred during litigation with a partner in a subchapter S corporation. The IRS determined that the deductions were not allowable and sent the Bermans a bill for $62,000. "During the years that my husband was in litigation our marriage became troubled," Josephine told us. "In 1970 we separated. Needless to say, communication between us became even more sparse than it had been before." Josephine did not become aware of the tax problems until three years after the separation, when an IRS agent showed up on her doorstep and threatened to post tax sale posters on the trees in front of her home.

By that time, Josephine's husband was not working, and she had taken a job as a dental assistant to support their three children. The family, according to Josephine, subsisted on her $13,000 a year salary and welfare assistance. "I cannot overstate the desperateness of our situation," she testified. "The only thing that kept me going was my responsibilities to my children." Josephine had never been involved in her husband's business, nor was she ever included in business and tax decisions. "I did not understand the intricacies of the tax laws or why I was being held responsible for the debts of my husband's business," she testified, describing for our committee how she had been treated brutally by the first of many revenue officers who tried to collect from her the debt owed by her husband. "He repeatedly harassed and bullied me in front of my children," she said. "Under the threat of eviction I signed the first of several waivers and a lien was put on my home. These conditions allowed us to at least keep the roof over our heads."

For almost 30 years, Josephine and her children have been pursued by agents from New York, Pennsylvania, and New Jersey. IRS personnel have come to her place of work, called her employers looking for information, and threatened to levy her wages. "My personal affairs have been exposed to my employers and coworkers," she told me. "Not only is such conduct humiliating, it also serves to strain my relationship with my employers. My private life has become totally public."

As if this harassment was not enough, in 1995, federal revenue officers—in violation of regulations—stepped in and seized the only asset Josephine had, a $40,000 IRA that she had struggled for years to build. Will it come close to satisfying the original $62,000 debt? Not a chance. As Josephine testified before our committee, the agency claimed that her husband's original debt had ballooned to $400,000. "Short of winning the lottery I will never be able to pay," she said. "Twenty-five years ago I worked my way off welfare. With the final indignity of stealing my retirement money, the IRS ensured that is where I will end up."

Now living from paycheck to paycheck, Josephine said that nothing stands between her and abject poverty. "I cannot adequately describe the horror of the position I'm in and knowing that it is my government that put me there," she testified. "I have lived nearly half my life under the weight of this crushing debt. Now, at the end of my life, I live in a home that I paid for but don't own. What little I was able to save has been seized, and I don't know how much longer I will be able to work to support myself."

Josephine Berman put her plight in a context that still troubles me. "Senators," she concluded, "not long ago I heard a story about a man who had been sentenced to 15 years to life for manslaughter. He was released on parole for good behavior after serving just under eight years in prison. A killer gets released from prison after eight years but I'm serving a life sentence. The laws as they exist now are unjust and immoral. You have the power and responsibility to change this."

For Josephine Berman, Elizabeth Cockrell, Stephanie Toth, Svetlana Pejanovic, and the thousands of women like them, we made dramatic changes to the law. First, we eliminated all of the complex understatement thresholds that had to be met in order to qualify for innocent spouse protection (these are outlined in chapter 7). To qualify under the new law the understatement of tax must be attributable to an error made by the spouse filing the returns, and the innocent spouse must not know of the understatement. We also created a separate liability election that an innocent spouse can claim if she is divorced or separated from the husband with whom she filed the joint return. By claiming separate liability, the innocent spouse becomes responsible for taxes associated only with her portion of income claimed on the return. The bill also gives the agency authority and greater flexibility to relieve an individual of liability if relief is not available under the expanded innocent spouse rules or the separate liability election, and if the agency determines that holding the individual liable would be unfair. These important changes were provided not only for future innocent spouses. We made them retroactive, covering all innocent spouses whose income tax liabilities remained unpaid on the date the new law was enacted.

Penalties, Interest, and All that Remains

"The new law to protect innocent spouses should work phenomenally well," explained Jay Freireich, a tax attorney who has taken innocent spouse cases all the way to the Supreme Court. "Tens of thousands of women who were on the verge of bankruptcy will now have no liability at all. They've been given back their lives." Freireich described one client who burst into tears when he told her that a $5 million assessment the

IRS was trying to collect would be erased because of the Restructuring and Reform Act of 1998. The woman's ex-husband had taken deductions for tax shelters that the agency later denied; she was saddled with the bill. "Liabilities don't start out in the hundreds of thousands or millions," he explained. "But after the agency adds penalties and interest, the assessments eventually grow to be many times higher than the initial tax deduction that the IRS disallowed."

It would be difficult enough, and unjust, for innocent spouses to pay even the understatement, or the original tax owed by their former husbands, but once penalties and interest are added, paying the assessment most often becomes impossible. For example, the $650,000 liability the agency tried to collect from Elizabeth Cockrell began as an $80,000 liability due to deductions claimed by her former husband and his accounting firm *before* the two were married. Cockrell, who has spent a quarter million dollars fighting the IRS, tried on several occasions to have the penalties and interest abated, agreeing that she would pay the original liability if the agency would leave her alone. Her offers were rejected. The agency, in violation of policy, was using penalties and interest to raise revenue and punish taxpayers rather than to enhance compliance, the purpose for which they were originally intended.

At times, the misuse of penalties and interest borders on the outrageous. James Bovard reported a 1993 incident in which the agency tagged a taxpayer with a penalty of "$46,806 for an alleged underpayment of 10 cents." Correspondence I received from the Heritage Foundation reported another case in 1995, where a penalty of $155 was added after the IRS readjusted a taxpayer's return and found it to be a penny too light. Most often, they are simply excessive. Katherine Hicks, who had been told by the agency that it could not take her payment until she received a bill, ended up being forced to pay $8,195 for a tax liability that was originally a little over $2,700—all because of the agency's own negligence and delay. The original alleged underpayment on the return filed by her former husband had almost tripled in the 18 months that she waited for the bill to arrive.

The Senate Finance Committee heard one witness after another testify concerning how the Internal Revenue Service began using penalties and interest to raise revenue. Indeed, Congress had even come to depend on the application of penalties and interest in its budget projections, allowing the agency to increase the kinds of penalties that could be applied to taxpayers from 13 to over 150 and changing the interest structure from simple interest on the original amount of delinquent tax owed to interest that compounded daily, not only on the delinquent tax but on the penalties as well. The result: inside two decades, dollars assessed in penalties increased over tenfold; interest owed on taxes and penalties more than doubled liabilities, and—in fact—ran counterproductive to the original objectives of enhancing compliance and raising revenue, as the backbreaking financial burden destroyed the taxpayer's ability to stay viable within the system.

"It's legal usury," Bruce Strauss told me. "And the federal government is the only establishment that can get away with it." It is not uncommon for agency personnel to apply several penalties—complex and unexplained—on a single case, and the interest does not begin at the time of the audit but from the date that the taxes were due. In this way, an honest mistake or disallowed deduction on a tax return filed years earlier can burst into a deluge of unpayable assessments many times greater than the amount of the original underpayment. Individuals and small businesses can quickly find themselves buried beneath cascading liabilities as they struggle to climb out from under annual and quarterly obligations, only to fall deeper and deeper into debt. Struggling to pay off principal, penalties, and interest on past returns, they fall short on current assessments; these, in turn, are laden with penalties and interest all their own—while interest is still accruing on the unpaid portion of previous liabilities. Soon, there is no way for the suffocating taxpayer to survive.

In an effort to restore equity, the Internal Revenue Service Restructuring and Reform Act of 1998 includes several provisions to address penalties and interest. The most significant change in the law requires the agency to suspend interest and penalties unless a notice of deficiency is sent to the taxpayer within 18 months. Individuals who are not audited or informed of additional assessments until years after their returns were initially filed will only be liable for penalties and interest that accrued during the first year and a half. This will protect taxpayers and promote efficiency in the agency, but it covers only those returns which are filed on time or given appropriate extensions. After January 1, 2004, the 18-month period will be shortened to one year.

Two other important protections in the new law require supervisors to approve all noncomputer-generated penalties before they are assessed and to provide taxpayers with specific information concerning the name and application of penalties and how they are calculated. Taxpayers are also given the right to have payments earmarked for specific liabilities. In this way, they will be able to stay on top of current obligations and take care of prior assessments as they can, thus eliminating the application of cascading penalties and interest.

Each of these will be an improvement to the system as we found it, but much more needs to be done. The process of applying penalties is still chaotic. Penalties should not be used to retaliate, punish, or intimidate. They must be fair, consistently applied, well understood, and never considered—along with interest—to be revenue raisers within the federal budget. It had been my hope that we could have eliminated many of the penalties now on the books, simplified the system, and pushed for more relief in specific areas. One such area is the failure-to-pay penalty, which needlessly shackles individuals who are trying to comply with an installment agreement with continued penalty payments on top of their interest payments. (We were successful in cutting the failure-to-pay penalty during installment agreements in half, though it would have been better to eliminate it altogether.) Refusing to give up the fight in this area, we did call for a study on the administration of penalties and interest, requiring the Joint Committee on Taxation and the Treasury to separately examine the penalty provisions in the tax code and to return with recommendations to improve conditions and reduce taxpayer burdens.

Other issues that remain to be addressed include the need to mitigate the harsh results that occur in the lives of innocent men and women who are held personally liable for an employer's failure to pay employment taxes. While it is appropriate and necessary to hold officers, owners, and directors responsible for the tax liabilities of their companies, the so-called "Responsible Person" penalty has been used recklessly (see chapter 4: The IRS vs. Small Business), the agency holding employees accountable whose only authority is to have check-signing authority at the local bank. Not only are innocent individuals like Larry Westergard and Nathan Unger given "economic life sentences," but, according to a recently released report from the General Accounting Office, the IRS has no way of assuring companies that it is not collecting the full liability from each employee or officer of the companies it is pursuing. Privacy laws disallow one individual from knowing the tax-related information of another, and the agency's business and individual master files operate off independent and incompatible data bases.

"We found instances where all parties liable for one assessment were not given credit for payments received from other liable parties," noted the GAO. "In fact, in 53 of 83 trust-fund recovery penalty cases reviewed involving multiple assessments for unpaid payroll tax withholdings, we found that payments were not accurately recorded to reflect each responsible party's tax liability reduction. In one case, two of three officers were due a refund for at least a portion of the $1.5 million in trust-fund recovery penalties they paid, because the bankrupt corporation subsequently settled its payroll tax liabilities. More than two years after the corporation paid, IRS records still show multimillion-dollar balances on these three officers' accounts and liens on their personal property, despite the fact that it appears these accounts should be reduced to zero."

Small businesses also need consistent and easy-to-understand rules regarding contract labor. Worker classification is a complex issue with proponents on all sides. Small businessmen benefit from the flexibility and accessibility of independent contractors; they are unencumbered by tax requirements and regulatory paperwork. Labor groups are concerned that allowing easy designation of such contractors will erode the collective power of employees and threaten benefits like health insurance and retirement. The Internal Revenue Service sees the dynamic in terms of efficiency, as employees are easier to track for tax purposes than are independent contractors. Keeping balance in mind, Congress must work to reform worker classification rules, making them easier to understand, more consistent in their application, and less cumbersome in the time and energy it takes for taxpayers to resolve related disputes with the IRS.

Of all that remains to be done, three governing principles are most important: Simplicity. Simplicity. Simplicity. There is no question that the majority—if not all—of the abuses we uncovered could have been obviated by a tax code that is easy to understand, fairly applied, and efficiently administered. As we move closer to Election 2000, we're bound to see as many different proposals for tax simplification and reform as there will be candidates. From flat to VAT, we will see proposals to modify the current income tax with a healthy cut and major simplification, proposals for a value-added tax that will be built into the cost of goods, proposals for flat taxes that place a single rate on businesses and individuals, and a multitude of hybrid proposals that take and use a little from each. Just as Jack Kemp and I succeeded in getting our twenty-five-percent across-the-board tax cuts passed in 1982, after Ronald Reagan embraced our plan as part of his economic program, we will most likely see a new attitude for reform take shape as Americans line up behind their candidates in the coming presidential campaign.

10

Protect Yourself

The two most frequent comments I've heard since we began our oversight and restructuring efforts have been: (1) Let me tell you about my own horror story with the IRS, and (2) How can I protect myself?

It's discouraging to think that, in America, honest men and women have to be concerned about protecting themselves from their own government. Certainly they have better, more productive concerns to occupy them. On the other hand, the stories that have surfaced—and continue to surface—in our ongoing effort make it clear that a little trepidation may be a good thing, at least until we can be sure that every examiner, agent, and officer within the IRS is playing by rules that protect those who are complying with their legitimate obligations.

Some may be quick to say that the IRS audits only about two percent of all tax returns a year. That's true. And seen this way, the number appears to be rather insignificant. But consider that two percent of 200 million returns represents four million taxpayers. And if you happen to become one of them, you'll quickly find yourself receiving what feels like 100 percent of the agency's attention.

The best defense against an audit and a long-term relationship with a collections officer is knowledge and a few precautions. Know how the IRS works. Know what to expect. Know where to respond to questions and correspondence you receive. And know what to keep in your files and for how long.

Legitimacy has nothing to do with flagging you for an audit. When notice arrives that your return has been pulled, take it seriously but don't panic. Every filed return gets what the IRS calls a DIF (Discriminate Information Function) Score, and for the majority of audits this has been the sole determinant of why they have been chosen. DIF Scores are calculated by assigning mathematical values to areas of the return that might signal whether or not the agency will be able to assess a higher liability to the taxpayer. How this is done remains one of the agency's most well-kept secrets. We do know that the process is carried out by computers at the Martinsburg, West Virginia, Center and that the higher the DIF Score the more likely it is that you will be audited.

Once your DIF Score has been established, it will be sent to the service center and matched with the hard copy of your return. The decision will then be made whether or not to contact you. Most of the time, you will simply receive a computer-generated notice requesting additional information or letting you know that an adjustment has been made to your tax liability and an assessment is due. At this point, you can elect to provide the information or pay the assessment, or you can request a meeting to explain your side of the story. Either way, you must know that once you've been contacted by the IRS, your best friend is not a tax attorney, not a CPA, and not an enrolled agent. It's paper.

Most taxpayers are forced to meet the demands of the agency from the point of first contact simply because they do not have the receipts, invoices, pay stubs, and financial notices necessary to make their case. Often several years have passed since the tax return was originally filed. Old records have been thrown away. The calculations that were used to determine the deduction for moving expenses have been forgotten, or perhaps they were nothing more than a few penciled equations on a piece of scrap paper that mean nothing five years later. Throughout our investigation, I've heard it time and again: Paper, paper, paper—the three most important words when it comes to protecting yourself from the IRS!

According to the experts with whom I spoke, forget all those who tell you that you should keep your records for only three years. There have been cases where 20-years later a taxpayer wants to depreciate a home and the IRS demands to see original documentation. Keep those records. The best rule of thumb is ten years—especially for documents pertaining to the acquisition of major assets (valued at more than $1,000).

"But wait!" you say. "I want to know what I can do to keep from being audited in the first place."

According to the experts, the most important precaution that can be taken to avoid an examination is to refrain from doing anything that would flag the audit. If the DIF criteria are so secret, how do we know where these flags come from? By comparing similarities between tax returns that have been selected for audit. For individual audits these include:

- Excessive noncash charitable contributions.

  The best way to protect yourself in an IRS audit is to show the receipt and the original price of the gift to prove its worth. If you are going to donate a particularly valuable item to charity, such as a collectible or a work of art, make sure to have a qualified appraisal.

- Schedule Cs with little or no income but with numerous expenses.

   These flag more audits than anything else, and the two toughest barriers on the Schedule C are depreciation and substantiation of travel and entertainment. For depreciation you must have your acquisition documents to show your basis. Travel and entertainment are favorite areas for examination. The IRS knows it can nick just about everyone, because even if you can produce all of your bills you are going to have to prove the business purpose of the expenditures. For these reasons, the smart business person keeps an ongoing expense journal. If you're audited and haven't kept a journal, you can go back and create one. It's not illegal, as long as you tell the agent that it is a reconstruction. Never represent a back-dated item as an original record.

   Even if you don't keep a diary, you are still allowed a certain amount of travel and entertainment expenses per day, but don't expect the IRS to tell you anything it doesn't have to.

- Hobby losses.

   The IRS is concerned as to whether what you claim to be a business is actually a hobby. If you file several consecutive returns showing a loss on a Schedule C you're going to attract attention.

- Excessive itemized deductions.
- Excessive unreimbursed employee business expenses.
- Excessive moving expenses.
- Large casualty losses, without explanation.

   Always suspect that you might be audited. The best way to protect yourself is to attach a simple and clear explanation. If a contractor has done repair work on the bathroom of the apartment you rent out to a tenant, have the contractor write a letter, explaining what happened and how much he charged.

- Informants.

You may not believe that you have an enemy in the world, but just be advised that many audits are the result of someone bringing you to the attention of the IRS. The three biggest types of informants are disgruntled employees, an angry spouse, and a former business partner.

- Home office.

Though Congress recently liberalized the law establishing the criteria necessary to claim a home office deduction, this is still an extremely sensitive issue for the Internal Revenue Service. My best advice here is to be careful and see a practitioner.

From our investigation and this quick overview of what draws attention from the Internal Revenue Service, we can list six rules for dealing with the agency:

Rule No. 1—If there is something unusual on your tax return, attach a letter of explanation. Make sure you keep a copy for your records, and never send original paperwork to the agency.

Rule No. 2—Always file your tax return by registered or certified mail, or use another carrier like Federal Express, Airborne, or UPS. But it's not enough simply to send the return in this manner; you should also prepare a written statement that you sign, stating what was inside the envelope you sent. All that the receipt for a certified or registered letter will say is that something was sent on a particular day. On the day you mail the tax return you should prepare a declaration of mailing, a statement that says, "On [specify the date], I filed my state and federal returns and sent them via certified mail." List receipt numbers.

Make sure you send the right returns to the right governments. Your state government will not forward your federal return, and vice versa.

Rule No. 3—Keep your records neat and readily available.

Rule No. 4—Conduct your financial affairs in such a way as to expect an audit.

Rule No. 5—Don't make the mistake of thinking you're not going to be audited if you don't file a return. Failure to file a tax return can lead to criminal prosecution, not to mention years of self-inflicted torment. The IRS has such information-sharing capabilities that it can and will construct a substitute for your return. When it does, you will not be given credit for any itemized deductions, multiple exemptions, or specific credits.

Rule No. 6—Get professional assistance when the IRS presents you with something you don't *fully* understand. Try to select a representative who is either a tax attorney, an enrolled agent, or a CPA. You may have to pay $50 per hour or more, but you'll be surprised how many problems can be solved with a one-hour consultation. Simply pay the professional to look over your concern and give you advice. When you arrive at the consultation, take all the correspondence and documentation that you have received from the IRS. You should also be prepared to discuss your financial situation with the professional. For example, if you are insolvent, let the professional know so that he can tell the IRS that it will be a waste of government time to audit you. And be prepared to offer proof.

Most practitioners know their limits. If your problem is over your CPA's head, he or she most likely will know of another CPA or tax attorney in your community who has the expertise to solve your problem. If you feel that your situation has the potential to lead to a confrontation with the IRS, you should consider consulting a tax controversy attorney. The best place to start is to ask your own accountant for a recommendation. The second best place is to contact your local bar association through the yellow pages.

Demand proof that the person you are seeing is currently licensed and in good standing with their professional association. There are too many examples of charlatans holding themselves out to the world as CPAs and attorneys. Be leery of anyone who tells you that they have "inside connections" with the IRS and will be able to solve your problem instantly and completely. Tax problems take longer to resolve than most people would like to believe.

How to Prepare for an Audit

The first thing you should do when you receive a notice of audit is to call the IRS appointment clerk and get a firm time and place for the examination. There are two types of audits: field (the IRS employee goes to the taxpayer) and office (the taxpayer goes to the IRS). Field audits are generally for corporations and office audits are for individuals. It is not unreasonable to expect the IRS to give you a time that suits your schedule. It is also not unreasonable to ask how long the audit will take. The best way to approach the IRS is in a businesslike but courteous manner.

Most IRS auditors want you in and out of the office within about two hours. If the audit is going to run over two hours you can ask that the audit adjourn and resume at a later date. You should also ask the IRS to send to you a checklist of what the examiner will want to see. If you feel that the checklist is too broad and burdensome you should consult a tax professional immediately. Many IRS requests are simply fishing expeditions in an attempt to find something wrong. Most auditors when they get your case have no idea what to look for or where to find the errors. Supplying the IRS with absolutely everything it requests is usually a bad idea, because the examiner will discover areas that he or she had no intention of reviewing in the first place. Therefore, always try to narrow the scope of the IRS examination by questioning the purpose and the relevance of what the IRS wants to see.

If you get someone who's not cooperative, and who will not work with you on narrowing the scope of the audit or confining the examination to relevant documents, ask to speak to that person's immediate supervisor or manager. Remember, everyone in the IRS has a boss, and if you are not satisfied with either the information you are receiving or the way you are being treated you should immediately ask to speak with a supervisor. If you are told that the supervisor is in a meeting or not available, leave your name and phone number but do not comply with the demands of your assigned agent until your concerns are addressed. You also have the right to postpone the audit, or any IRS conference for that matter, and consult with an enrolled agent, CPA, or tax attorney. Your auditor may encourage you otherwise—and may even appear to offer an incentive to continue—but if you are feeling uncomfortable, don't hesitate to postpone the proceedings until you can get a professional practitioner.

There are times when the IRS will not get to a case immediately, or a supervisor will not return phone calls in a timely manner. If this happens to you, it may cause your audit to drag on or seem to fall between the cracks. When the agency eventually gets back to your case you may be asked to give the IRS an extension of the statute of limitations for examination. The agent may tell you that you *must* sign a statute extension. Be careful. No taxpayer is required to grant the IRS a statute extension of any type. In fact, the Internal Revenue Service Restructuring and Reform Act of 1998 requires the agency to inform you of your rights regarding statute extensions.

Why does the auditor want an extension, and what are the hazards to you? The agent most likely has a large inventory of cases to work. It's only human to procrastinate. He or she wants to manage as many cases as possible, but keep the daily caseload under control. The statute extension gives a window of time the agent would not otherwise have. However, weeks have ways of turning into months, and many months can go by before the agent again picks up the file. By that time much has been forgotten and there is high risk that the documents you provided can no longer be found. It is not unusual for the agent to ask you to resubmit documentation; this will take additional time to review.

In the meantime, what buys the agent more time on one side of the equation costs you more on the other side. Daily compounding interest accrues on any ultimate assessment you may receive. You'll be responsible for the underlying tax deficiency and the interest on that deficiency, and both will earn additional interest every day the audit is in question. Your only recourse, should you disagree with the agent's ultimate determination, is an attempt to have the excess interest abated under recent tax legislation. However, this usually requires the involvement of a tax-controversy expert. And those costs could reach more than the amount of interest involved.

We learned that some IRS agents are taught to bully and harass a taxpayer who refuses to grant a statute extension by making such comments as 'Your failure to give us an extension will result in our issuing penalties against you' or 'Your failure to grant us an extension will cause us to disallow all of your deductions.' This is abuse, and it should not be tolerated. If you have all of your paperwork and your records are in order, you will eventually be given an opportunity to present your case. Never sign a statute extension out of fear or because of intimidation. The conventional wisdom of tax-controversy experts is to avoid granting an extension to the IRS unless it can be seen that the result to the taxpayer will be favorable.

The Audit Process

If you're ready to go forward with the audit, the best way to be prepared is to have photocopies of all receipts, invoices, and other documentation and photocopies of proof of payment, such as a check or money order, attached to the invoices. All items coming from a specific category—such as interest deductions—should be placed in a single manila folder or envelope together with an adding-machine tape that ties in with the enclosed invoices, and those invoices should tie in to the deduction taken on the return. In this manner the agent will see that you are highly organized and efficient and not one to be bullied.

The IRS may try to pressure you into making statements or other disclosures that you are not willing to make. It is in the auditor's best interest to expedite the examination and close the case. Remember, IRS agents are on a clock. You, on the other hand, do not want to contribute one dime more than you absolutely legally have to, and you are the only one in the room who is looking out for your interests.

If the agent or auditor pressures you, simply stand up, excuse yourself, and state very clearly that you are discontinuing the examination in order to meet and confer with a tax adviser. This should end the discussion.

Far too many taxpayers, in an attempt to please the IRS, make unnecessary disclosures that open the audit into areas the IRS never intended to look into in the first place. Conduct yourself in a businesslike manner. Always keep your cool no matter how outrageous you feel the agency's position is, or the manner in which you are treated.

One of the positive features of the IRS examination process is the many levels of review you are allowed if you disagree with the agent. The best place to obtain a fair hearing within the IRS structure is with the IRS appeals division. Under the new law, you are entitled to an independent reviewer, an experienced representative who will take a fresh look at your documentation and your arguments. As a matter of fact, most experienced tax professionals such as tax attorneys would prefer to resolve a taxpayer's case with a member of the appellate division rather than with the auditor.

Many times during the audit the agent will ask the taxpayer to leave documents so they can be reviewed in more depth at a later time. While there is nothing wrong with the agent making this request, *under no circumstances give the IRS the original documents*. IRS agents are frequently transferred from one group to another, or from one office to another, and taxpayers' files often get lost in the process.

According to one tax professional who spoke with me, "A client allowed the IRS to take custody of his original general ledger and employment records only to have them lost. When the IRS subsequently issued an assessment many times larger than what the taxpayer had originally envisioned, the taxpayer had no way to disprove the IRS' figures. He wound up paying more taxes, a negligence penalty, and interest for not having adequate records."

The Audit Ladder

Both Congress and the IRS have taken great pains to create and strengthen a system of checks and balances during the audit process. Regardless of whether your audit is the traditional office audit or the more complex corporate field examination, all audits have in common several levels of review in order to protect taxpayers' rights and guarantee objectivity and fairness in the examination process. However, don't expect your auditor or the manager to tell you this.

You do not have to agree with the agent's findings. Most taxpayers are under the impression that IRS agents are well-trained technicians. Some are, but many aren't. An IRS agent's findings and opinions should always be suspect. Never allow yourself to be pressured into agreeing with the audit report by putting your signature on the dotted line.

A prudent taxpayer will consult with an experienced professional to review the accuracy and propriety of the audit report and to get an opinion on whether it pays to appeal the agent's findings. For example, we heard testimony that many agents are told by their managers to add a 20 percent negligence penalty. This is "water." Most IRS appeals officers will remove that penalty in the interest of settlement, but only if you haven't signed. Once your signature is on the line it is very difficult to rescind your consent. Most taxpayers having "signer's remorse" wind up paying the assessment and filing for a claim refund.

Many times the assessment made by the auditor will not disclose the interest that has been compounding daily since the due date of the return (this could be three years or longer). Before you sign, ask the agent for a printout of the entire deficiency, including taxes, penalties, and interest. Many taxpayers have agreed to the outcome of an audit, only to find later—when it's too late—that the amount they owe is substantially larger because the IRS did not tell them the effects of daily compounding interest.

If you and the auditor agree to disagree, the examination process is not over. The taxpayer has several rungs left in the audit ladder. The first is to inform the agent that you disagree with the findings and you wish to appeal. You will soon receive a 30-day letter, providing guidelines for appeal. This letter informs you that if you disagree with the auditor's findings you may ask to have your case reviewed by the Appeals Division.

Care must be taken here.

You *must* file a protest within 30 days of the date of the auditor's report. No particular form is necessary to file the protest, but do not assume that the auditor has told your side of the story. As a matter of fact, assume otherwise. It is incumbent upon you to file a timely protest, setting forth the facts as you see them and any supporting argument and documentation. You send these, along with the audit report, to the name and address set forth in the instructions. Read those instructions carefully!

Perhaps the most important point in filing a protest is to make certain that you send it by registered or certified mail, again placing a notice of documentation in your own files. Protests have a way of getting lost in the system, and the only way you can prove that you filed a protest on time is to have proof of mailing together with a copy of the protest in case it becomes necessary to assert your rights to an appeal at some future date.

Within a few months of sending the protest you will receive a letter from the IRS Appeals Division inviting you to a conference where you will meet an assigned appeals officer. You are entitled to an independent and objective review. These appellate conferences are informal. They are usually held in a conferee's office on a one-to-one basis. The appeals officer will have had an opportunity to review the entire file and to do research on any points of tax law needing to be discussed and resolved. Most IRS disputes are settled at this level; very few wind up in court.

The distinction between an examination agent and the appeals officer is one of education, experience, and point of view. The appellate conferee is generally a professional. He or she has proven experience with the agency, and the objective is to consider the hazards of litigation as opposed to bringing money into the Treasury and satisfying a quota-driven personal agenda.

The appeals officer is there to settle your case, if reasonable settlement is possible. This is the best place within the IRS to settle a dispute. However, don't go in expecting the appeals officer to give the store away. Remember, a settlement means give and take on both sides. A settlement is going to cost you something. The chances are you are not going to come out of the process owing nothing.

Your Day in Court

Suppose you and the appeals conferee agree to disagree. The next step is litigation. The choice of court is up to you. If you choose not to pay the tax, you may elect to have your case heard in the U.S. Tax Court. This court is unique in that it is the only federal tax forum where you can have your case heard without first having to pay what the IRS alleges is owed.

If you have not yet sought the advice of a tax attorney, now is the time to do so. With experience and research, the attorney may be able to tell you that the Tax Court in a previous case has ruled in your favor. If so, file your case in the Tax Court. If, on the other hand, research discloses that the Tax Court has not previously ruled in your favor, you may wish to pay the deficiency and file a suit for refund in either the U.S. District Court or the U.S. Court of Federal Claims.

Litigation, no matter which court you choose, is going to be expensive. You are going to need a lawyer to pursue your case formally in federal court. The U.S. Tax Court, on the other hand, was originally created to be an informal forum where lawyers were not necessary. However, over the years things have become more sophisticated, and a wise person does not go to Tax Court without competent tax counsel. If you are successful against the IRS in any court, you may be entitled to at least a partial reimbursement of costs and professional fees.

How long does all of this take? Figure on an average of three years from the time you are audited until a judge hands down a decision. Remember, during this time interest continues to compound daily on any owing and unpaid liability. You can protect yourself by prepaying all or a portion of your liability, but you have to be careful. If you want to go to Tax Court you must not fully prepay the IRS' assessment, or the court will not be able to hear your case. You may be able to make a deposit in the nature of a cash bond by following the provision set forth in Internal Revenue Procedure 84–58. Again, it is best that a professional guide you through this process.

Many people ask, "If you take the IRS to court, do you antagonize them in such a manner that they repeatedly audit you?" According to at least one tax attorney I spoke with, the opposite happens. "The harder you fight the IRS," he told me, "the more they respect you and tend to leave you alone." He cited the example of a client who was audited for civil tax fraud in the late 1970s. The case was bitterly contested in the Tax Court for four years and was finally settled by the IRS just moments before it was scheduled to go to trial. Much time and energy was spent by the IRS with little to show in return. The attorney continued to represent the taxpayer for 14 years, with the taxpayer never again being audited for any reason.

"I believe that the IRS truly respects any taxpayer or taxpayer's representative who fights like hell in a legal and ethical way," he concluded. "But if you anger the IRS because of unethical actions, the agency will have a memory like an elephant."

Protecting Yourself in Collections

As illustrated in chapter 3, there is no federal law enforcement official with more authority to carry out his mission than a revenue officer working for the IRS. The tools he or she has been given can turn your life upside down before you even know what's happening. However, there are still many protections you have even if your case has been handed over to collections. Before we review these, let's begin by looking at why your file may be with Collections in the first place. Among the possible reasons are:

1. Filing a return and not paying the deficiency in full.
2. Failing to pay an audit assessment.
3. Not filing at all and having the IRS prepare a substitute for your return.
4. Being assessed a penalty and not paying it.
5. Neglecting to pay child support or to repay a student loan.
6. Being personally assessed for the failure of a corporation to pay employment and withholding taxes.*

---

*Failure to deposit employment taxes prompts a more aggressive collection effort than an individual tax matter, because these are funds paid out of the Treasury whether they are deposited by the employer or not. Under the law, the employer is deemed to hold these taxes in trust for the U.S. government, and failure to deposit is seen as a form of theft. As noted in chapter 3, the IRS has a policy of closing down businesses that have chronic payroll tax violations, and occasionally the agency will criminally prosecute those who have failed to withhold, account for, and deposit federal employment and withholding taxes.

Once your case has been given over to Collections, you can—as you can at any stage in the process—contact the Taxpayer Advocate (made more independent under the new law). You would also be well advised to have a knowledgeable tax professional on your side. Revenue officers doing their job and following the law, no matter how harsh the results, cannot be stopped by a legal order even from the Chief Justice of the Supreme Court. Within the law, however, there are ways to protect yourself and to stop illegal or overzealous tax collectors:

1. Understand the power of the revenue officer. He or she can make your life miserable or tolerable. While the recent legislation strengthened due process in collections, there are very few rules and much of what will occur will depend upon your one-to-one relationship and whether you are perceived to be acting honorably.

What are some of the things the revenue officer can do?

- File a notice of tax lien, or remove a tax lien after it has been recorded.
- Seize anything belonging to you that is not specifically exempt under the Internal Revenue Code. The revenue officer can seize your business, your home, your car, or levy your bank account and your paycheck, if you ignore your rights to a hearing.
- Recommend criminal prosecution for failing to file tax returns.
- Suspend collection completely due to hardship.
- Grant an installment payment arrangement.
- Abate penalties.
- Treat you as an innocent spouse and abate assessments of taxes, penalties, and interest.

- Recommend the acceptance of an offer-in-compromise.
- Issue summonses.
- Grant an audit reconsideration.

2. Always keep the lines of communication open. Do not bury your head in the sand when dealing with the IRS. Your problem will not go away by itself. Carefully read all correspondence from the IRS Collections Division. If you believe the IRS is wrong, you will be allowed a hearing prior to any seizure, providing you act in a timely manner.

3. When approached by representatives of the IRS Collections Division be honest. Avoid sarcasm and hostility. Be accurate about your ability to pay. Don't hide assets. Don't play games.

4. Know your rights. Once you have given a professional representative your power of attorney, the IRS must deal with your representative. Any contact with you is improper, and you should notify your practitioner at once. Politely decline discussing your case, and under no circumstances should you let the IRS talk you into revoking your power of attorney or your rights against improper IRS actions.

5. If you want any concessions from the revenue officer you must get current on filing returns and paying your taxes, and you must stay current.

6. Whenever legally possible, try to reduce your taxes, interest, and penalties by filing an amended return or making an abatement request.

7. Never lose sight of the fact that the revenue officer's job is to protect and collect the revenue—not to help you solve your financial problems. Don't depend on the IRS to tell you your procedural rights. Remember that you have new rights

under the '98 law. Read all notices that are given to you by the revenue officer and do some research on your own. Again, an hour spent with a practitioner could be one of the most important hours of your life.

8. Beware of inconsistencies between groups and individual revenue officers. Whenever possible, get it in writing. Send letters confirming your understanding of what was said to you. Ask for promises, statements, and requests by the IRS to be put in writing.

9. Never assume that the revenue officer is correct about what you owe. If in doubt, order a copy of your computer transcript from the IRS disclosure office in your district. Sometimes the revenue officer will give you a copy upon your request. Have a tax professional review the transcript and do an independent calculation of your tax liability.

10. If you suddenly receive a statement from the IRS without first having been audited, ask the revenue officer for an audit reconsideration. This could lower or even eliminate what you owe. The IRS will not try to collect from you during reconsideration. You are also entitled to a pre-levy and pre-wage garnishment hearing before an independent Appeals Division. You can even take the IRS to court before paying anything you feel you do not owe, but you must act in a timely manner.

11. Never send the IRS anything you don't want haunting you in the future. Be respectful in your communications. Again, the vast majority of IRS personnel are professionals doing the best job they can under difficult conditions.

12. When you get a statement from the IRS, you must do four very important things to protect your rights: (1) make sure the assessment is legal; (2) make sure the amount you owe is correct; (3) make sure the statute of limitations for the IRS to assess or collect the taxes has not expired; (4) decide if you wish to challenge the IRS' position in an administrative hear-

ing or in court before you have to pay. You must find out these things yourself. Don't expect the IRS to volunteer this information without your asking.

13. If you have been making payments to the IRS make sure you are furnished periodically with data to show how your payments have reduced your liability. You must request this information from your regional service center.

14. You may wish to make an offer-in-compromise. This is an attempt to negotiate the payment of a smaller sum when a larger sum is owed. Of course, if you can pay what the IRS maintains you owe it is unlikely that your offer-in-compromise will receive serious consideration. When making an offer-in-compromise:

- You do not have to submit money with your offer.
- If your offer is accepted, all tax liens should be removed, even though you are making payments on your delinquency.
- Taxpayers owing income taxes should consider seeing a bankruptcy attorney before submitting an offer-in-compromise. Contrary to popular belief, federal and some state income taxes may be dischargeable in bankruptcy under the right circumstances.

15. Finally, if you disagree with a revenue officer, or feel you are not being treated properly, do not hesitate to ask to speak to the officer's supervisor. Just as I explained in exams, every revenue officer also has a boss.

In a collection proceeding, it's important to know your rights and what is exempted under the law from collection activities. While the IRS may seize your home, your business, and your automobile there are certain categories of assets that the agency is prohibited from taking from you. According to Internal Revenue Code 6334, the IRS cannot take:

1. Wearing apparel and school books.
2. Fuel, provisions, furniture, and personal effects that do not exceed $6,250.
3. Books and tools of a trade, business, or profession that do not exceed $3,125.
4. Unemployment benefits.
5. Undelivered mail.
6. Certain annuity and pension payments.
7. Workmen's compensation.
8. Judgments for support of minor children.
9. Exempted wages, salary, and other income. (The amount exempted is limited by how often you are paid, your standard deduction, and the number of personal exemptions allowed.)
10. Certain service-connected disability payments.
11. Certain public-assistance payments.
12. Assistance under Job Training Partnership Act.
13. In some cases a principal residence. (For specifics, consult a professional tax practitioner to discuss your rights.)

You may also protect yourself from IRS collection activity through a hardship suspension. If you can show the IRS that you are either financially, physically, or mentally unable to pay an assessment, the agency is *required* to suspend collection due to hardship. However, it is important to understand that collection suspension does not mean debt forgiveness. Interest continues to accrue on the amount that you owe. And eventually the IRS will reopen your case and take a fresh look at your financial circumstances. For many cases, a hardship suspension is the least desirable avenue to take.

One final avenue to protect yourself if the tax liability relates to an understatement on a joint return is to seek innocent spouse relief. As outlined in chapter 9, the Internal Revenue Service Restructuring and Reform Act of 1998 made major changes in the law relating to one's ability to seek this protection. These new laws apply to any outstanding income tax liability in existence at the time the act was signed into law on July 22, 1998. Congress has created new Internal Revenue Code Section 6015. The IRS has been given much greater flexibility in granting innocent spouse relief. However, you must petition for this relief in a timely manner; it is not automatic. You are entitled to an administrative hearing before an independent appeals officer. If you are not satisfied with the officer's determination, you may take the IRS to the Tax Court by filing a petition. You do not have to pay the agency anything until the court adjudicates your status as an innocent spouse. New rules are also provided for those who are separated or no longer married to be relieved of joint and several liability.

These final insights and guidelines are provided not from the vantage point or experience of a practitioner but from the insights that emerged during the course of our investigation and congressional hearings. You can protect yourself from many of the situations that came to our attention; others you may be able to control and remedy. Don't hesitate to seek professional counsel. Work cooperatively with IRS agents and officers, but remember that the two of you have vastly different agendas. The IRS employee should be professional. If this is not the case, ask to see another. You should be courteous and well-prepared. Know your rights. Review the new protections created by the Restructuring and Reform Act of 1998, and take time to reread the many cases that have been documented in these pages. Let the experiences of these individuals give you wisdom as well as courage.

Epilogue: Taxation *with* Representation

A tax system that is impartial and fair has been the objective of America since its founding. The colonists themselves were descendants of tax protesters. As Edmund Burke, the eighteenth-century English statesman, pointed out before his House of Commons, there should be little surprise that a colonial revolution was fomenting against English levies and imposts as the historical "contests for freedom in [England itself] were from the earliest times chiefly upon the question of Taxing.

"The Colonies," he told his colleagues in Parliament, "draw from you, as with their life-blood, these ideas and principles. Their love of liberty, as with you, fixed and attached on this specific point."

America won its freedom from taxation without representation. With it came the opportunity to build not only a new nation with new political institutions but a more just and less onerous system of raising revenue for government responsibilities. However, taxation with representation has never been free from criticism and attack. Our national history is filled with incidents of rebellion. Most often they have been followed by corrective measures and constructive reforms. The investigation and hearings I launched in 1997—and which continue to this day—fit seamlessly into this historical dynamic. The personal horror stories of taxpayers and agency employees that surfaced, many of which I have included in this book, galvanized the attention of Americans and demanded action from Washington.

But there were many other stories and a wealth of documented evidence of IRS shortcomings that I have not included in this book. For example, we learned that some agency employees were involved in theft not only of taxpayer assets but government property. One manager in the Criminal Investigation Division who was responsible for overseeing undercover operations in his region managed to steal up to twenty government vehicles and get away with the crimes. We heard testimony from one international examiner who, following a lengthy and complex audit of a multinational corporation, arrived at a $24 million assessment. The corporation agreed to the issues the examiner proposed and was in the process of negotiating the penalties and interest when the examiner's manager ordered that the case be dropped "no change," or without assessment, and the work papers be purged. The witness testified that today there is no evidence of the case, or her $24 million assessment, despite the fact that the procedures within her division is to keep a file of all closed cases.

Several agency witnesses testified about other cases where major corporations had their tax liabilities dramatically reduced or zeroed out, and they hinted of a disparity in treatment. "All taxpayers are not treated to a no-change," one testified. "Small

taxpayers are written up unagreed and penalties are assessed."
We also learned about the agency's computer problem, how
over $4 billion has been wasted in a fruitless attempt at mod-
ernization, and we reviewed evidence from the General Accounting Office that documented a basic breakdown in the
Service's ability to accurrately account for its budget. This,
despite the fact that Americans are held responsible—with the
threat of criminal prosecution—for every penny of their income.
We reviewed evidence concerning what some call the IRS's
"no-pay policy," how taxpayers who do win judgments against
the agency fail to receive payment. We heard about the threat
of politically motivated audits, and sent related evidence to
the Joint Committee on Taxation for a thorough review. And
we listened to testimony involving discrimination within the
Service.

It is not that each of these issues is somehow less important than those detailed in these pages. Indeed, each one of them
could merit and fill a book all its own. But the objective of
this work has been to focus on problems within the Internal
Revenue Service that touch the vast majority of Americans,
because these were the anecdotes that resonated in the taxpayer's heart and successfully drove Congress to pass the
Restructuring and Reform Act of 1998. And it will be the
agency's influence on the lives of taxpayers that will assure
continued efforts toward improvement. The new law will not
solve all of the problems we have uncovered—and those that
continue to come to our attention. Congress must press forward with vigilance and reform.

I was very concerned to hear one revenue agent, Minh Thi
Johnson, testify that despite Congress's efforts to disclose abuses
and change the agency's culture, "IRS management has openly
flaunted the fact that it is not concerned . . . and that it will carry
out business as usual when things quiet down." Similar com-

ments came from others, and even Commissioner Rossotti has been clear about the herculean effort and length of time that will be required to modify entrenched behaviors.

But if success can happen anywhere, it can happen here. As Burke pointed out, fundamental to our temper and disposition is the quest to be free from the tyranny of heavy taxation and the threat of abusive collectors. However, not even Burke understood, nor could he articulate, this emotion as well as Thomas Jefferson. Twenty-five years after penning the Declaration of Independence, Jefferson delivered his first inaugural address as president of the United States, fully aware that the catalyst for independence was still pervasive throughout the land. Asking what is "necessary to make us a happy and a prosperous people," he eloquently answered, "A wise and frugal Government, which shall restrain men from injuring one another, shall leave them otherwise free to regulate their own pursuits of industry and improvement, and shall not take from the mouth of labor the bread it has earned. This is the sum of good government, and this is necessary to close the circle of our felicities." He passionately added that "the wisdom of our sages and blood of our heroes have been devoted to their attainment. They should be the creed of our political faith, the text of civic instruction, the touchstone by which to try the services of those we trust; let us hasten to retrace our steps and to regain the road which alone leads to peace, liberty, and safety."

My commitment to improve the Internal Revenue Service, and my pledge to push for tax reform—a tax code that is fair, simple, and economically constructive—are borne by my sincere belief that this spirit, and the conditions articulated by Jefferson, are alive and well in America today, and that by working together we can succeed.

Source Notes

INTRODUCTION

Auden, W. H. *Collected Poems.* Edited by Edward Mendelson. New York: Vintage Books, 1991.

Shirley Barron, interviews by the author, September 1997 through March 1998.

Letter from John Cardone, U.S. Department of Justice to Federal Magistrate-Judge James Muirhead, U.S. District Court in Concord, 24 September 1997.

"Derry Lawyer's Widow Tells U.S. Senate Prober Her IRS Horror Story," *Union Leader,* 26 September 1997.

"IRS Admits Irregularities in Barron Case," *Union Leader,* 27 September 1997.

"IRS Admits Breaching Procedures," *Sunday Monitor,* 28 September 1997.

CHAPTER ONE

Poll, *USA Today*/CNN/Gallup, 21 December 1997. Demonstrates that 95 percent of Americans are angry about the current tax system and demand change.

Wattenberg, Benjamin J. *Values Matter Most*. New York: Free Press, 1995.

Dubasky, Mayo. *The Gist of Mencken: Quotations from America's Critic*. Lanham, Maryland: Scarecrow Press, 1990.

Dostoyevsky, Fyodor. *Crime and Punishment*. New York: Modern Library, 1996.

U.S. House Subcommittee on Government Operations. *IRS Senior Employee Misconduct Problems*. 101st Cong., 1st sess., 25–27 July 1989.

U.S. House Subcommittee on Government Operations. *Followup on Investigation of Senior-Level Employee Misconduct and Mismanagement at the Internal Revenue Service*. 101st Cong., 2nd sess., 9 May 1990.

U.S. House Subcommittee on Government Operations. *Continued Investigation of Senior-Level Employee Misconduct and Mismanagement at the Internal Revenue Service*. 102nd Cong., 1st sess., 24 July 1991.

"IRS Criticized for Possibly Misleading Congress on Fraud in Housing Program," *Wall Street Journal*, 11 November 1996.

Dobrovir, William A., "IRS Secrecy Draws Growing Attention," *New York Times*, 20 November 1996.

U.S. Senate Committee on Finance. *Practices and Procedures of the Internal Revenue Service*. 105th Cong., 1st sess., 24 September 1997.

Senator Daniel Patrick Moynihan, interviewed on *Face the Nation;* CBS, 29 September 1997.

Davis, Shelley. *Unbridled Power: Inside the Secret Culture of the IRS.* New York: Harper Business, 1997.

Internal Revenue Service. *1995 Data Book.* Washington, D.C., 1996.

Burnham, David. *A Law Unto Itself: Power, Politics, and the IRS.* New York: Random House, 1989.

Senator John Williams, *Congressional Record.* Washington, D.C. 28 May 1948.

Shelton, Dr. James Hill. "The Tax Scandals of the 1950s." An unpublished dissertation.

Senator David Pryor, *Congressional Record.* Washington, D.C., 21 October 1988.

"IRS Secrecy Draws Growing Attention from New Government Panel," *New York Times,* 20 November 1996.

"Internal Revenue Service: Historical, Agencywide Budget Authority and Outlays, fical years 1970–1998," Budget of the United States Government, Appendix, FY 1998.

"IRS Admits Harassing Taxpayers," *Wilmington News Journal,* 26 September 1997.

CHAPTER TWO

"Barlows Epitomize Modern-day Pioneers," *Idaho State Journal,* 17 July 1979.

"Ferrol Barlow (today's David) vs OSHA (today's Goliath)," *Arizona Republic,* 14 February 1977.

Editorial, *Idaho Statesman,* 26 May 1978.

"Bill Vindicated: Inspectors May Need Warrants," *Time,* 5 June 1978.

Internal Revenue Service. *Internal Revenue Manual.* "Examination Division Guidelines and Procedures."

U.S. Senate Committee on Finance. *Practices and Procedures of the Internal Revenue Service.* 105th Cong., 1st sess., 25 September 1997.

U.S. Senate Committee on Finance. *Practices and Procedures of the Internal Revenue Service.* 105th Cong., 1st sess., 24 September 1997.

Internal Revenue Service. *Internal Revenue Manual.* "Audit Income Tax."

U.S. General Accounting Office. *Tax Administration: More Criteria Needed on IRS' Use of Financial Status Audit Techniques.* Washington, D.C., December 1997.

Kinsey, J.C. *Working for the IRS.* Cutten, California: Iris, 1997.

Bovard, James. *Lost Rights: The Destruction of American Liberty.* New York: St. Martin's Press, 1994.

"Family Saga Depicts Battles of Citizens vs. Government," *Idaho Falls Post Register,* 23 January 1997.

CHAPTER THREE

Adams, Charles. *Those Dirty Rotten Taxes.* New York: Free Press, 1998.

U.S. Senate Committee on Finance. *Practices and Procedures of the Internal Revenue Service.* 105th Cong., 1st sess., 25 September 1997.

Interview with former audit branch chief who desired to remain anonymous, 21 August 1997.

Transactional Records Access Clearing House (TRAC). "Outcome When Taxpayer Contests IRS Audit Results." Syracuse University: Internet Site. www.trac.syr.edu.

"IRS Takes Further Action in Response to Internal Audit Review of the Use of Enforcement Statistics in the Collection Field Function," Internal Revenue Service, press release, 13 January 1998.

"Statement of Treasury Secretary Robert E. Rubin," U.S. Department of the Treasury, press release, 13 January 1998.

"Use of Enforcement Statistics and Performance Measures at the IRS," Internal Revenue Service, press release, September 1998, FS 98–16.

U.S. Senate Subcommittee on Taxation and IRS Oversight of the Committee on Finance. *Oklahoma Field Hearings into the Practices and Procedures of the Internal Revenue Service.* 105th Cong., 1st sess., 3 December 1997.

Internal Revenue Manual, National Policy Statement P-5–38 (approved 2/13/78).

Internal Revenue Code, Section 6334 (e).

Internal Revenue Code, Section 5323.

Internal Revenue Manual, 57(10)1.

U.S. Senate Committee on Finance. *Practices and Procedures of the Internal Revenue Service.* 105th Cong., 1st sess., 24 September 1997.

Internal Revenue Manual, 57(10)1.1.

Internal Revenue Manual, 57(10)9.3.

U.S. Senate Committee on Finance. *IRS Restructuring.* Hearings. 105th Cong., 2nd sess., 28, 29 January and 5, 11, and 25 February 1998.

CHAPTER FOUR

"IRS Sends Couple $300 Million Bill," *CNN Internet,* 16 February 1998.

Bovard. *Lost Rights.*

"But I'm a Nobody," *Forbes,* 24 March 1997.

U.S. Senate Committee on Finance. *Practices and Procedures of the Internal Revenue Service.* 105th Cong., 1st sess., 24 September 1997.

Kinsey. *Working for the IRS.*

U.S. Congress, House Committee on Government Operations. *Improving the Administration and Enforcement of Employment Taxes-.* Washington, D.C.: Government Printing Office, 1992.

"Sympathetic Judge Suggests Taxpayer Should Flee Country," *The Journal of Taxation,* November 1994.

"Annual Readers' Poll," *People,* 8 January 1990.

National Survey conducted by The Polling Company, 17–24 March 1997.

CHAPTER FIVE

"Pair Expected to Testify They Were Told to Lie to Save IRS Reputation," *Atlantic Journal and Constitution,* 27 July 1989.

"Don't Whistle While You Work: At the IRS, Tattling Can Be Hazardous to One's Career," *Time,* 16 July 90.

Goldberg, Fred. Internal Revenue Service Memorandum. "Action Plan: Congressional Hearings on IRS Intergrity," 16 February 1989.

"Wiping Out Reprisal at IRS a Top Priority, Hill Members Told," *Federal Times,* 21 May 1990.

"Pervasive Fear' Dulls Internal IRS Probes, Witnesses Say," Federal Times, 7 August 1989.

Joseph and Edna Josephson Institute of Ethics. *Internal Revenue Service Survey of Managers' Values, Opinions, and Behaviors.* Marina del Ray, California, 1991.

Joseph and Edna Josephson Institute of Ethics. *Ethics, Principles and Practices: Survey of IRS Employee Opinions, Values, and Behavior.* Marina del Ray, California, 1992.

Michael Josephson, interviews by the author, September 1997 through May 1998.

"Infernal Revenue Disservice," *Newsweek*, 6 October 1997.

"Internal Audit Review of the Use of Statistics and Protection of Taxpayer Rights in the Arkansas-Oklahoma District Collection Function," Internal Revenue Service, press release, December 1997, FS 97–27.

U.S. General Accounting Office. *Tax Administration: IRS Inspection Service and Taxpayer Advocate Roles for Ensuring That Taxpayers Are Treated Properly.* Statement of Lynda D. Willis, Director, Tax Policy and Administration Issues. Washington, D.C., 5 February 1998.

U.S. Senate Committee on Finance. *Practices and Procedures of the Internal Revenue Service.* 105th Cong., 1st sess., 25 September 1997.

Internal Revenue Service. *SFA 95: Survey Feedback Action Survey Booklet.* Washington, D.C., 1996.

Internal Revenue Service. *SFA 95: Survey Feedback Action Employee Guide.* Washington, D.C., 1996.

CHAPTER SIX

Internal Revenue Service. *SFA 97: Survey Feedback Action Working Group Report.* Washington, D.C., 1998.

U.S. Senate Committee on Finance. *Practices and Procedures of the Internal Revenue Service.* 105th Cong., 1st sess., 25 September 1997.

U.S. Senate Committee on Finance. *Practices and Procedures of the Internal Revenue Service.* 105th Cong., 1st sess., 24 September 1997.

Davis. *Unbridled Power.*

Davis, Shelly, "The IRS Is Out of Control," *Wall Street Journal,* 15 April 1996.

Internal Revenue Service. "Seizures: Southeast Region—FY 1997." Atlanta, Georgia, 12 January 1998.

CHAPTER SEVEN

"Kitzman Guilty of 7 of 8 Charges," Daily Globe, 21 June 1996.

U.S. General Accounting Office. *Tax Policy: Information on the Joint and Several Liability Standard.* Washington, D.C., March 1997.

U.S. General Accounting Office. *Innocent Spouse: Alternatives for Improving Innocent Spouse Relief.* Statement of Lynda D. Willis, Director, Tax Policy and Administration Issues. Washington, D.C., 24 February 1998.

"Ex-spouses Seek Relief from IRS," *USA Today,* 5 February 1998.

U.S. Senate Committee on Finance. *IRS Restructuring.* 105th Cong., 2nd sess., 28, 29 January and 5, 11, and 25 February.

"Joint Returns Can Be Disaster for Ex-Spouses," *USA Today,* 5 February 1998.

"Tax Report," *Wall Street Journal,* 31 December 1997.

Beck, Richard C. E., "Joint Return Liability and Poe v. Seaborn Should Both Be Repealed," *Tax Notes,* 22 October 1990.

CHAPTER EIGHT

Internal Revenue Service. *Seventy-Five Years of Criminal Investigation History–1919–1994.* 7233 (Rev. 08–95), Catalog Number 64601H.

Kennedy, Robert F. Address to the graduates of Intelligence's Special Agent Basic Training School, 13 April 1962.

U.S. Senate Committee on Finance. *IRS Oversight.* 105th Cong., 2nd sess., 28, 29, and 30 April and 1 May 1998.

"A Poster Child for IRS Foes: In a Tax Shelter Inquiry, Did Agents Go Too Far?" *New York Times,* 18 October 1995.

"Seven Point Plan to Improve the IRS Criminal Investigation Division," Internal Revenue Service press release, 27 April 1998.

Brown, Ted F., "Assistant Commissioner's Message," *CI Digest,* Spring 1998.

Transactional Records Access Clearing House (TRAC). "Outcome of IRS Criminal Investigations." Syracuse University: Internet Site.

CHAPTER NINE

"Tax Test: Mistakes Even the Tax Pros Make," *Money,* March 1998.

U.S. Congress, House Committee on Ways and Means. *Overview of the Federal Tax System,* 1993 Edition. 103rd Cong., 1st sess., 14 June 1993.

Internal Revenue Service Restructuring and Reform Act of 1998. 105th Cong., 2nd sess., H.R. 2676.

Bovard. *Lost Rights.*

Davis. *Unbridled Power.*

"IRS Cheated on Ethics, Panel Told," *Atlanta Journal and Constitution,* 26 July 1989.

National Commission on Restructuring the Internal Revenue Service. *A Vision for a New IRS.* Washington, D.C., 25 June 1997.

U.S. Senate Committee on Finance. *Nomination of Charles O. Rossotti.* 105th Cong., 1st sess., 23 October 1997.

"Lone Ranger at the IRS: New Commissioner Rossotti is Making His Mark," *Time,* 15 December 1997.

U.S. Congress Joint Committee on Taxation, "Summary on the Conference Agreement on The Internal Revenue Service Restructuring and Reform Act of 1998," 24 June 1998.

CHAPTER TEN

Schriebman, Robert S., interviews by author, September 1997 to January 1999.

Schriebman, Robert S. *How to Practice IRS: No Tricks, No Magic.* Chicago: Commerce Clearing House, 1990.

Kaplan, Martin, and Weiss, Naomi. *What the IRS Doesn't Want You to Know: A CPA Reveals the Tricks of the Trade.* New York: Villard, 1994 (Rev. 98).

Adams, Charles W. *For Good and Evil: The Impact of Taxes on the Course of Civilization.* New York: Madison Books, 1993.

"$4 Billion Later, IRS Admits Its New Computer System Is a Failure," *Charlotte Observer,* 31 January 1997.

U.S. General Accounting Office. *Internal Revenue Service: Immediate and Long-Term Actions Needed to Improve Financial Management.* Washington, D.C., October 1998.

U.S. General Accounting Office. *IRS Management: Improvement Needed in High-Risk Areas.* Statement of Lynda D. Willis, Director, Tax Policy and Administration Issues. Washington, D.C., 14 April 1998.

Index